René Daumal

SUNY Series in Western Esoteric Traditions

David Appelbaum, editor

René Daumal

The Life and Work of a Mystic Guide

Kathleen Ferrick Rosenblatt

State University of New York Press

Published by
State University of New York Press, Albany

©1999 State University of New York

All rights reserved

Printed in the United States of America

No part of this book may be used or reproduced in any manner whatsoever without written permission. No part of this book may be stored in a retrieval system or transmitted in any form or by any means including electronic, electrostatic, magnetic tape, mechanical, photocopying, recording, or otherwise without the prior permission in writing of the publisher.

For information, address the State University of New York Press, State University Plaza, Albany, NY 12246

Production by Bernadine Dawes
Marketing by Dana Yanulavich

Library of Congress Cataloging-in-Publication Data

Rosenblatt, Kathleen Ferrick, 1947–
    Rene Daumal : the life and work of a mystic guide / Kathleen Ferrick Rosenblatt.
    p. cm. — (SUNY series in Western esoteric traditions)
    Includes bibliographical references and index.
    ISBN 0-7914-3633-0 (hc : alk. paper)
    ISBN 0-7914-3634-9 (pbk. : alk. paper)
    1. Daumal, Rene, 1908–1944. I. Title. II. Series.
    PQ2607.A86 Z86 1999
    841'.912—ddc21
    [b]   98-41577
                                                        CIP

10 9 8 7 6 5 4 3 2 1

To Camille and Adam

May you feel the difference this day,
as the galaxy whirls you by
some estimates 29 million miles away
from yesterday.

Contents

Introduction   xi

I BIOGRAPHY

   1 An Anarchist of Perception   3
   2 Daumal and Renunciation: The Imbecility of Individualism   31
   3 Drug Experimentation: Asphyxia and Absurd Evidence   35

II THE PATAPHYSICAL PURSUITS

   4 Surrealism and Le Grand Jeu: Living on the Pataphysical Edge   43
   5 The Avant-Garde and Party Politics: Marginal Marxism   71

III EASTERN STUDIES

   6 The Influence of Hindu Thought:
      Renunciation and Transformation   83
   7 Daumal in the Labyrinth of Pathways:
      The Influence of René Guénon   97
   8 Daumal and Hindu Poetics: The *Rasa* of the Word   113

IV GURDJIEFF AND THE DE SALZMANNS

   9 Daumal with Gurdjieff and the de Salzmanns: Finding a Path   127

V MAIN WORKS

   10 The Poetry of *Le Contre Ciel* : Death and Her Consort   161

   11 La Grande Beuverie: A Night of Drunken Delusions   179

   12 Mount Analogue: Non-Euclidian Mountain Climbing   197

Conclusion   213

Notes   217

Bibliography   233

Index   241

*Chaque fois que l'aube parait
le mystère est là tout entier.*

Each time the dawn appears
the mystery is there in its entirety.

—RENE DAUMAL

Introduction

> For the Hindu, all applied teachings are linked by a common goal, call it deliverance or consciousness; in learning archery or grammar one learns to know oneself.
>
> —René Daumal

Why has the Musée d'Art Moderne in Paris recently celebrated a lesser-known literary figure with an exhibition of writings and photographs? Indeed, today, as in the 1930s, René Daumal enjoys a growing renown among literary circles as well as New Age readers. The measure of his worthiness, however, lies not in his public acclaim but rather in the originality of his thinking. Born in the Ardennes in 1908, Daumal died of tuberculosis in 1944, at the age of thirty-six, two weeks before the Allied landings in Normandy. Throughout the five decades since his death, the legend of this shadowy figure has only grown. Amid the plethora of romantic figures in the Parisian literary scene of the 1930s, Daumal stands out as a modern proto-saint, a seminal figure at the crossroads of the East and West. As a young avant-garde writer in league with the Surrealists, Daumal went beyond the kind of dabbling in mysticism that was fashionable at that period. At the age of sixteen, he taught himself Sanskrit in order to better understand the form and content of the language. He is one of the first Western writers to truly decipher the essence of Hindu philosophy and poetics, as well as to successfully apply these concepts to his own writing. His essays, poems, novels, and translations all had one singular aim: to examine the purpose of human existence. In 1932, at the age of twenty-four, he became press secretary to Uday Shankar, a master of Indian dance who was the first to introduce this art form to the West, and traveled with him to the United States. But it was the teaching of the modern sage, G. I. Gurdjieff that truly gave René an intimate and practical knowledge of Eastern esoteric thought and changed his life.

This book seeks to follow Daumal's unique explorations of three major areas: his collaboration in the surrealist world of literature and politics, his study of Hindu philosophy and poetics, and his active participation in the Gurdjieff teaching. We will examine Daumal's collected poetry, *Le Contre-Ciel* and his two novels, *La Grande Beuverie* and *Mont Analogue*, in light of these influences.

In recounting the story of Daumal's life, we glimpse through the eyes of this man-child the world of the French avant-garde and the perturbations of two world wars; we also glimpse, through his psychic eye, the contours of his soul and the cosmos beyond. For that is where Daumal lived in spirit—in the vast emptiness of space. His early encounters with "the Void" (*le néant*) filled him with anguish and despair, yet throughout his life he always yearned for oneness with "the Beyond" (*l'Au-delà*). Fortunately, there were earthly ties that moored him and kept him on the liminal threshold of the Void—the bonds of family and friends, his mountain climbing and gymnastic skills, and his acumen in science and literature. Within these bounds, he was known for his selfless concern for others, his psychic abilities, and his otherworldly gaze, which created an aura of energy that drew people to him.

Daumal had many of the characteristics of a twentieth-century modern poet: the social and political conscience, the metaphysical yearnings, the *desinvolture* or sense of unrestricted freedom, and especially, the crazy absurdist humor mixed with despair, in the face of the meaninglessness of modern existence. He came of age at the moment when there suddenly burst forth an interest in the common man, and the belief that governments could legislate peace and prosperity for all. Although poets had touched upon these issues in centuries past, certainly no generation had grappled with all of them so intensely as the interwar generation. Even the burst of creativity of the 1960s and the absurdist lyrics of new-wave music are only variations of what was first posited by the Surrealists and the original *enfants terribles*, the Dadaists, in the 1920s.

What determines Daumal's unique position among them is not the fact that he formulated parallel theories and parapsychic experiments while still in his teens, independently of the Surrealists, but rather that he recognized that the unconventionality of the Surrealists was only a minor step on the long road toward self-evolution and self-liberation. The depth of his quest during his teenage years allowed him to see the value in Eastern traditional teachings. This provided him with a profound, positive construct at a time when he and his peers were rejecting traditional European values.

In the mid-1920s, Daumal and his coterie of friends began experimenting with avant-garde forms of writing, before they even knew that the Surrealists existed. They delved into psychoanalysis, dream interpretation, automatic writing, psychic phenomena, and sociopolitical involvement. Together they launched a literary review, *Le Grand Jeu*, which expressed their revolutionary ideas about life and literature. These years represent the embryonic stage of Daumal's development, when he first explored the metaphysical realm. He went so far as to experiment with the ingestion of the toxic substance carbon tetrachloride in order to experience the loss of consciousness and glimpse other dimensions of the Beyond. He then described his near-death experience at length in visual, mathematical, and acoustical detail. His early poetry, collected in *Le Contre-Ciel* (for which he received the *Prix Jacques Doucet* in 1936), reflects his desperate ardor as he grappled with the mystery of these other dimensions.

As a group, the members of Le Grand Jeu ("The Big Game") were drawn toward Eastern philosophy, but only Daumal pursued it beyond the surrealist parameters, seeking its source. At the age of sixteen, he began to study Hindu philosophy through the writings of the metaphysician, René Guénon. This led to a direct study of Hindu poetics and the Sanskrit language itself. He applied the teachings of this tradition to his literary endeavors as well as to his life. He believed that transformation could only be attained through a stripping away of personality and ego through renunciation. Although this is one of the foundations of Hinduism and Buddhism, it was hardly a current, let alone a popular idea in contemporary Western thinking. His practice of personal asceticism and self-abnegation led him to what he described as the experience of Tad Atman. This is a Vedic term for a spiritual communion between the individual soul and the great Universal Soul, resulting in an enhanced perception of the spiritual nature of reality.

In Sanskrit, the word *kavi* stands for both poet and priest. In many ancient cultures the essentially sacred nature of poetry was the domain of the priest; all poetry was basically prayer and all prayer was poetic. In one of his many essays on Hindu thought, Daumal contrasts this image with that of most European writers, whom he perceived as being temperamental and self-absorbed.

The ancient treatises on theater and poetics that he translated, the *Sahitya Darpana* by Visvanatha and the *Natya Sastra* by Bharata, describe the writing of poetry as a spiritual endeavor involving inner work. These writings suggest that if the poet is able to connect with his innermost essence, then his creative effort will achieve the true purpose of art, which is not to distract but to awaken—to awaken the reader to a higher state of consciousness. The quality of art thus attained was known as *rasa* or savor—it creates "the moment of awareness that a true work of art should evoke in whoever has an interior being," according to the *Sahitya Darpana*.[1] The presence of *rasa* brings to poetry the essential qualities of clarity, fluidity, and ardor, the qualities of water and fire so prized by the Hindu poets and also seen throughout Daumal's work.

The most pivotal event in Daumal's life was his encounter with the teachings of G. I. Gurdjieff and his associate disciples, Alexandre and Jeanne de Salzmann. These three individuals helped Daumal to deepen his understanding of Eastern teachings as they applied to his writing and his life. Although the Gurdjieff Work did not derive from Hinduism, it shared kindred theories and techniques and moved toward a shared final goal. With the guidance of living teachers, the support of fellow seekers, and a practical life discipline, Daumal was able to mature as a man and poet.

Although Surrealistic imagery abounds in both Daumal's novels, *A Night of Serious Drinking* (*La Grande Beuverie*) and *Mount Analogue*, it is Hindu philosophy and the teachings of Gurdjieff that form the raison d'être of both books. The first book is a satirical underworld tour of the modern-day intellectual elite, a surrealistic passage through "Hell" and "Purgatory." The second, *Mount Analogue*, is a short allegorical tale about a group of seekers searching for the elusive holy mountain. The imagery of his writing evolved from the dark, heavy, obscure images of *Le Contre-Ciel*, "The Counter-Heaven" (which retained its French title in the English translation), to the humorous irony of *A Night of Serious Drinking*, then finally to the bright, clear, flowing imagery of *Mount Analogue*. These three phases correspond to the three Hindu *gunas* which represent the negative, neutral, and positive aspects of reality (*tamas*, *rajas*, and *sattva*, respectively).

We can observe Daumal's growth process from the early years full of naiveté, anxiety, and curiosity, to his subsequent excessive experimentation, over-intellectualizations, disillusionment, and despair. Even as he harangued against the intellectualizing of modern thinkers, his own early writing was sometimes equally so. The Hindu writers, especially Bharata and Visvanatha, showed him avenues of expression that allowed him to communicate in a less tortured way. He learned to maintain a clearer state of mindful attention and from this state create works of art that transmitted an immediately felt experience or *rasa* to his readers.

By the end of his life, Daumal had developed a more positive view of human evolutionary potential. He was able to let go of much of his angst and found a greater peace, but he never completely abandoned his belief in the necessity for struggle and hard work. One could say Daumal had to pass through the dark night of the soul in order to climb the peak to Heaven. In his early poem "Civilization," he expressed his discouragement—"I no longer have the breath (strength or inspiration)" (*Je n'ai plus de souffle*)—but years later, after being introduced to the Gurdjieff Work through the de Salzmanns, he added a footnote to a later edition of the same poem, stating, "I have since found it" (*Je l'ai trouvé depuis*).[2]

By integrating what he perceived to be the essence of Hinduism with the teachings of Gurdjieff, Daumal was able to create original works of art channeling the most subtle expressions of spiritual reality.

To study Daumal's life is to stand at a threshold and gaze in both directions at his inner and outer life. According to Porphyrus, a threshold is a sacred place. The Hebrew mezzuzah placed on a doorpost and the special Tibetan mantra spoken at doorways reflect a universal recognition of the sacredness of passageways. Standing at this threshold, I looked to see if the deeds of Daumal's outer life reflected the writings of the inner life. I sought to maintain an objectivity about his theories and beliefs, to collect the anecdotes and opinions of his contemporaries, and to suggest theories of mine and others about his motivation, without presuming to pass judgment. From this, I hope to have distilled the essence of this remarkable man.

During the first five years of research into Daumal's life and work, I was limited to the hard-to-find printed word. Then in 1977, with the help of Lord John Pentland, and the cinematographer René Zuber, I was able to track down some of Daumal's surviving colleagues, most of whom were still actively writing.

When I went to interview these individuals, I wanted to listen with more than my ears and extract more than just the facts of Daumal's life. Consequently, neither the use of a tape recorder nor excessive note taking seemed appropriate in the presence of these individuals, all spiritual, elderly, and French "old school." Hopefully, I have transmitted the essence of their conversations.

In every case, each colleague struggled to find words to describe René. They all seemed to convey the same awe and devotion when speaking of him, which often resulted in superlatives or utter silence. They put little stock in the efficacy of words to describe the indescribable. Their testimonies all seemed to confirm that among his colleagues, Daumal was considered no ordinary man.

Daumal's teacher, Madame de Salzmann, was very open and generous, sharing her personal letters from Daumal. Being in her presence, in her own surroundings, was an opportunity to experience firsthand the energy that Daumal so revered. As she spoke of the lessons of the past, she related them to the present moment as my husband and I sat with her, then engaged us in an intense exercise of energy concentration. Jeanne de Salzmann remained a great support to all the followers of Gurdjieff's teaching up to the time of her death in 1991, at the age of 101.

Geneviève Lief met me at the Paris Mosque where we could talk over a meal of couscous. For her, René had been both teacher and patient when she took care of him during the war years. She shared letters from their extensive exchange, many of which have recently been collected in the third volume of his correspondence. In spite of failing health, she avidly followed the same spiritual path as René until her death in late 1996.

Liselle Reymond, a close friend of René, invited me on several occasions to her Tai Chi Chuan studio where we talked and practiced Tai Chi together. As the author of several firsthand accounts of her experiences with Indian culture and philosophy, including her classic work, *To Live Within*, she was a thoughtful judge of Daumal's character and accomplishments. She passed away in 1993.

Daumal's friend and colleague, Henri Tracol, a journalist who had covered the Spanish Civil War, received us in his home. In 1986, he was still teaching and writing about the Gurdjieff ideas. His current reading was the latest book of Carlos Castañeda, *The Fire Within*. He continued to meet with small groups to discuss the Gurdjieff teaching that he had adhered to for so many years, until his death in August 1997.

Another friend and colleague, Philippe Lavastine, a writer on Eastern religion, was a very animated conversationalist who revealed the personal sides of Daumal. He sketched Daumal's own sad image of himself: a balloon on a string—a brain with no body. As one of Daumal's companions in the Gurdjieff Work, he felt that Daumal had provided a tremendous support to him and others. The book-lined walls of his flat in the Quartier Saint Germain reflected his lifelong interest in literature and Eastern thought in particular. Ever a storyteller, he still found time to go and converse with the denizens of local Paris cafes. He was no longer actively involved with the Gurdjieff groups.

Claudio Rugafiorri, the primary editor of Daumal's work, and Helen Maxwell, an expert on Le Grand Jeu and coeditor of Daumal's correspondence and many books about him, both lived in garret apartments in an ancient building around the corner from Lavastine. In 1977, Rugafiorri showed me the vast library of all Daumal's handwritten manuscripts, including his Sanskrit notebooks.

Helen Maxwell also authored a book about Roger Gilbert-Lecomte and edited his correspondence as well. She was a colorful, heroic woman, passionate about the subject of these young poets. We met several times through the years. In 1986, I helped her run a stall at a Parisian book fair where Daumal's new Sanskrit dictionary was for sale. The last time I saw her, we visited the Grand Jeu exhibit at the Musée d'Art Moderne that she herself had put together. We lunched on the patio of the museum as she pointed out the little inaccuracies that had survived her scrutiny, and how, in her mind, Daumal was uniquely endowed from birth, and never needed Gurdjieff for his personal evolution. After many years of health problems, she passed away in 1994.

I first met with Jack Daumal, René's younger brother, in 1985. Upon receiving the original version of this book, he immediately began to translate it into French and seek out a publisher. It was published in 1992 by Editions José Corti, and entitled *René Daumal: au-delà de l'horizon*. In these last thirteen years, Jack's energy and intellect has been matched only by his sensitivity and care in helping to bring his brother's work to a greater audience. A deep friendship has grown from our efforts together. His wife Jacqueline entrusted me with a gold Egyptian scarab from around her neck. The shape of this sacred beetle resembles the form of the brain's cranium, with its two hemispheric cerebral lobes, yet, for the Egyptians, it also symbolized the intelligence of the heart—a knowledge that comes through merging. Hopefully this power object provided some of this corresponding intelligence needed for studying a poet like Daumal.

During a two-year stay on the island of Grenada, an acupuncture patient of mine, Dennis Malin-Smith, turned out to be the last remaining member of a Gurdjieff enclave that had thrived in the 1970s on the tiny Caribbean island of Carriacou. This enterprising group had functioned as a sort of farm and lay monastery, living according to Gurdjieff's precepts for spiritual growth. It took the violent 1977 political revolution and Communist takeover by the Cubans to bring it to an end. This wonderful old man spoke with great enthusiam and fervor about his years spent living on this self-sufficient farm. He seemed to have incorporated something alive and lasting into his being. This encounter renewed my interest in exploring the history and essence of the legacy of Gurdjieff.

During a two-year stay in Bath, England, I continued to contact many avid Daumal readers on both sides of the Channel. Since then, the original version of my book has been extensively revised and expanded for this present edition, to include recent interviews with Dr. Michel de Salzmann, Natalie de Salzmann d'Etiévan, Maurice Desselles, Jack Daumal, and his daughters, Miriam and Jijhad. I also conferred with writers and publishers interested in Daumal, such as George Quasha and Charles Stein of Station Hill Press, Barrytown, N.Y., Jean Louis Accarias of *L'Originel* and Xavier Dandoy of Editions Eolien in Paris, who were of enormous help.

I am very grateful to all these people who took the time to speak with me. Likewise, I am eternally indebted to those who helped me in the physical labor of typing, editing, and turning out the two books: Dr. David Langmuir, Virginia Parsel, Dr. Marc Lebel, Allyson Dal Ponte, Dr. Fran Shaw, Dr. Glenn Williams, Gordon Chessmar, Janet Wass, Keith Kirts, Thomas Canny, Arthur Godotti, David Applebaum, and Bernadine Dawes. I also thank those who gave me encouragement and advice: John Pentland, Lucille Pentland, Dr. Tilo Ulbricht, Dr. Jacob Needleman, Paul Reynard, Dr. Margaret Higonnet, Professor Roger Shattuck, Dr. Joseph Cary, and finally, most of all, my husband Steven and my children, Camille and Adam.

Through all these years of immersion in René Daumal's mind, his presence was often tangible. In the endless discussions about the work of this one human being, the energy that he cultivated has often been palpably felt. As I pass through this threshold, I am grateful to him for being such a faithful companion and personal guide.

A NOTE ABOUT THE TRANSLATION

I have worked primarily with the original French texts and translated them myself. Wherever possible, I have tried to provide the references for those books recently available in English and retained in some places the original French references.

I
BIOGRAPHY

1
An Anarchist of Perception

> LUC DIETRICH: How would you describe Daumal (in body and spirit) to someone who has never seen him?
>
> LANZA DEL VASTO: He resembles a vial full of moon milk into which an alchemist has placed an elf.

According to the French meteorological archives, it was a sunny, cold, thirty-degree day on March 16, 1908, when René Daumal was born in the Ardennes mountains of France, near the Belgian border. He inherited from his mother certain Mongolian facial features—slanted eyes and high, broad cheekbones—traits that were even more prominent in his elder sister Marianne. The Mongols had settled in the Ardennes mountains when they invaded Gaul in the fifth century A.D.; and consequently many Ardennais natives share these same facial features. His mother Zelie was a convivial, outgoing woman, according to René's younger brother Jack (born 1916). She had no intellectual pretensions and was an excellent cook. The three children were raised without any formal religious upbringing, for their father, Leon, a learned instructor and a politically active socialist, was also a confirmed agnostic. Jack Daumal reports that there was virtually no dissension in the family, ever. The basic integrity of his parents is evident in the brief glimpses gleaned from René's writings: "The familial anticlericalism was honored by receiving the esteem of the abbot, who in his sermons often referred to my father as the only honest man in the county even if he was an atheist and socialist."[1]

By contrast, the paternal grandfather, Antoine, with whom René was very close as a child, was more attuned to the spiritual and psychic realm. He was a healer, magician, amateur occult Mason, and beekeeper, who severed ties with the Freemasons in order to establish an occult Masonic lodge. From this distance of eighty years we will see how the strands of influence from both his father and grandfather were woven neatly together; they entwined with yet other strands and then interfaced with René's own innate nature.

In many ways Daumal's life mirrors that of his idol, the great nineteenth-century Symbolist poet Arthur Rimbaud, who was born in Charleville, very near Daumal's birthplace. As youths they had in common an intellectual precocity, a revolutionary attitude toward poetry, passionate inner lives, and premature deaths that were due in part to the effects of dangerous exploits. They both sought a language capable of translating the Absolute.

From the beginning it appears that Daumal was not quite of this world. By all accounts it appears that even as a child his gaze was turned inward. René's younger brother Jack recalls:

> At a family reunion, René remained deep in his own reflections during the meal, indifferent to everything going on around him. When a plate of food was offered to him, he did not respond. When his name was called, "René, René!" he responded, "Oui, oui," reaching out his hand, but when the plate was placed in his hands, he did not support it. He let it fall, splattering himself and everyone around him with sauce. He apologized, excused himself, went to his room, and did not appear until morning.[2]

Although his behavior might sound like typical modern teenage apathy, in 1920 in France it was regarded as very strange.

René's introversion did not preclude a deep commitment to his close friends and family. He was well known for his kindness and generosity. From his earliest years until the last days of his life, Daumal had an alert, inquisitive mind. His brother reports that René taught himself to read at age four. Upon discovering the existence of such a thing as a dictionary, he is reported to have exclaimed, "I'm saved!" As a precocious child and adolescent he read extensively, exploring traditional science, chemistry, and the occult. At age eleven, he was an avid chemist and beetle collector, displaying his treasures artistically in specially constructed boxes. His brother Jack reports that shortly before the war he presented these specimens to a primary school in Gonesse, near his parents' home.

In his 1932 Surrealist-style *Treatise of Pataphotogrammes*, he gives a brief but fascinating glimpse into his childhood imaginary world:

> Thanks to the flying machines that I kept in my attic (under a hinged roof that opened up) I have made numerous trips to my native Africa.
>
> At age ten I discerned the curvature of space according to the Einsteinian laws of astronomy, and I vanquished the fear of death that had devoured my epigastrium each night for many years. In Auvergne I frequented witches, nocturnal pigs. . . .
>
> Paris 1915. Bombardments. Basements . . . Boum Boum, like the Medrano Circus where I tried my young talents. . . . I tamed a Burgundian snail. I invented ovoid space. I had hallucinations.[3]

Daumal was a being who was often painfully aware of other dimensions of existence. He was born in a period of shifting patterns, a slackening of traditional belief and a gradually growing interest in various forms of spiritualism. A large majority of the French at that time were anti-Catholic and antireligion. (The official separation of church and state occurred in 1905, at which time the French government confiscated all the assets of the Catholic Church and expelled numerous congregations.) In this milieu, René was left to interpret his inner visions on his own. With his early exposure to his grandfather's occultism and Freemasonry and his lack of formal religious training, he took it upon himself to discover the strange "other world" alone, outside the Christian framework of a "God," "Heaven," or "Hell."

During his childhood René seemed to be unusually susceptible to oneiric influences, yet lacked the vocabulary or knowledge to describe or understand them. Furthermore, (from age six to ten) he lived close to World War I's worst battlegrounds. Jack Daumal wrote in a recent letter that his parents succeeded in sparing them the worst echoes of the war. Yet their elder sister, Marianne (ten years René's senior), was traumatized by the bombardments and haunted by memories of "Big Bertha," the large cannon that repeatedly bombarded Paris, Liège, and other nearby cities. René never spoke of having suffered from war-provoked anxiety, and yet his early childhood experiences of the "Infinite" often occurred as terrifying nighttime encounters. For him, God equaled not love but terror or death. Lacking the support of ordinary religion, which might have calmed him and allayed his fears, he channeled all that intensity into an obsession with death; this seemed to be the only state in close approximation to the Infinity for which he yearned. Later, in his essays and letters, he refers to the physical experience of the terror-filled "Infinite," likening it to a rope tightened around his stomach. In one essay, "On the Life of Basiles," he writes:

> A childhood without religious upbringing put me prematurely face to face with the fear of death. It was, as I finally realized, a tightening in the pit of my stomach, which a simple relaxation of the abdominal muscles could dispel. Then the tightening went up into the chest in the form of a knot of dread, then further up to the brain in the form of a problem: to be or not to be? This tightening turned over and over in my brain, and remained there for a good number of years. It proliferated in metaphysical speculation and almost resulted in complete decapitation.[4]

During the war years (1914–1918), the Daumal family eventually left the Ardennes, which were dangerously close to the war front, and relocated several times in different parts of France. Finally they sought refuge in Paris, where René's father Léon accepted a position with the Ministry of Finance. After completing several dangerous and delicate missions to areas devastated by war, Léon Daumal requested transfer to the nearly destroyed region around Charleville and Reims.

At age eleven, René attended the Lycée Chanzy in Charleville (Rimbaud's birthplace) from 1919 to 1922. His classmate Luc Périn described him as

> very calm, even phlegmatic. He talked very little and was not interested in ball games. He was not outgoing but with his close friends he was charming and funny. There was a particular expression about his smile although I never saw him laugh. The originality and quality of his humor struck me. I did not know at the time nor did he, that this variety of humor was called black humor.[5]

In 1921, when René was thirteen years old, he entered the lycée at Reims. There he established what were to become lifelong friendships with Roger Gilbert-Lecomte, Robert Meyrat, and Roger Vailland. In a city more than half destroyed by war, these four boys passed their adolescence exploring ancient churches and abandoned war ruins, always on the lookout not only for adventure but for examples of curious architectural detail and obscure symbolism. They shared a common mania for escapades, farce, and subversive prankery, yet this did not impinge upon their scholastic achievement. They were not typical of the *âge ingrat*, the ungrateful, unfruitful teenage years. All four were budding young intellectuals and poets—high-spirited, with a flair for the bizarre and a growing disregard for societal norms.

Daumal described the experience of being the new kid at the lycée: "The others scared me. I was the tooth that hadn't yet broken through the gums, the future gunshot through attic windows, a hard working, sad, good little boy, given to infernal debauches of reveries in his solitude."[6] Robert Meyrat, the only surviving member of the group of four friends, described the impact that René's arrival had on himself and the others:

> [His arrival] completely changed everything. We had been nothing more than three jokers. René brought our minds together and was the catalyst for the group. He taught us how to view things from a much deeper point of view. In spite of his dreamy, expressionless demeanor, he thought and saw much further than we did, and he got us to read new things—Maeterlinck, Alfred Jarry, Rimbaud, authors that were not yet accepted by the academic syllabus—and to reflect on problems that had been foreign to us.[7]

As the group of four began to gain notoriety for their strange behavior, they decided to change tactics: they would present a conventional exterior so as to be free to pursue unconventional avenues of thought and behavior, unfettered by professors and less adventurous classmates. They continued to rank highest in class (since they collaborated on homework assignments) but no longer expressed their unusual ideas in their written work. Instead they discussed their true interests among themselves, and, according to Meyrat, the most original ideas usually came from René. At one point the group inaugurated their own secret society, which they called "Les Phrères Simplistes," a name derived from the spelling technique of one of their heroes, the earliest absurdist, avant-garde writer Alfred Jarry (1873–1907). As Simplistes, they sought to attain the intuitive and spontaneous simplicity of childhood. They established special codes and elaborate rites that fortified their bond. Their experimental projects included astral projection, telepathy, extra-retinal vision, lucid dreaming, meeting in planned dreams, and automatic writing. They sought to explore disassociated, intoxicated mind states that they referred to in "Simpliste" terms as "le Maelstrom pigmé" ("the pygmied Maelstrom").

The group grew in size and cohesiveness as the years went by. In a letter to Maurice Henry, a young poet about to join the group in 1926, René (now eighteen years old) disclosed his admiration for his friends, especially the brilliant, charismatic Lecomte, leader of the group. He describes how shy he himself had been at first, intimidated and yet irresistibly drawn to these three eccentric companions:

> When they named me "Nathaniel," I recognized my father in the one they call Lecomte; the two others [Meyrat and Vailland] were my brothers. Little resemblance in bodies and character, but a thousand mystical affinities rapidly bonded us together: childhood dreams or a sudden word would set off the resonance of four souls, long silences of the four of us together when the Being regenerated by our union took us as witnesses of its happiness. Then the discovery that we were angels, "agglutinated angels." Angel brothers or perhaps a single angel in four bodies. Our union was an accelerated gravitation of the four cardinal points of one soul, and the resplendent cohesion of a star being born.[8]

The Simpliste aim was to attain a kind of astral state, be it postmortal or prenatal. They saw themselves as visionary angels without bodies of flesh. Meyrat, in a 1978 interview, said: "We weren't angels, but we did not have flesh-and-blood bodies, in the sense that we forbade ourselves to talk about any physical contingencies; we never mentioned being hungry or sick."[9] For the most part, Daumal carried this stoic tendency to his death.

Drawing on the strength of their homogeneity, the four proclaimed their fundamental axiom, "the imbecility of individualism."[10] Their affirmation of the collective soul was realized by a whole fabric of interpersonal relations, special rites, obscure jargon, and clever, cryptic letters. In a 1927 letter, Daumal wrote, "Simplism is a religion of which all members are heretics."[11]

As for the attitude of the Simplistes toward religion, Daumal wrote:

> Rites and doctrines, you need them—rite: rhythm of life, proof that one gives oneself one's faith and liberty. We have created, or rather, they were born naturally from our union—doctrines: our reading of the mystics (Vaisya, St. Teresa, Swedenborg, the

theosophists, etc.) was a shock that clarified the revealed word. Through diverse symbols, according to the various races, all religions teach several great ideas that we recognize. (Vailland prefers the Christian language; Lecomte and I, the Buddhist language; Meyrat, primordial agnosticism.) But the dogmatic formulas are of secondary interest to us.[12]

In 1924, at age sixteen, René's childhood obsession with the Void and his desire to "possess" death led him to ingest the toxic substance carbon tetrachloride, an experience he describes in two later essays. This hallucinatory experience validated for him the existence of a greater reality, one that has been described by mystics, seers, and poets throughout the ages. He believed he had finally touched "une révélation sensible" (a felt, tangible revelation). For him it was a firsthand experience of what he called the "Absurd Evidence" (or "absurd obviousness") of another world. (The term *L'Evidence Absurde* was later chosen as the title of the first volume of Daumal's essays, published in 1972.) His experimentation with various drugs is alluded to in *A Night of Serious Drinking* (*La Grande Beuverie*), where he disparages "the beatific mummification via opium, the theatrical and turbulent transmutation of everything by hashish, the respiratory vertigo of cocaine, the metaphysical dizziness of ether, and the disintegrating effects of several other drugs."[13]

Through a natural gift for experiencing superordinary dimensions of reality, sometimes through the addition of psyche-enhancing drugs, he saw that this earthly existence for the average person has become "unglued" or disconnected from its heavenly counterpart, its greater half. He had a vision of the two halves making a whole, the fusion of opposites that make up the greater reality that he sought after all his life. Perhaps because of his agnostic upbringing, he turned toward a purely spiritual view of existence that was far removed from any traditional religious viewpoint. Ribemont-Dessaignes, another Surrealist poet who defected and allied himself with Le Grand Jeu, quoted Daumal as saying, "Je suis religieux à me faire tuer,"[14] which translates as "I am religious enough to be the death of me." He sought only after the Absolute.

After finishing his baccalaureate at age seventeen, René entered another lycée, Henry IV in Paris, in October 1925, where he established a friendship with his classmate Simone Weil. Here he began preparing for the qualifying examinations for entrance into the prestigious Ecole Normale Supérieure while his family remained in Reims. (They later moved to Paris to be closer to him.) In June 1927, just prior to the exam,

René suffered a temporary bout of amnesia caused by a fall while doing gymnastics. Because of this he failed the examination. This seemingly unfortunate incident played a definitive role in shaping his life and changing his destiny, allowing him to pursue "free" studies in philosophy at the Sorbonne. He would later regard the accident as very "fortuitous." He enrolled at the Sorbonne in October 1927, and earned one certificate in psychology and another in ethics and sociology.

While studying in Paris, he enlarged his horizons further by making contact with the artistic avant-garde of Montparnasse, yet he continued a lively correspondence with his friends in Reims and frequently returned to visit them. In *Le Quotidien des Livres*, Jean-Jacques Levêque reviewed an earlier French edition of the present book, and discussed Daumal's vast poetically sophisticated correspondence with the Simplistes: They were "the fiery horsemen of the absolute who smashed themselves on the hard exigencies of life. It was a correspondence oscillating between humoristic rebus, coded signs, and hidden references, a kind of stock car race where the friendships of these provincial Rimbauds criss-crossed and chased each other."[15] Ever in league with one another, their escapades continued. They began to refer to themselves as "Pataphysicians," that is, students of Alfred Jarry's "Pataphysics," an absurdist worldview defined as the "science of imaginary solutions."[16] For the next seven years, the Simplistes continued to delve into literary and parapsychological research, exploring the subtle relationship between the visible and invisible worlds. Vailland referred to the group as "anarchists of perception."

They were all in their late teens when they published the first of three issues of a literary journal called *Le Grand Jeu*. In it they proclaimed their intention to "make men despair of themselves and society for from this massacre of hope will be born a Hope, pitiless and bleeding. To become eternal by refusing to merely survive."[17] Given their age, this intense quest for eternity was remarkable. Their efforts spawned a review that was acknowledged by the Parisian intelligentsia. Yet even within this group of educated and ardent young writers, Daumal stood out as having a distinct passion. There was a driving quality to his search. He, more than the other members of Le Grand Jeu, provided the key intellectual ideas, the religious fervor, and the motivating force to complete the endeavor.

During this three-year period Daumal experimented with narcotic and hallucinogenic substances. Like Aldous Huxley and the poet Henri Michaux, his intention was to somehow comprehend their chemical effects on his brain. René soon realized that this method could not work to advance him on his chosen path. He eventually gave up the use of drugs and strove to heal his psyche and resolve his metaphyical quandaries within a supportive intellectual community of artists, writers, and free thinkers.

Many writers interested in Daumal have exaggerated the extent of his drug taking. According to his brother, his usage was minimal and always used as a tool for his inner vision. Very early on he became an antidrug proponent. In one of his final visits with his brother Jack, then involved in planning postwar education reform, René declared: "and above all, you must warn the youth against mind-altering drugs. Some of the best and most superior young people are lost through these drugs."[18]

As the thirties approached, René embarked upon a period of prolific literary production within a supportive intellectual community of artists, writers, and free thinkers. His group Le Grand Jeu remained committed and intact until 1932. All through these years, Daumal truly believed in the magical effect of their camaraderie and their mission as a group. He put great energy into guiding the group through its endeavors, especially the publication of *Le Grand Jeu*. He was not afraid to act in the world, but neither was he caught up in it. In later years, Daumal would look back on this period with amusement and even scorn, as if it were all part of an adolescent lark; yet many of the seminal ideas that became crucial to his adult thinking were beginning to germinate during this period and only later found richer, more mature soil in which to take root and flower.

In Daumal's youth, his fascination with death fostered a rather cavalier attitude toward the value of life. Like many young people who feel invincible in their teens, Daumal was fearless and reckless in the face of dangerous challenges. The physical body was expendable; only the spirit mattered. Everything that he undertook had a spiritual aim. As a teenager he seemed to have had the selflessness and detachment of an aged sage. Apparently he was freer from the usual driving force of the ego. This lack of ego involvement allowed him to identify much less than most people with his surroundings, associates, and belongings. Instead, he viewed them as very detachable extensions of himself. The energy usually spent in bolstering and protecting the ego seems to have been available to him for other intellectual and psychic pursuits, in a manner unusual for someone so young. At age seventeen, René went through a psychological crisis, but it did not seem to stem from the usual life concerns of lost love, poor self-image, competition, or personal ambition. His crisis stemmed from his distress at the futility of the existence that he was expected to pursue. He was extremely disenchanted with the current bourgeois structure of society and hated the capitalist goal of self-aggrandizement. He looked at the lifelong race to create a career, family, wealth, pleasure, and satisfaction and considered it trivial and absurd. He felt that there was a greater purpose for man's life on Earth.

During this period in Paris, the dominant influence on Daumal's world view came from his study of Hindu poetics and philosophy, begun in 1922. This fostered in him a rich appreciation for Eastern mystical thought as he attempted to synthesize Eastern and Western ideas in his essays for *Le Grand Jeu*. He continued to view these traditions through a political lens and was hypercritical of the priestly caste and the secular influence on pure religious thought. But gradually he dwelt less on the final outcome of popular religion and more on the original texts. He became engrossed in René Guénon's books on Indian thought, such as *An Introduction to the Study of Hindu Doctrines* and *Man and His Becoming According to Vedanta*. This interest was shared by his colleagues, though he alone proceeded to study Sanskrit. Through rigorous discipline, he was soon able to translate sections of ancient Sanskrit texts, including the Vedas, the Upanishads, and the *Bhagavad Gita*. This achievement earned for him the admiration of the top Sanskrit scholar, Renou. Some of these translations, as well as various essays on Hindu thought, have been collected into a single book entitled *Bharata: L'Origine du Théâtre, la Poésie et la Musique Hindoues* (1970). Later, in 1982, this collection became available in English, published under the title *Rasa*, with a new edition soon to appear.

In deciphering Sanskrit, Daumal believed he had discovered his mother tongue. He meant this in a double sense: he saw Sanskrit as the mother of all languages, one based on a scientifically constructed grammar, making it the prototypic link between sound and meaning for all Indo-European languages. He also found in Sanskrit a "matrix" (Latin: womb) that gave meaning to other aspects of his life. The ancient writers he translated described the mysteries of life that interested him most: the interaction of the inner and outer worlds and how that affects the development of one's soul. He learned that the idea of renunciation and self-abnegation that came so naturally to him was a recurring theme spanning over two millennia of Hindu writings and could be understood on many levels. For some it meant an actual rejection of home and family and a formally structured discipleship. For others it encompassed a more subtle form of self-abnegation and did not include a withdrawal from the world, but rather an internal awakening concomitant with a renewed way of seeing reality. Daumal discovered in the area of poetics and language that ancient Indian sages had already explored this full range of nuance. By comparison, Daumal felt that the attempts of the European Surrealists to forge a new language were merely pale reflections of an earlier, nearly perfect bridging of sound and sense that had been expertly realized by Sanskrit poets.

Daumal's gradual penetration of the Vedic mysteries resulted in a diminished sense of anguish and despair in his own writings, and an expanded feeling of fulfillment and serenity. As he entered his early twenties, Daumal became a veritable disciple of these ancient Hindu teachings. The only thing lacking was a living teacher. In his search for such a person, Daumal became the press agent for an Indian dance group led by Uday Shankar, a master dancer and elder brother of the musician Ravi Shankar who also danced in the troupe. In two essays, Daumal expressed his awe before "the immemorial beauty" of Shankar's dance and "Shankar's perfect control of the 450 muscles of his body."[19] But the teacher he finally chose to follow was not an Indian at all, but rather a Georgian artist of German origin named Alexandre de Salzmann, himself a proponent of the teachings of G. I. Gurdjieff. For Daumal the "Gurdjieff Work" seemed to synthesize essential teachings of both Eastern and Western esoteric traditions. Since he had come to the conclusion that the core of Hindu teaching was essentially one with that of all great religious traditions including Christianity, Judaism, Islam, Taoism, and Buddhism, the teachings of Gurdjieff gave Daumal a practical method along with a well-defined theory of development.

In *The Heart of Philosophy* Dr. Jacob Needleman[20] describes how a seeker must go beyond the realm of philosophy and accept the next level of inquiry: self-confrontation. Here a guide or "school" is indispensable in order to overcome the transitory concerns of the ego. For Daumal it was time to give up struggling on his own and learning only through books and to start working directly with a teacher. This suited Daumal well and he eventually shed his feelings of alienation from the world and learned to use the external world to nourish his inner life. Working toward this aim with a small group of committed people provided an environment for him conducive to spiritual awakening.

In November 1932, as Le Grand Jeu began to run out of funds and energy, its members convened for what was to be their last meeting. One week later, Daumal left Paris to spend four months on the road with Uday

Shankar's dance troupe as they toured the United States. This was the first tour ever by an Indian dance troupe in Europe and America. Upon his return, Daumal reentered the Sorbonne to complete his *License de Lettres* and reestablished his friendship with the woman who was to become his wife, Vera Milanova. Shortly thereafter he was drafted into military service. Several letters from his father refer to the latter's efforts to arrange a deferment. After three months, he was released due to ill health.

Back in Paris and now in his mid-twenties, Daumal was recognized as a serious poet, essayist, critic, and philosopher. His work was published in the leading journals of the day—*Bifur, Variétiés, Les Cahiers du Sud, La Nouvelle Revue Française,* and *Commerce*—but his true consecration came with the inclusion of his writings in the prestigious *Anthologie des Philosophes Contemporains,* published in 1931.

Throughout 1934 and 1935, Daumal wrote a regular column of short reviews and anecdotes on the contemporary Parisian scene for the *Nouvelle Revue Française.* He also wrote a regular page-long commentary on what he found to be absurd scientific discoveries, called "Pataphysics This Month." In 1936 he began working for *l'Encyclopédie Française,* preparing the first eleven volumes to appear before the war. Because of his erudition in several fields, including natural and human science and mathematics, he was given the task of transcribing and editing scientific data. He translated numerous texts such as *Death in the Afternoon* by Hemingway and three volumes of Suzuki's *Zen Buddhism* from English to French. Several of his essays were published in French journals and reviews. Concurrently, he continued working on his compilation of Sanskrit poetics, a monumental undertaking that was finally published posthumously in 1985 under the title *La Langue Sanscrite.* In 1936, twenty of the sixty poems that he had written over the previous decade were collected and published in *The Counter-Heaven* (*Le Contre-Ciel*). For this he won the Prix Jacques Doucet, awarded by the eminent writers Paul Valery, André Gide, and Jean Giraudoux. Part of the award consisted in the publication of the book one year later. *A Night of Serious Drinking* (*La Grande Beuverie*), a caustically humorous tale in which Daumal satirizes our modern-day professional and artistic elite, came out two years later.

Even in his pursuit of income work, in such varied avenues as writing, editing, and translating, Daumal always sought out pieces that would expand his knowledge of the world and the inner world of man. He continued to pass through several developmental phases, each with its own particular characteristics. Certain themes remained constant, reflecting his lifelong interests: the relentless inner search for gnosis—the indirect, experiential knowledge of reality and the renunciation of outward manifestations—in order to attain what he perceived to be a heightened state of Oneness with the universe.

⁓✣⁓

In his personal life René enjoyed a close bond with his family and was particularly fond of his younger brother Jack. Since he shared his father's radical political viewpoints he never felt the need to rebel against his family.

As an adolescent and young man René was generally indifferent to romance. Yet, according to Natalie de Salzmann d'Etiévan, the daughter of Alexandre and Jeanne, René was in love with a young classmate in Reims during his early teenage years. René confided to Natalie many years later that one day, as his train pulled into Reims, he had a sudden feeling that this girl was no longer alive. In effect, his mother was awaiting his arrival with the sad news that the girl had died unexpectedly the previous day.

After this relationship, the only other woman in his life was Vera Milanova. She was born in Siberia, the daughter of an exiled Jewish revolutionary intellectual. As a journalist and teacher, she was a supportive member of Le Grand Jeu along with her first husband, the poet Hendrik Kramer. As the friendship developed, and after her marriage dissolved in 1929, she gradually fell in love with Daumal and vigorously pursued the pensive poet. Eventually he became extremely attached to her. From 1931 onward, she joined Daumal in becoming more and more actively involved with the Gurdjieff teaching. Conversations with Gallimard editor Claudio Rugafiori and with Daumal's colleague Philippe Lavastine in 1977 suggest that his relationship with Vera was primarily a deep love between soul mates. Only in one poem, "Mémorables," does he refer to the concept of earthly love and it is clear in the context of this autobiographical poem that he is referring to his own experience with Vera.

> Remember that love triumphed when she and you learned how to submit yourselves to its jealous fire, praying to die in the same flame. But remember that love belongs to no one, that in your heart of flesh there is no one, that the sun belongs to no one, blush while regarding the quagmire of your heart.[21]

In 1932, his position with Uday Shankar's dance troupe allowed him to join her in the United States. He returned after four months, while she stayed on eleven months with her family. Daumal exhibited an obvious distress when they were separated for long periods during their relationship. In September 1932 he wrote to her "Verachka, ma Sohehinah," "Ma Vivante, ma Vraie Vera" ("My living, my true Vera"), and described spending hours with his brother Jack in the Hindu rooms of the Guimet Museum of Oriental Art, then added, "Vera Vera Vera your name dances in my head until I become dizzy." Two pages later he spoke of the difficult period of her absence and added:

> During that period when you were truly absent, I could not think about you with this continuity (like air that one breathes) as I do now. Then it was more like sudden violent blows which tightened my heart, sometimes with a kind of rage: thus more passionately (in the exact meaning of the word) and painfully. Today your light looks down at me and bathes me always.[22]

They voluntarily separated for one year in order to test the strength of their bond and subsequently found that their relationship was still strong. According to Lavastine, René and Vera completed each other very well. Since René was often off writing somewhere secluded, she would use a whistle to call him to lunch. When Vera tried whistling for Lavastine, he retorted, "Ah non!! You can whistle for your husband, but not for me!"[23] Daumal, on the other hand, explained to Lavastine that he saw absolutely no offense in being whistled for, and that it was a perfectly fine arrangement. Lavastine saw this as an example of René's supreme intelligence and lack of egoism.

Vera was a hardheaded, blunt woman who protected her gentle poet husband. If the Gallimard editors failed to pay him for his translations, he would never ask them for payment. It was she who hounded the publishers to collect his writing fees. Through all the hardships their bond grew in strength. Jack Daumal feels that if Vera had been able to have children, it would have forced René to deal more effectively with the material and practical aspects of life in order to better support a family.

※

It is difficult to summarize Daumal's early character and personality with only his work, his letters, and anecdotal information available to us. Sometimes there are seeming paradoxes when his subtle humor is juxtaposed with his apparent shyness, or his political vehemence with his expressionless demeanor. His friends and Grand Jeu colleagues have left poignant descriptions of him.

André Rolland de Renéville wrote:

> When I first met René Daumal in 1928, I was struck initially by his beautiful face, oval and immobile. In spite of his silence and modest demeanor he gave me an impression of extreme superiority. I noticed that the most ordinary among our group could not help but feel a certain timidity at his approach. In effect, it was not possible to interact with him without feeling suddenly deprived of one's mask. In speaking with him, one suddenly became sincere with one's self and with him.[24]

The writer Monny de Boully was a former Dadaist and Surrealist who went over to the Grand Jeu camp in 1929. He does not mince words in describing Daumal's character:

> Daumal was what one calls a saint, a pure being, an angel. Never did Daumal say "Impossible, I can't, I don't have the time, I'm tired." Never, never, NEVER. Such that those who loved him felt a reticence to speak because we knew that he would never refuse anything that was asked of him. No one could ask him for money since he had none. He would have just enough to get a train back to his parents' home in Gonesse. But naturally, no one was too shy to ask him for the help of a higher order. I asked him for many things in my life, essential things. He never spared any effort.[25]

Daumal's exceptional qualities emerge, yet it is hard to isolate the causal factors that might explain them. Like most "saints," his extreme lack of concern about the physical plane of existence caused unnecessary damage to his body, in particular his teeth, ears, and lungs. From a medical point of view, according to the paradigm of classical homeopathic diagnosis, Daumal had the symptoms of a constitutional tubercular type. He had a severe tubercular miasm (predisposition) that in his case, was aggravated by the inhalation of carbon tetrachloride. Many individuals can carry this miasm for years and transmit it to succeeding generations without ever contracting tuberculosis. One sample profile of the tubercular type is often the brainy, disembodied romantic who burns himself out by forgetting to live on Earth and take care of himself. This seems to apply to Daumal's absorption with the life of the spirit and his total disregard for health concerns.

The implication of his nickname may throw some light on his personality. His friends called him Nathaniel, a name coined for him by Lecomte, and based on Nathaniel, the main character in André Gide's *Les Nourritures Terrestres* (*The Fruits of the Earth*). In this novel, Nathaniel was a spiritual seeker who has frequent dialogues with his elder teacher. In the early days of Daumal's friendship with Lecomte, the latter was the bolder father figure for René, the "Papa" to René's "Nathaniel." In many of his letters to his wife and close friends, Daumal signed his name as "Nath" or "Natha," even well into his thirties. Since *Les Nourritures Terrestres*, published in 1897, was the "Bible" or underground classic of an entire earlier generation of students, it had a great effect on Daumal and his peers. When, at age seventeen, he took the name Nathaniel, he fit the description in the book of the perennial listener, the archetypal student, soaking up any information he could gather about the secret of life.

In *Les Nourritures Terrestres*, Gide provides a poetic vision of how God is in the world and everything is God: "Nathaniel, the only way to talk about God is naturally."[26] The book is filled with precepts on the art of what Gide called "la disponibilité" ("openness" or "readiness")—always being receptive to God in the world. This is perhaps the first of Daumal's encounters with a nondualist philosophy. "Understand that at each instant of the day you can possess God in his totality. Let your vision be new in each instant. The wise man is he who is surprised at everything."[27] These are insights that seem to have been impressed upon Daumal's being; Daumal was the ingenuous Nathaniel, spontaneous in his response to many layers of meaning in the world around him.

A 1927 letter to Richard Weiner provides a glimpse of the buoyant yet sensitive side of Daumal.

> All is well and I am happy. With the same facility that I cross from one sidewalk to another—while the street remains the same—I now leave Paris and Roger to join you: I sketch out a tango step as I cross the street. I laugh a lot in the cafés, writing short ineptitudes while waiting for Roger. You would never suspect how much Roger and I can laugh. I also have overwhelming moments of sad happiness at the sight of certain insignificant objects: a white wall, a flower, a cloud or dead leaf; a pebble or a piece of string that I hold in my hand can become

a very dear friend. That distracts me a lot from working, but so what.[28]

Given his psychic sensitivities, which we will discuss later, it is most likely that here he was not only responding to the literary and metaphysical symbolism of these images but also to the beauty, physicality, and magnetic frequencies of the actual substances.

Why was he so able to perceive the other spiritual dimensions of reality in the midst of his daily life? Why was he so unsatisfied with the common pursuit of happiness? One of the reasons was that he was not a very sensual, pleasure-oriented person. Except for some tender words written to his wife, nowhere in his writings is there a hint of romance or frivolity. It is not to say that he was sullen or morose; but in his writing Daumal was never interested in depicting the ordinary, personal aspects of life—man's personal joys and woes—except as they contributed to his allegories. Although he enjoyed deep spiritual bonds with his friends and with Vera, as evidenced in his letters, he rarely discussed personal relationships. Even in his later works, his two most well-developed characters—"Totochabo" in *A Night of Serious Drinking* and "Sogol" in *Mount Analogue*—are both teacher figures, fleshed out sufficiently to serve as sources of great wisdom. With minimal brushstrokes Daumal sketches in just enough details to project the power and essence of these two men. Likewise, another, fainter personage, Mugle, is the main character/teacher figure, and the title of a 1927 short story, "Mugle," published as a novella in 1978. The narrator/protagonists of these stories are even more ambiguous with their vague, ever-changing identities. Thus one sees that Daumal's characters are deliberately allegorical figures—mouthpieces for expressing an important message. The ordinary life of the narrators as mere human beings was either satirized or omitted altogether.

Daumal blatantly rejected human sentimentality and voluptuousness in his poetry. He never composed poetry about purely sensual or naturalist themes. Yet he borrowed earthy, visceral language to discuss his obsession with the beyond. In contrast, André Gide writes: "Each perfect action is accompanied by voluptuousness. TO BE became enormously voluptuous for me. I wanted to taste all the forms of life, those of fish and plants. Of all the joys of the senses, I most envied that of touching."[29]

Yet, for Daumal, under the influence of the Hindu philosopher Sankhya, the world of the senses was an illusion, a source of distraction from the concentration on one's interior being. In contrast to Gide, he wrote: "Everything we adore is a cadaver, except God; the idols to which I give my life."[30] And in the poem "Nénie" he wrote:

> Speak no more of plains with that tenderness
> Speak no more of snows, speak no more of the heart
> [and the incantatory phrase "speak no more" repeats another eight times].[31]

From childhood onward, Daumal the nature lover was not impervious to the loveliness of the physical world, but he never wrote of it until the late thirties—in *Mount Analogue*, in one poem, and in some letters. His distrust of the material world, so inculcated by the Hindu Sankhya philosophy, gradually abated as his understanding matured. Just as his physical health began to waver, he returned to the nature-loving tendencies of his earliest years. He began to appreciate the physical plane of existence, seeing it as a legitimate source of inspiration for inner development.

There are some letters, dating from 1938 onward, where he praises the joy of mountain climbing and describes the mountain scenery. Published in the periodical *Argile* in 1977, "Lettres de la montagne" (1938–1941) expresses the excitement of mountain climbing and the beauty of the landscape. He describes in minute detail the scenery, flowers, food, alpine skills and techniques, and his emotional responses to all of them. In a letter to his friend, the Surrealist poet Jean Paulhan, we find one of Daumal's pagelong, action-filled sentences where he alludes to the beauty before him:

> hoist yourself, secure the rope, pull up, shout "I made it to the top," undo the ropes, dry them out, have a drink, have a snack, drink in the entire countryside, 'til it could make you cry, remain in perfect silence, name the peaks, point out Mont Blanc . . . (etc.).[32]

In another letter to Vera, Daumal exclaims in capital letters: "THE RHODODENDRONS! Finally I see the Rhododendrons in bloom."[33] Then he discusses them for five lines and sketches them freehand in the margin. But this renewed earthly delight was yet another vehicle for an expansion of his visionary capacities. Mountain climbing allowed him to be alone, above everything earthly, breathing a more rarefied metaphysical air.

Emile Dermenghen described his last visit with René, at the foot of the highest mountains of Daughiné.

René passionately loved the mountain, with a love both physical and metaphysical. Although his body was already affected by illness, it seemed to gain relief and a definite freedom from mountain climbing. He had just made a solitary effortless climb of the Barre des Ecrins; nobody could believe it possible. He came down the mountain as if from Sinai or Tabor, his vision purified from the snow; or from Mount Meru, center and pillar of the world, the immutable axis around which circles the multiplicity of appearances.[34]

Yet Liselle Reymond, a close friend of Daumal, would later assert that even in the 1940s Daumal was not at all rooted in the material plane. Liselle Reymond had lived many years in India and was an authority on Hinduism, a teacher of Tai Chi Chuan, and later a follower of the Gurdjieff teaching. In several interviews with me in 1977 and 1983, she took issue with the premise that Daumal was interested in total renunciation. She insisted over and over that he had nothing to renounce, nothing to give up because he was interested only in God. During the war, he shared a villa in Provence with Reymond and her husband, writer and publisher Jean Herbert, an authority on India and to whose publications Daumal contributed various articles. Reymond described how Daumal would drill her on Sanskrit vocabulary, saying a new word for each row of crops and vines that they would pass. She reported that his intense search never let up for a moment, a dogged study to uncover his truer, inner self.

Likewise, during my interviews with him in 1977 and 1983, the writer Philippe Lavastine recounted his memories of René and incidents that shed light on some of Daumal's character traits. In 1931, Lavastine was anxious to meet the author of the intriguing journal *Le Grand Jeu*, but the quiet, self-effacing Daumal was not at all what he expected. Daumal had little interest in discussing *Le Grand Jeu*. He referred to it all as merely "des betises et des mensonges" (stupidities and lies), and told Lavastine not to bother with it. Instead, he urged him to accompany him and Vera to a lecture that same evening given by Alexandre de Salzmann. After the lecture, de Salzmann discussed Gurdjieff's ideas of the cosmos with them until nine o'clock the following morning. Immediately, Lavastine was drawn into the Gurdjieff Work and they became close friends.

This was Lavastine's first exposure to Daumal's inimitable ability to just listen. Lavastine ascribes his vast intelligence and store of knowledge in great part to this single ability. He was the archetypal listener. Lavastine felt that he himself talked all the time so that he never listened enough or wrote very much.

> Daumal was not a man full of himself; he was empty of himself. Thus he could listen—there was room inside for something to enter. Daumal and [the Surrealist leader] André Breton, although very different from each other, had one thing in common: neither man spoke much. Both men could write all night, yet I would often have to force responses out of René.
> Even at meetings with Madame de Salzmann or Gurdjieff, he would not ask many questions. He listened, then actively practiced what he learned. On the other hand, when he did speak, he could encapsulate such and such a person or situation in one sentence. He had "la dent dure" ("a hard tooth"), that is, he was incisive and harshly honest.[35]

Lavastine reported that Daumal was not particularly concerned about money matters. Before the war, it did not matter much if he had little ambition to earn money, but during the privations of the war years, in failing health, he had to work very hard for little recompense. Lavastine recounts how his extreme penury was matched only by his intense honesty and fear of imposing on friends. One night he walked seven miles in the snow rather than ask a friend for train fare. It seemed to Lavastine that René was following the Hindu concept of *vinaya* (discipline and humility), which Lavastine (who lived in India and wrote extensively about it) felt was one of the most valuable elements in Hinduism.

Finally, Lavastine felt that what most characterized Daumal, besides his intelligence, humility, and ability to listen, was his extreme sense of continual wonder. He quoted Aristotle: "The wise man is he who is amazed at everything!"—the same phrase incorporated by Gide into Les Nourritures Terrestres (a phrase that had affected me in my life and that I too had applied to Daumal). Lavastine saw him as a child first perceiving the phenomena of the world.

Monny de Boully gives another personal recollection of Daumal's character:

> In the world of experimental metaphysics, Daumal had something special, a "neo-will," a "super-will" or power to affect things. He was an absolute master. Even in a drug state or in a dangerous experiment, he had the innate power to decide to stop.

I saw this when I worked with him daily. He was never one who just slid down a slope. He was more and more the master of himself, more and more a master at putting on the brakes. You would have to have known him as well as I did to realize how much power he had, because in day-to-day living he was *absolutely* at your service. At your service for the most humble tasks, no matter what his state of fatigue, extreme, apparent or real. If you expressed the least sign of lassitude, he would say, "No, relax, I'll do it for you." Daumal never refused any request for assistance or help, he was "disponibilité totale" ("complete readiness") constantly. He was the "supernatural incarnated." He is the only person in my whole life that appeared to me disincarnate and I still have a burning and shining memory of this. Daumal, with his extremely peaceful demeanor, his round face, a certain suppleness, almost acrobatic yet never "performing." He would climb trees like a squirrel and he knew how to perform all sorts of feats and slights of hand that bordered on actual yoga, but he never showed off. He did it with humor, and a humor specifically his own. And Daumal could always say "no." At any moment he could stop and leave. Whatever the situation, he was present to himself. He is the most present human being that I ever met.[36]

In conversations with me, Maurice Desselle, an old friend of René and an authority on the Gurdjieff teaching, gives an interesting historical glimpse of his connection with Daumal. Desselle had been actively involved with the Surrealists and with politics, while he pursued his studies. Upon meeting Daumal in 1925, he was immediately impressed by "the limpid rigor" of his intelligence. He exchanged letters with Daumal, followed his career, and read all his works. Upon his return to Paris he would have contacted Daumal except for one obstacle: Daumal's apparent opposition to Krishnamurti. Deselle had met Krishnamurti, an encounter which totally changed his life, turning him away from politics to follow a strictly spiritual path. He then met Madame de Salzmann through his neighbor, Philippe Lavastine. When he joined her group on the rue de Four, Madame placed him under Vera's direction to prepare him for the movements class. In a recent letter to me he wrote, "At this point to my great astonishment, I discovered that my old friend Daumal, formerly communist to the teeth, had followed the same strange itinerary as I."

Daumal and Vera worked closely with Alexandre de Salzmann in Paris during the early 1930s. De Salzmann remains for us today an illusive figure with very little written work extant. Born in 1874 into an aristocratic family from the Balkan provinces, his family moved to Georgia where his father became the chief administrator and architect of the city of Tiblisi. One of seven children, he was kidnapped by brigands as a child and returned to his family several weeks later. After completing his studies in Tiblisi, he spent many years in Munich, the center of arts and letters for all of Eastern Europe. Closely aligned with the poet Rainer Maria Rilke, he painted, exhibited, and did cover illustrations for two principal avant-garde reviews, *Jugend* and *Simplicissimus*. He was an authority on lighting and stage design, having patented a lighting installation in Hellerau, Germany, that was destroyed in World War II. In order to give a brief glimpse of the man's spirit, the following excerpts are quoted from *Der Rhythmus* (1912), where he discussed the theory of diffuse lighting for the theater:

> Light conforms to music, music animates movement. Light clarifies movement. Only through light can movement take on form and expressiveness. However, this is only possible when light plays the role of milieu. Light must be for movement what a sounding board is for a musical tone. It must so affect the movements that it and the music together comprise one psychic force.[37]

It was in Tiblisi, in 1919, that Alexandre and his wife Jeanne began to commit their lives to working with George Gurdjieff. In 1922 they helped him establish the Institute for Harmonious Development near Fontainebleau, south of Paris. It was an experiment in communal living that flourished for ten years.

Upon the death of Alexandre de Salzmann in Leysin, Switzerland, in 1934, René and Vera became students of Jeanne, a renowned teacher and theorist of dance movement. They lived with Madame de Salzmann for three months in Evian, near Paris, then in Geneva, Switzerland, for one and a half years. Starting in 1936 they lived communally for three years in a large house with Jeanne, her children Natalie and Michel, and several others in the town of Sèvres, a western residential suburb of Paris. Under Jeanne de Salzmann's deft hand they lived and worked together according to the inner path or "Work" brought by Gurdjieff. Natalie de Salzmann, a teenager at the time, has clear memories of living with René during this period. She remembers him as extremely warm, serene, and self-effacing. In a telephone interview from her home in Caracas, Venezuela, she said that he had an astonishing intelligence and sense of humor, and that he was never negative.

In 1937 Daumal's health began to deteriorate. He became deaf in his left ear following a poorly treated case of otitis. In this same year, Daumal had ten teeth pulled and suffered greatly from a subsequent infection. He was weak looking and pale and finally at Jeanne de Salzmann's insistence he consulted a doctor. He was diagnosed with tuberculosis. In a letter dated May 1939, when all of Europe was on the brink of World War II, Daumal wrote a rare description, remarkable for its ultimate optimism, of his deteriorating physical and material state.

> While at Sèvres, I would walk to Paris, carrying old books to sell in exchange for the return metro fare. Lately, my eyes have been aching; I'm cross-eyed, I see double, I see smoke rise up before me, I fall asleep while I'm unlocking my door. I pull my hair to wake myself; my feet burn and I have trouble keeping my breakfast down in the morning. But I would be an idiot to complain because all this is eclipsed by *the fantastic luck* to have found a path (difficult as anything is that is real) that I have searched for all these years—a real possibility to get out of this *vicious circle* that we are in *naturally* [sic].[38]

Three years later, in 1942, he described his difficult living conditions in two letters from the south of France:

> All is well except for my carcass, which, for lack of sleep, and the shock of this abominable provençal climate (mistral wind, heat, labbé wind, tempest, glacial cold, mistral, sun, frost, storm, mistral) has come down with a bad case of bronchitis.
> And the rest of the time I spend looking for wood to burn, and things to cook on it, chopping my index finger. (Alep pine wood is not as straight as Mélèze pine.) My wife is even busier because the wood I bring her is green and she has to go beg the neighbor's hen to lay an egg for her sick husband, etc.[39]

Later, relocated to the Plateau d'Assy, he wrote:

> In spite of the thermometer, the cold is much more tolerable than in Provence. (I won't forget that "douce Provence!") Here there is no humidity or wind. The mistral (which emptied me and suffocated me) is now only a bad memory. Here the houses are well provided with heating systems (while the people of Marseille don't want to admit that they have a winter), and the friends with whom I'm staying are pharmacists [Geneviève and Louis Lief] and they shower me with care. The apartment I am planning to rent is far enough away from all those cadaver factories [sanitariums] which have invaded this plateau. What luck I had to escape from that world of organized illness, all those poor people who have their lungs punctured, ribs cut up, bodies needled and inoculated, like guinea pigs, playing bridge.[40]

The following is extracted from a letter to René from Jean Schlumberger, one of the founders of the *Nationale Revue Française*. Although only an acquaintance, he admired Daumal's work and wanted to give him financial support during these difficult war years.

> Vienot alerted me to the bad conditions in which you are convalescing. We agreed that a means had to be found to resolve this problem. I could have expressed this more diplomatically in person; excuse me for going right to the point and asking you simply, between friends, how much you would need in order to go spend two months in the mountains, where you can find better food and lodging than in Marseille. It is inadmissible that you should spend the whole summer in such unfavorable conditions. You are one of those people that we sorely need and who brings to French literature certain rarely discussed issues. I would be sad if you did not answer just as simply as I have written to you. It is necessary that you gain some weight, and that cannot happen on the diet of Milarepa. It is not admissible that a simple pecuniary consideration should prevent you from staying as long as is necessary. Show me your friendship by making use of me with as much simplicity as you might with one of your friends. We must reach the end of the war in as solid a state as possible.[41]

Daumal survived the hardships of World War II but lived under continuing conditions of severe deprivation and poverty. Although his career as journalist and editor foundered when the war forced the closure of many publishing houses, he derived a minimal income from freelance editorial work and the publication of A *Night of Serious Drinking*. He often bemoaned his inability to provide more comfortable housing for his wife. She chose not to seek the safety of her parents' U.S. home. Instead, she returned immediately from a U.S. visit (required for visa purposes), to continue overseeing his health requirements, adapting meager rations to his dietetic needs. Their life was further complicated by Vera's Jewish background and naturalized American status. Partly for this reason the two decided to formally wed in December 1942.

As the war dragged on and René's life gradually drew to a close, his wartime correspondence reveals a web of friendships that struggled to remain intact. Many colleagues were also in difficult or even life-threatening circumstances (Hendrik Kramer, Vera's former husband, died in a concentration camp). In spite of the harsh conditions and poor communication lines, certain longtime friends, near and far, continued to depend on René's friendship, and they remained a support to him. His expression of *carino* and fraternity is ever present in letters to such friends as Jean Paulhan, Georges Ribemont-Dessaignes, and the Liefs.

The eminent French writer Simone Weil, a former lycée classmate of René's, became a good friend to both René and Vera in 1941. He would lend her his Sanskrit notes and the *Gita*, which he had hand copied. She wrote to them:

> I thank you for having been the wellspring of a precious stimulant that brought many things—Sanksrit and everything connected to it. When we met again, it was the moment when I began to have a great thirst for this language and for this teaching. From now on, the memory of both of you and the joys and pains of these months will be forever melded with these Sanskrit characters. I hope never to stop loving them, these characters so sacred and such vehicles for the higher.[42]

It seems clear that in the domain of friendships, Daumal had always given of himself with great intensity. In his earliest years, his strongest bond was with Roger Gilbert-Lecomte and this endured from his lycée days until his meeting with Alexandre de Salzmann. At this point their paths began to separate, Lecomte falling deeper and deeper into drug-induced states of introspective euphoria, beyond the help of his closest friend. Daumal and Vera lodged and nursed him, but finally René despaired of any cure for him and broke definitively with the friend who had been such a strong influence in his life. In 1944, Lecomte died of tetanus, shortly before the death of René.

During his last five years, Daumal enjoyed a close friendship with Luc Dietrich, a charismatic young writer and follower of Gurdjieff. Dietrich would later become so despondent at René's death that, en route to the funeral, he had to turn and flee. Weeks later, he would needlessly place himself in danger and perish in the Normandy invasion, along with the only copy of a notebook filled by René over a two-year period at Luc's behest. Several months before René's final days, copies of a few pages of this notebook were made, in which he described their friendship in answer to Dietrich's formal query:

> Our friendship, all friendship consists in this: I can learn, acquire or attain something only when you also have learned, acquired or attained the same. Our friendship is for perpetual re-creation. Our first work for attaining friendship is to break with all that is ordinarily considered friendship: alliance in deceit, familiarity (complicity in the fall), commodity, connivance in sleep, rejection of responsibilities one for the other. Therefore, in front of you I must not allow myself any weakness. All our encounters must be sacred moments.[43]

Daumal wrote the poem "Mémorables" for Dietrich and dedicated it to him:

> Remember the friend who held out his intelligence to you
> > to gather up your tears,
> gushing forth from the frozen spring that the springtime sun
> > had violated.[44]

In their last exchange of letters, neither one mentioned Daumal's illness. Dietrich wrote:

> Nath, my brother, I am near you. Several times a day. I keep the best part of me for you. Thinking of you gives me courage, confidence. You are an example for me. I must tell you this again. Because next to your feeling of nullity—which you apply so

harshly against yourself—it is right that you should know your own value. And I want to tell you again that you give me an impression of gold.[45]

Daumal's last six months were one long agony according to Rolland de Renéville, during which he never ceased to remain superhumanly serene: "'Do not worry, it would take something other than this to get me down,' he murmured to me as I stared speechless at the frightening spectacle of his illness."[46]

On the third of May, Vera wrote to Pierre Granville and his wife:

Dear friends, I add a short note without René knowing. We are going through difficult times; the doctors can do nothing more for him. And as for him, the only thing he has left to count on is his own interior force. He begins the day with a temperature of 101 F (39 C), which rises to 104 F (40–40.2 C) or more by evening. At 3 A.M., I find him covered with sweat and torn apart by coughing; but he, he remains sweet, calm, patient—never a word or gesture that betrays his interior grandeur. His words are always noble. One would so like to help him. He continues to see one or two friends each day in order to have a real exchange, and then one can still see his eyes shine. He still maintains the hope of being able to pull himself out of this impasse. If only this miracle would happen! For now, my pain is great. Vera[47]

At the Daumals' Paris apartment on the rue Monticelli, near Denfert-Rochereau, Dietrich took the last photograph of René, looking strangely stronger and more peaceful than ever. On May 21, 1944, three days after this photo, Daumal's physical body gave out. He was thirty-six years old. He left behind an interrupted but important body of literature, but he had to leave his final work *Mount Analogue* unfinished. His wife Vera's pronouncement at his death was, "He was a prince."[48]

Fig. 1. René with his paternal grandparents in their native Ardennes in northern France. Antoine Daumal, a strong influence on René, withdrew from the local Masonic chapter to establish his own esoteric Masonic lodge.

Fig. 2. The Four Simplistes, circa 1926, clockwise from left: René Daumal, Roger Vailland, Roger Gilbert-Lecomte, Robert Minet. Pictured here with Bubu, their mascot fetish doll, they sought to retain the simplicity of childhood. In 1927, Meyrat would leave the group while André Rolland de Renéville would join, and a new name would be found: Le Grand Jeu [The Big Game].

Fig. 3. Eighteen-year-old René was the premier candidate for Professor René Maublanc's frequent experiments in extrasensory perception, then known as *le sens para-optique*. Tactile perception of the fingers and a focusing of the mind allowed the blinded subject to determine the contents of the sealed box.

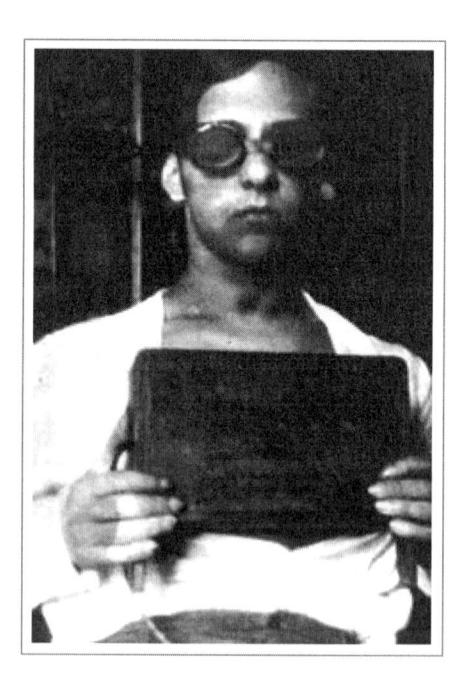

Fig. 4. Some members of Le Grand Jeu: André Rolland de Renéville, Monny de Boully, Roger Gilbert Lecomte, Vera Milanova [Daumal], and René Daumal.

Fig. 6. Arthur Rimbaud (1854–1893). The errant poet, emulated by the Simplistes. At age twenty-one, he rejected the world of Symbolist poetry and set out to find his way in the most primitive parts of the globe.

Fig. 5. Alfred Jarry (1873–1907). The initiator of pataphysics, the philosophy of the absurd, whose real-life antics were the basis of his works *Ubu Roi* and *The Exploits and Opinions of Dr. Faustrol, Pataphysician*. Here pictured in 1898, the year that *Dr. Faustrol* was completed.

Fig 7. André Breton (1896–1966), often called "the pope" of the Surrealists. As an early supporter of Daumal's group, he would later feel threatened by it. An erstwhile Communist, he is here photographed in Mexico in 1938, picnicking with Leon Trotsky, Stalin's foremost rival, two years before Trotsky's savage murder there.

Fig. 8. One of Daumal's many whimsical sketches, which appeared in *Le Grand Jeu*.

2

Daumal and Renunciation

The Imbecility of Individualism

> Thus, I truly am only in the act of negation, in the moment. My consciousness seeks its eternal self in each instant of time, in killing its successive envelopment, which become material. I am going toward a future that doesn't exist, leaving behind me at each instant a new cadaver.
>
> —René Daumal, at age sixteen[1]

Even at this early age, Daumal totally rejected living life for material goals and ordinary rewards. His precocious intellect and rebellious instincts led him to seek a more authentic purpose for living. In his article "The Spiritual Experience of Daumal and India" ("L'Expérience spirituelle de Daumal et de l'Inde"), Jacques Masui expresses the feeling of many writers that Daumal had an inherent understanding of the great truths and the importance of renunciation, or nonattachment, even before he read about Hinduism or Gurdjieff.

> Daumal seemed to me to be in complete possession of a message that he had perfectly integrated. This message was above all, the absolute veracity of an impersonal and ageless knowledge that we find in all the great traditions, a knowledge thanks to which we can awaken our true nature. In a word, be totally what we are. He did not initially come to this conviction through the holy books

of India. Long before making their discovery, he had acquired the certitude that there existed "another world": a consciousness more vast with which we can communicate when we place ourselves in the conditions required to perceive it.[2]

Daumal believed that methods and techniques existed that would allow man to reach a higher, more evolved state. His search led through many literary, philosophical, and spiritual avenues. Throughout his endeavors he adhered to an original understanding of two important theories: the possibility of experiencing the sacredness of one's inner self at any moment, and the importance of self-negation in the present moment. He believed these experiences heighten consciousness, immediately and cumulatively. As early as 1929, in *Le Grand Jeu*, he wrote:

> A man can, according to a certain so-called mystical method, attain an immediate perception of another universe beyond with his senses and understanding; knowledge of this universe marks an intermediary stage between individual consciousness and the other one.[3]

One of the first ramifications of self-negation that concerned Daumal and Le Grand Jeu was the necessity of giving up the autonomy of the individual. This was as important to Alfred Jarry's "Pataphysics" as it was to the theories of René Guénon. In the second page of *Le Grand Jeu*, Lecomte wrote: "We are not individualists; instead of locking ourselves up in our past, we go united together, each carrying his own cadaver on his back."[4] Further on he refers to "the imbecility of individualism."[5]

In his article "Freedom without Hope" of the same issue, Daumal outlined a theory of renunciation and self-negation as a means of attaining freedom. He seemed to be addressing the young "révoltés" of his day, as he discussed the commonly held beliefs about how to attain personal freedom: how to choose freely without being influenced by reason, desires, goals—that is, how to accomplish *a free act* (*un acte gratuit*). Daumal laments the typical first impulse, which is unfortunately to hold oneself apart from one's fellow man, achieving a sense of oneself through revolt, isolation, and pride: "And man thinks he has found salvation. Existence itself and worldly goods lose their value, there is nothing further to fear, and the soul continues its search for purity in this stiffening pride, that of a stoic."[6]

Rimbaud might qualify as a poet who embodied the self-lacerating snobbery of pain and exclusiveness of suffering. On the first page of "A Season in Hell," he wrote, "In order to strangle all joys I have sprung upon them like a wild beast."[7] When he abandoned his literary career at age nineteen, giving up one suffering and falling into many others, perhaps he was rejecting the prideful isolation of the literary elite, to join what he saw as the "real world" the camaraderie of merchants, tradesmen, and Third World people. Daumal seems to have viewed Rimbaud's life and his visionary genius in its most positive light.

So the revolt-for-revolt's-sake against society, even for the strong and earnest, is just as much an illusion and prison as is the total capitulation to society's conventions. Both positions entail isolating oneself from one's fellow men and continually making judgments about their conduct: "Nothing can enrich the soul in this exile; it is separated as much from heaven as from earth. The heavy boredom and dryness with their cortège of temptations will make him feel his immobility and his sleepfulness."[8]

To this kind of man who wants to affirm his being by disdaining society around him, Daumal offered another kind of freedom: "giving oneself wholeheartedly to every action rather than merely pretending to consent to be human,"[9] that is, truly noticing the miracle of the fact that you are alive. He wrote:

> Freedom is not *le libre arbitre* but liberation; it is the negation of individual autonomy. The soul refuses to model itself on the image of the body, desires, or logic. In whatever form I find myself, I must say: I am not that. By this abnegation, I reject all forms created by nature, and make them instead, objects; everything which tends to limit me—body, temperament, desires, beliefs, memories, I want to leave them to the vast world, as well as to the past. For this act of negation is the creator of consciousness in the present, a unique and eternal act in the instant. Consciousness is perpetual suicide. If it is aware of itself in the flow of time, still it is only in the present, that is, an immediate simple act outside the flow of time.[10]

Daumal went on to clarify that he is not speaking of renunciation or resignation in the ordinary sense of the word, an attitude taken by some persons who retreat from the world, seeking a milder, less troubled life. They become hypnotized by certain rules of conduct and achieve a kind of dulled interior calm. The act of renunciation that Daumal sought was not something that one could accomplish once and for all, but is rather something that is striven for, moment to moment.

Daumal dealt with this subject in an essay entitled "La Révolte et l'ironie"[11] with subsections entitled "L'Humilité et la grâce," "l'Abnégation, la Conscience" and "l'Union." He reiterates how the passage through these seven states of awareness can create an overall state that we might call "happiness." Quoting the *Bhagavad Gita*, Descartes, and Saint Theresa, he makes a strong case for giving up in order to receive. Most religions consider renunciation a necessary element in the process of salvation and the evolution of consciousness. In alchemical terms it is necessary to melt down the lead in order to make gold; in Christianity, it is necessary to die in order to be reborn to eternal life. For Daumal, it would be the tradition of Hinduism and the Gurdjieff teaching that would deepen his innate understanding of renunciation. Michel de Salzmann prefers the term *nonattachment* over *renunciation* because it is less extreme and more perfectly approximates the aim of the Gurdjieff teaching. Daumal employed the French term *renunciation* from the beginning, but gradually realized the point and purpose of Gurdjieff's and the *Bhagavad Gita*'s exhortation to strive for relaxed, mindful nonattachment.

The melting down of the lead, the fire of austerities, is sometimes seen as an atonement, a payment for our self-centeredness. The etymological dictionary tells us that the word *atone* comes originally from the phrase "at one," lexicalized as atone in early modern English, meaning "united, in harmony." By struggling with the projections of the ego one atones for one's isolating pride and one is unified—internally and with one's fellow man.

3

Drug Experimentation

Asphyxia and Absurd Evidence

> If the doors of perception were cleansed, everything would appear as it is, infinite.
>
> —William Blake

Of all the experimentation that Daumal would undertake, psychic or literary, none had a greater effect on him than his deliberate inhalation of poisonous carbon tetrachloride. At age seventeen, he discovered the strange, pleasant effects of this drug when he accidentally inhaled it while using it to preserve insects for his collection. After a few repeated trial inhalations, he realized that this substance could provide an opportunity "to see how consciousness disappears at the moment of dying."[1] He describes the experience in two essays, "Asphyxia and Absurd Evidence" (1930) and "The Determining Memory" (1943). This experimentation had a profound effect in orienting him toward the pursuit of a higher level of consciousness because it gave him a glimpse of that higher level, and a taste of what he calls a "certainty" that there *is* something more. This experience calls for a very detailed telling, just as he himself struggled to put into words the taste of "the Beyond." From this experience were born many of the most crucial obsessions and recurring themes of Daumal's work: (1) the dissatisfaction with our common foggy state of perception; (2) the need to find more conscious states of being, achieved through nonattachment and self-abnegation; (3) the fascination with death and nonbeing as the ultimate renunciation and transformation; and, most of all, (4) the attainment of the state of nondualism—the communion of the soul with the Universal Soul. He wrote:

> Around the age of six, not having had any particular religious belief instilled into me, the problem of death presented itself to me in all its nakedness. I spent horrible nights, clawed in the stomach and constricted at the throat by the anxiety of the abyss, of the "nothing more." Around eleven years old, relaxing my body at night, I pacified my organism's terror and revolt before the unknown, and a new feeling was born in me, the hope and the foretaste of something imperishable. At fifteen or sixteen, I began my experimental research, without direction and a little haphazardly. Not finding the means of directly experimenting with death—on MY death—I decided to study my sleep, supposing that an analogy existed between the two. One day I decided to confront the problem of death itself. I would put myself in a state as close as possible to that of physiological death, but would concentrate all my attention on remaining awake and recording everything that happened to me.[2]

He inhaled the poison on several occasions and each time he experienced the same results: being brutally catapulted into another world. His sensory experience of it was an intense mixture of expanding circles and triangles spiraling beyond three-dimensional space, a sound and a rhythm that he eventually realized was the vibration of his own organism. "I maintained my existence by emitting this sound."[3] He gave a detailed and fascinating description of these other-worldly dimensions of time, space, and number. But the essence of this experience was his conviction that an eternal world actually does exist, a higher state of comprehension, encompassing and surpassing the ordinary, waking state. The major difference between these two states is that the superior state is One—undivided and unified—and the inferior state is one of multiplicity. Here we have the core of Daumal's world view, as well as the essence of all Hindu thought: the One versus the many. The One contains the many, but man is blinded by the many and does not see the One. This multiplicity, the source of all anxiety and misdirection from the truth, was the source of the pataphysical notion of the absurd. Under the effect of the drug, he encountered multiplicity as a revelation:

> The indefinite multiplication of points, circles, triangles, instantaneously became regenerated and perfect Unity, Except ME, and this EXCEPT ME unbalancing the unity of All, engenders an indefinite and instantaneous multiplication . . . without the ALL being

altered.... I saw my abyss face to face, or rather, my perpetual dissolution in each instant.[4]

Except in the rare case of highly evolved beings, whether we call them saints, yogis, gurus, or *sannyasins*, one cannot achieve this victory over multiplicity—one cannot "stop the world" and maintain effortlessly the communion of the individual "I" with the Universal Principle. It requires a constant vigilance, a constant effort to see the One in the many. Even in drug-enhanced visions of other dimensions, there was, for Daumal, a continual fluctuation of the many into the One. And it was always the individual "Me" that seemed to create the imbalance of the whole and engender the multiplicity of the particulars.

How could he remain aware of the absurdity of this world of appearance, without being taken in by it? At the end of "Asphyxia and Absurd Evidence," he counsels:

You don't have to try this particular and rather exceptional experiment in order that your intuition of the absurd can attain the value of a metaphysical experience. But . . . the existence of persons and consciousness distinct from yourself, your own existence as an individual and finite creature, all that should, if you really wake up, appear to you intolerably absurd.[5]

Apparently it was the special circumstances and synergy of the Grand Jeu personalities that led some of them to inhale these life-threatening substances, but certainly, Daumal was driven to it ever since his childhood visions. His whole life up to that point was largely focused on catching glimpses of an alternative reality. His entire being was just waiting for the opportunity to glimpse the molecular world of his internal organism through these chemically induced visions. Also, his reading of Guénon and Hinduism seemed to justify for him his explorations, since the ancient tradition attested to the existence of another world.

In his biographical prose poem "Mémorables," Daumal devoted approximately three to five lines to each of the eighteen stanzas that recall an incident or a period in his life. Each verse invariably began with "And remember" ("*Souviens-toi*"). But this event merited fourteen lines, from which I have excerpted:

Remember the day that you tore open the curtain and were taken alive, stuck in the uproar of uproars, in the wheel of wheels. And remember the days that followed, when you walked around like a cadaver bewitched, with the certitude of having been eaten by infinity, canceled and voided by the single existing Absurd.[6]

This experience determined so much of Daumal's particular slant on life that one French writer, Phil Powrie claims in *René Daumal: L'Etude d'une obsession* [The study of an obsession] that this experience was the touchstone of his entire philosophic outlook. "This experience structured in an obsessional way both the thinking and the literary work of Daumal. Each work is, in fact, an attempt at dislodging the anguish that Daumal had felt during this experience."[7]

Many writers believe that this repeated ingestion of carbon tetrachloride seriously affected his lungs and provoked his subsequent tuberculosis. In the 1943 essay, a year before his death, he refers to the various levels of dangers involved with ingesting a poison. He accepts the physiological danger: "For if, in return for the acceptance of serious illnesses or disabilities, or of a very perceptible abbreviation of the physical life-span, we could acquire one certainty, it would not be too high a price to pay."[8] Daumal mentions the word *certainty* about eight times, often in italics—referring to this "certainty of the existence of something else, of a beyond," of another world or of another knowledge.

At the end of the 1943 essay, he mentions that many poets and mystics have had the same vision—sometimes horrific, sometimes peaceful or ecstatic, according to their level of development. Of his friends, only Lecomte ever had a similar experience. Regarding some of Daumal's references, one finds that O. V. de L Milosz, in his "Epistle to Storge" from *Ars Magna*, describes two extrasensory experiences. Most interesting was Milosz's vision of the infinity of time and space and how we are doomed to divide it up and thus create materiality.

> All our worries arise from our need to situate this infinite space itself and this infinite time; and the mental operation by which we assign them a place in themselves, multiplying and dividing them to infinity, does not take these terrible anxieties away. . . . One must multiply and divide infinity by infinity for an eternity of eternities with no rest, no memory, no love, no hope for you; multiply, multiply, divide, divide; these worlds will fall into chaos and you will replace them with others.[9]

Another example that Daumal refers to, likening it to his vision, is the revelation of the divine Being in the *Bhagavad Gita*. The following passage calls to mind his vision of an infinity of circles:

> Of a thousand suns in the sky
> If suddenly burst forth
> The light, it would be like
> Unto the light of that exalted one.
> The whole world there united,
> And divided many-fold
> Beheld in the God of Gods'
> Body, the son of Pandu then.[10]

To underline how momentous this drug experiment was for his life, we merely have to quote the last lines of his 1943 essay. There he alludes to how this experimental glimpse led to that other momentous experience of his life, his fateful encounter with Alexandre de Salzmann, the man who would become his teacher for four years.

> Not having become immediately and definitively crazy, I began to slowly philosophize on the memory of this experience. And I would have drowned in my own philosophizing if, at the right moment, someone hadn't appeared on my path to tell me: "Here is an open door; narrow and of difficult passage, but a door, and it is the only one for you."[11]

Was de Salzmann or Daumal recalling Christ's words in Luke XIII, 24, "Strive to enter by the narrow door," quoted by André Gide on the title page of his novel *La Porte Etroite* (*The Narrow Door*)? Like most escape hatches, the way out is narrow and the passage difficult. Daumal had the sensation of being in prison, a theme that runs through all his works, especially *La Grande Beuverie*. His drug experience had been like a cell window opening onto the greater world beyond this one. Alexandre de Salzmann figured as the liberator, the man with the key.

> And above all remember the day when you wanted to throw everything away but a guardian was watching over you in your night, he remained awake while you dreamed, he made you touch your flesh, he made you remember your own, he made you gather up your tatters—remember your guardian.[12]

II
THE PATAPHYSICAL PURSUITS

4

Surrealism and Le Grand Jeu

Living on the Pataphysical Edge

> *Plonger au fond du gouffre,*
> *Enfer ou ciel, qu'importe?*
> *Au fond de l'Inconnu*
> *pour trouver de nouveau!*
>
> [Plunge into the depths of the abyss,
> Hell or Heaven, what does it matter?
> To the depths of the Unknown
> To find it again!]
>
> —Charles Baudelaire

In recent years there has been growing interest in Daumal's group known as Le Grand Jeu ("The Big Game"), a group that paralleled the Surrealists in the style and content of their beliefs but managed to establish their own unique identity within the avant garde of post-World War I Paris. In the spring of 1993 the Musée d'Art Moderne presented an exhibition of photographs and writings of Le Grand Jeu, coupled with the paintings of Joseph Sima, a Grand Jeu contributor, whose portraits of these young writers captured their essence on canvas.

In 1927, having abandoned his experimentation with drugs and alcohol, Daumal joined with his companions, together known as the Simplistes, and founded a literary review in which they could express their revolutionary ideas. They called it *Le Grand Jeu* and began to refer to themselves as a group by the same name. With great virulence they proclaimed the metaphysical nature of life and the urgency of total commitment: "One must put oneself in a state of complete receptivity, a vacuum inside. From this proceeds our project to put everything in question at every moment."[1]

This passionate undertaking comprised four issues (including the final unpublished one), featuring poems, drawings, and essays on revolution, renunciation, politics, science, religion, psychoanalysis, and of course, poetry and literature. Highlighted are essays on Rimbaud, Nerval, Lautréamont, Montherlant, Jean Prévost, André Breton, Victor Hugo, and René Guénon. Throughout, one finds references to thinkers as diverse as Appolonius of Thanes, Balzac, Blake, Claudel, Darwin, Freud, Epicureus, Goethe, Kant, Thomas Aquinas, and Nietzsche. The first three issues were financed by the literary critic Leon Paul Quint and produced by publisher Jose Corti.

The fourth issue was completed and made ready for printing in the fall of 1932, but, lacking financing, it was never published. Nevertheless, it was included in the 1977 publication of all four volumes. Sixty years later, Editions Jose Corti continues to publish works of literature, philosophy, and literary criticism, especially about Surrealism. In 1992, they published the French version of the present book under the title *René Daumal, au delà de l'horizon*.

※

In order to adequately gauge the significance of the group, Le Grand Jeu and their publication, it is necessary to place them within the literary context of the1920s and 1930s and discuss them in relation to their elder brothers, the Dadaists and especially the Surrealists. Even before World War I, many writers such as Jarry, Conrad, Mann, Kafka, and Proust were exposing the decayed state of sacred and secular institutions and societal conventions in Europe. Then the advent of war itself had tremendous consequences. It was more than just a conflict between countries (or between the various relatives of Queen Victoria, cousins sitting on the thrones of Europe). The renewed butchery, brutality, and orderly deployment of endless carnage made possible by new technology caused a profound crisis of values that was to transform European consciousness.

The Dadaist movement, begun in Zurich in 1916, was a radical response to this multinational insanity. Living in a world seemingly emptied of all transcendence and meaning, the Dadaists challenged every aspect of this discredited culture, and ridiculed all traditional beliefs. The founder of the movement, Tristan Tzara, had a new recipe for writing poetry—to cut up words from a newspaper and randomly paste them back together. This was anti-art in its earliest incarnation.

Dadaism burst forth in Paris in 1919 and attracted such writers as André Breton, Louis Aragon, Paul Eluard, and others. In just a few years these men developed the Surrealist movement, building on the foundations of Dadaism but eschewing its total nihilism. Surrealism was intended to be revolutionary but constructive, in both its aesthetic and political agenda.

In this same postwar era, the young Simplistes were exploring new forms of thought and creativity. Their ideas were challenging and, like those of the Surrealists, were developed as a reaction to the rationalism and formalism of traditional European thought, which, they felt, held human consciousness in submission, stifling a freer form of expression. Le Grand Jeu emphasized the originality of their own beliefs and stressed their differences from the Surrealists and all that went before. Nevertheless, the two groups were fraternal twins and heirs to the same literary past.

Although Daumal was greatly influenced by Hindu literature, he was nevertheless a Western man, the product of modern literary society and with modern Western concerns to face. In spite of his growing preoccupation with Eastern philosophy, as a young man he paid glowing homage to both his French antecedents and his contemporaries. In 1926, at the age of eighteen, he expressed his affinity for certain Symbolist writers in a letter to Maurice Henri: "Here are my favorite writers: Baudelaire, Verlaine, Malarmé, Poe, Rimbaud, Lautréamont. Rimbaud is, I feel, the closest to me. Sometimes I dream of taking long silent walks with him. I still feel the violent impression that two painters made on me (although very different from each other): Gustave Moreau and Picasso."[2]

Daumal's early work was influenced by the nineteenth-century poets and even more by the current general milieu of surrealism. It is also true that a number of Surrealists were likewise influenced by Eastern metaphysics, which created rich parallels with Daumal's writings. To understand better the activities of Le Grand Jeu and the public and personal role of Daumal, it is worthwhile to examine general Surrealist concepts within the context of the time.

Anthony Hartley described Surrealism as a "continuation of the effort to make art a substitute religion which runs through the whole French nineteenth century."[3] This belief in the hallowed omnipotence of poetry, as well as a taste for extraordinary states of awareness and dreams, had found its way into literature with Romanticism, and continued to develop among the symbolist poets. Nerval, Baudelaire, Rimbaud, and Alfred Jarry were the literary ancestors the Surrealists honored, the first three elevating the poet to priest, dreamer, and seer, and Jarry contributing the elements of absurdity and humor to the poet's store of magical potions.

There were several important tenets that the Surrealists held in common with Daumal's group. Some of these had evolved in various forms from the nineteenth-century poets mentioned above, but were developed to an even greater extent by the Dadaists and Surrealists during the twenties and thirties. The main ideas were:

1. The necessity of destroying the rigid dualism between reality and dream, life and art, the physical and metaphysical, thus acknowledging the influence of Hegel, Guénon, and Eastern philosophy;
2. The acknowledgment of the essential ambiguity of experience and the deliberate use of ambiguity (equivocal interpretation) in art and literature;
3. The inadequacy of conventional logic in life and literature;
4. The importance of pure chance in life and as a literary technique;
5. The humorous and absurd nature of existence, and humor as the most appropriate response to the absurdity of existence;
6. The importance of parapsychic experiments with telepathy, hallucinations, mind-altering drugs, and out-of-body experiences;
7. The value of automatic writing to allow the pure dictation of the psyche's expression, unprogrammed by the calculation of rational thought;
8. The validity of Freudian psychology, the direct use of the unconscious and dream material for creative purposes and the melding of the "bizarreries" of the unconscious into one's life;
9. The preeminence of the cult of childhood and the cult of woman as the embodiment of magic;
10. The urgency of the social and political commitment of the artist.

Although many of these concepts and categories are deeply intertwined, it is possible to discuss them individually with their historical antecedents and to illustrate how the Surrealists and Le Grand Jeu put them into practice.

In 1922, while still at the lycée (high school), Daumal and the Simplistes were already experimenting with what they called half-conscious, half-automatic writing. They were unaware that the Surrealists were doing the same sort of thing until 1924, with the appearance of La Révolution Surréaliste by André Breton, leader of the Surrealists. Although the Simplistes were approximately twelve years younger than Breton and company, they initially felt a great affinity for the elder group. In a letter to Maurice Henry in 1926, Daumal writes:

> It is because of this sliding on one's back toward a vertigo of souls that we love Surrealism—just as much as opium. We are Surrealists, with just a few qualifications. The nature of Surrealism is to place man in an exceptionally receptive and unstable state.[4]

In another letter to Henry, Daumal describes their preexisting brand of Surrealism avant la lettre (before it existed):

> We think from immediate intuition and we look to pure dream for this revelation, these absolute memories of eternity, which is what made us Surrealists before this term was known. Breton's Manifesto simply gave us the shock of realizing that we truly were of our times.[5]

Given this initial acknowledged identification of Le Grand Jeu with the Surrealists, we can assume that, in all subsequent discussion of the Surrealists, their beliefs and tenets apply as well to Le Grand Jeu, except in the cases where the two groups establish separate identities. In time the slowly emerging contrasts created a true divergence of the two groups.

LIVING IN A SURREALITY

> God is the tangential point between zero and infinity
>
> —Alfred Jarry

It was through the deliberate "confusion or derangement of the senses" à la Rimbaud, and through ingesting hallucinogenic substances that the Surrealist poets came to incorporate the ineffable and the bizarre into both their writing and their lives, an experience Alfred Jarry refers to as "living in a Surreality." Gérard de Nerval (1808–1855), an early nineteenth-century poet, lived in this way, tragically melding his poetic dream life with his waking state until his hallucinations led him to suicide.

Jarry, known as the grandfather of both Surrealism and the Theater of the Absurd, is referred to in many of Daumal's writings, and appears as a character in A *Night of Serious Drinking* (*La Grande Beuverie*) along with Rabelais and Léon Paul Fargue. Jarry was the initiator of the cult of childhood and the cult of humor. In his book *The Banquet Years*, Roger Shattuck entitled his chapter on Alfred Jarry, "Suicide by Hallucination."[6] Maurice Nadeau writes in the *History of Surrealism*, "Jarry, confusing in a perpetual hallucination his own experience with that of [his fictional character] Père Ubu, signifies the eruption into life of humor, the supreme value of 'those who know.'"[7] When Jarry's masterpiece *Ubu Roi* was first staged in Paris 1896, it caused a major scandal. The lyrical, obscene black humor of the play reflects the real-life strangeness of Jarry. Père Ubu, the monster king, represents the most cruel and stupid forces of bourgeois law, order, and respectability. The laughter he produces, though antisocial and subversive, has for the viewer the moral function of a purge. In Jarry's later works *Le Surmâle* (*The Supermale*) and *The Exploits and Opinions of Dr. Faustroll*, humor was catapulted into the realm of the purely irrational and absurd. Jarry's work completely epitomizes the Surrealists' confusion of life and art. Shattuck writes:

> He [Jarry] installed a little marionnette theatre to entertain his guests, and invented the sport of bouncing chickpeas off the stovepipe hats of gentlemen on the boulevard below. The universe of total hallucination ultimately absorbed all of Jarry's life and writing. Primitive destructiveness was converted into an extravagant vision.[8]

Several lines from *Ubu Cuckolded* illustrate Jarry's absurd humor. Père Ubu, the main character, and still today a well-known personage in French literature, has a conversation with another character, his own conscience:

> PERE UBU: Hornstrumpot, by our green candle, let us consult our conscience. There he is, in this suitcase, all covered with cobwebs. As you can see, we don't overwork him.
>
> (*Conscience emerges from suitcase wearing a shirt.*)

PERE UBU: How do you have the insolence to appear before us in shirt tails?

CONSCIENCE: Sir, and so on and so forth, Conscience, like Truth, usually goes without a shirt.[9]

The juxtaposition of disparate images and the introduction of fanciful new language such as "Hornstrumpot" came to be common practice among the Surrealists, but in the 1890s this was considered bold, outrageous, and shockingly unconventional. Jarry well earned his infamous reputation among the Surrealists and Le Grand Jeu. His later disciples took their cue from him and reveled in public buffooneries and farcical exhibitionism.

The Surrealists found new ways to incorporate the strange and humorous into their lives. They were given to the same public antics as their Pataphysical "grandfather," Alfred Jarry. Their search for the unexpected found a new theory "Objective Chance" to explain and justify it. Living their lives in a perpetual "dare," they systematically sought out strange coincidences by changing their names, accosting strangers, and otherwise behaving erratically and randomly. Shattuck writes: "Driven by extreme inquisitiveness and self-imposed daring, they dropped everything else and affirmed these moments as the only true reality, as expressive of both the randomness and the hidden order that surrounds us."[10] They were looking to create cracks in conventional reality in order to experience a truer reality within. Breton considered "objective chance" to be the locus of these coincidences, embodying the interrelatedness of necessity and freedom. The Surrealists felt that to create a life entirely made up of startling synchronicity would be to attain surreality. Salvador Dali, in turn, had his own particular vision of the irrational and created a "perfect and coherent systematization of confusion in order to contribute to the total discrediting of reality."[11]

Daumal's own particular fusion of art and life evolved throughout his lifetime. In his adolescence, he sought out the inane and the weird in the tradition of Jarry. Along with Lecomte, he led his comrades to shock themselves and the citizenry, and in general, to "épater [shock and impress] la bourgeoisie." He wore his hair unfashionably long and was considered a strange clown by his peers. Michel Random describes some of the Lycée chicanery:

> Daumal's disorderly character and his taste for student pranks were famous at the Lycée. He wrote his freshman exam in surrealistic style and was given a grade of zero. At Reims during the school

holidays, he found his old friends and got into the spirit of pataphysical demonstrations. As a group, they paraded down the street holding up a banner composed of an inflated prophylactic contraceptive suspended with corncobs, straws, flutes, blow pipes, and spouts, and hawked these wares to the women in the streets.[12]

According to Robert Meyrat, it was Daumal who had the most developed sense of humor among the Simplistes. "He would draw caricatures and sketches that were intelligible only to him which he then would explain to us."[13] Pierre Minet, another lycée friend, remarks that René often wore a Moroccan fez over his long hair, and a photograph shows him in just such a hat.

> He walked like no one else, soberly, but with a quality so comical that he was irresistible. Humor for him was a special domain, never grating or mean; it was the outflowing of his goodness, the farcical expression of his love. For him, humor was a real talisman, thanks to which he triumphed over everything including his own weaknesses.[14]

Some of the group's activities were carried to radical extremes, especially when they seemed to be playing with fate. They made a pact among themselves called "the pact of the Absolute": this meant that each had the power of life and death over each other. This commitment was tested by their experimentation with Russian roulette, as described by Robert Meyrat:

> After a few rums and a residue of opium mixed with tobacco, they each took a turn. Daumal the youngest went first. He put the revolver to his temple then said "No, I can't, it is you Meyrat who are going to kill me." He knelt down and quickly recited a Hindu prayer. Meanwhile I held the revolver in my pocket and very gently removed the single bullet without their knowledge. Then gravely, I pressed the revolver against his forehead and pulled the trigger. He got up without manifesting any emotion. [After they all took turns] I finally told them it was empty. I was clobbered with reproaches. Were these reproaches really sincere? I think that, without doubt, Daumal would have liked to die in order to penetrate one of his other universes. Lecomte also took the game very seriously.[15]

In "Mémorables" (1942) Daumal evokes memories of these attempts at liberation: "Remember your accomplices and your tricks and this great desire to get out of the cage."[16]

AUTOMATIC WRITING

Automatic writing was a technique used by both the Surrealists and the Simplistes. Both experimented with language as a way to tap into the power of dreams and the unconscious and to express their perception of the absurdity of existence. They did not believe in the idea of talent, but felt that anyone could liberate his or her subconscious mind to produce art and poetry. This view eliminated the artistic elite and made poetry accessible to the masses, creating a broad new consciousness in society. They had an almost superstitious faith in language as a magic incantation. In their attempt to do away with literary style, they gradually developed automatic or free association of words as a general technique. According to André Breton, this allowed them to "seize the mysterious and marvelous moment when immaterial thought unites with the concrete word, and in a leap, is carried back to the birth of the meaningful element."[17] Robert Vitrac's line is an excellent example of their unexpected juxtapositions: "Cephalopods have more reason to hate progress than quadrupeds." Or Max Morise's line, "In the burning forest—The lions were fresh."[18]

In his "Treatise of Style" (1928), Louis Aragon includes what could be considered a lay manual for automatic writing:

> Put yourself in the most passive or receptive state you can. Forget about your genius, your talents, and everyone else's. Tell yourself that literature is the saddest path that leads to everything. Write quickly, without a preconceived subject, fast enough to remember and not be tempted to read over what you have written. . . . If silence threatens to overtake you because you have made a mistake . . . following the word whose origin seems suspect to you, put down any letter, the letter l for instance, always the letter l, and restore the arbitrary by imposing this letter as the initial for the word that will come next.[19]

These rebels were ostensibly anti-literature and anti-culture. Tristan Tzara writes:

> The poetry which expresses either ideas or sentiments no longer interests anyone. To it I oppose poetry as an "activity of the mind." . . . It is perfectly evident today that one can be a poet without ever having written a line. That there exists a quality of poetry in the street, in a commercial performance, anywhere, the confusion is great, it is poetic.[20]

Accordingly, the Surrealists established a "Bureau of Surrealist Research," open to all who had something to say, to confess, or to create. They encouraged revolutionaries, madmen, inventors, misfits, and dreamers. They also launched *La Révolution Surréaliste*, a literary magazine with the severe appearance of a scientific periodical, for they often borrowed from the world of science the methods (and veneer) of objective investigation and collective team work. This magazine emphasized revolutionary research and experimentation, and included a systematic listing of all cases of suicide currently reported in the newspapers, as well as automatic texts and accounts of dreams. In 1928 they grandly celebrated the fiftieth anniversary of a scientific publication on the phenomenon of hysteria written by Dr. J. M. Charcot. They considered this the greatest poetic discovery of the nineteenth century. Breton and Aragon insisted that hysteria was not just a pathological phenomenon but a valid means of expression.[21]

Daumal and his friends experimented extensively with automatic writing during the mid 1920s. In 1925, at age seventeen, René wrote a letter to Roger Vailland, describing automatic writing as

> a means of attaining, by the fatigue of lingual connections, that instability of expression which allows—it is intoxication—the passage of the soul. Automatic writing makes possible liaisons not of ideas . . . but of movements sketched by the body and determined by the image. I write: "The cistern of melted nights leaves for the port of butterflies."[22]

In a letter to Rolland de Renéville (1932), Daumal discusses the various procedures:

> The surest method of doing it is to describe, after the event, associations spontaneously surging up; in a dream or in any conversation, one wonders how we were led to speak of such and such. These procedures for remaining in the poetic domain cannot help but uncover raw, non-directed, poetic material, which only has

value if used by a directed thought. . . . To give birth in oneself to diverse directions of thought while remaining conscious of the one direction in which thought does not risk dying in repetitions of automatism: the active doubt. Active critique of the personality, to feel all the human personalities that are possible in you.[23]

Le Grand Jeu, in keeping with their contempt for highly polished cerebral poetry and their enthusiasm for the cult of childhood, included a short poem translated by Jack Daumal, then age twelve, in the first issue of their magazine: "The little green spider plays music . . . ."[24]

DUALITY AND THE ABSURD

> Time spent laughing is time spent with the gods.
>
> —Japanese proverb

The avowed aim of the Surrealist Movement was to reduce and finally dispose of the flagrant contradictions that seemed to exist between dream and waking life, the unconscious and the conscious, the "unreal" and the "real." They sought to merge and comingle all contraries until these formed a single whole. At the same time the Surrealists recognized the impermanence of any state of duality or of resolution. One must always be open and ready, they said, having "la disponibilité," for their parallel emphasis on freedom and dizziness (le vertige) demands that no resolution be permanent. They were proud to point out that this movement from contradiction to resolution found support in Marxist dialectical theory.

Le Grand Jeu shared with the Surrealists an obsessive preoccupation with the absurdity of life. What they could not know at the time was that their intuitions were correct: currently the most advanced scientific research reveals that the subatomic universe behaves absurdly and follows no known logic. In that era, however, what was it that they found absurd? For Jarry as well as Le Grand Jeu, the absurdity was the apparent dualism inherent in Western philosophy and the foundation that this created for the perception of reality. Dualism is the very substructure of the Western mode of perception; and this creates a separation of mind and body, material and ephemeral, reality and dream, continuity and discontinuity, the physical and metaphysical. The Dadaists, Surrealists, Le Grand Jeu, and their predecessors Nerval, Jarry, and Rimbaud all saw themselves as victims of this mode of perception; they perceived it as absurd, and strove to break through the rigid partitions of this either-or way of seeing. Rather than being caught in the dualist description of a "real" or an "unreal," they proposed a "surreal" that would encompass both. In the Western philosophic tradition, reality is described as a multitude of different analyzable elements. By contrast, Surrealists looked at this "ridiculous multitude of things," each with its attached value, and found it absurd.

Delving into Western philosophy, Daumal and the Grand Jeu avidly espoused Hegel's mystical belief in the interconnectedness of everything in the universe, making up one totality, which Hegel called the "Absolute Spirit." Many discovered in Eastern spiritual traditions the same description of reality as a single unity with merely a proliferation of forms. They declared the Western dualistic tradition—which focused on the particular, the individual, and was blind to the One—to be absurd. According to Daumal, "Everyone will experience the revelation that any form is absurd as soon as it is taken seriously."[25] For these "new thinkers" the best response was laughter.

Independent of the Surrealists, Le Grand Jeu delighted in the humor of this absurdity and revived Jarry's concept of Pataphysics—the study of the inherent humor of this absurdity as first introduced in the "The Exploits and Opinions of Dr. Faustroll, Pataphysician." They called themselves Pataphysicians and made it a major element of their ideology. Jarry defined Pataphysics as "the science of imaginary solutions."[26] Daumal's essay, "Pataphysics and the Revelation of Laughter" ("Le Pataphysique et la Révélation du Rire") explains:

> The pataphysical laughter is the striking awareness of an absurd duality which knocks your eyes out [and cites] the great principle that all things evident in the world are clothed with the absurd as their only manner of appearance. Whence the humoristic appearance of pataphysical reasoning, which at first seems grotesque, then upon a closer look seems to contain a hidden meaning, then seems grotesque again, then profound, etc.—the truth and the ridiculous endlessly crossing and reinforcing each other.[27]

Pataphysics was a major interest for Daumal; it became his chief way of looking at the world and interpreting the absurdity of existence. He wrote many pataphysical essays between 1929 and 1932, including "The Treatise of Patagrammes" (*Traité de patagrammes*) made up of "pataphotogrammes," "des Sphynx patagraphiques," and "le patascopie sommaire des liqueurs patascopiques" ("the summary patascopy of patascopic elixirs"). Later between 1938 and 1941, he wrote three more essays on the "Pataphysics of Phantoms." Some of the nonsensical essays had titles such as "Intellectual geloids except prunes," "Acoustical anaglyphs, still but in guinea pigs," "The use of the Cabbage Cutter," "How the Ecumenical Council of the Chew-Culottes veil their face."[28]

These treatises are very dense and colorful potpourris of sound and sense, corrosive parodies, alternately vamping the language of science, the arts, and religion. They are the motherlode of humorous nonsense that would become the material for *La Grande Beuverie*. During these years, it is only in his pataphysical writings that Daumal deals with ordinary, mundane objects. In his *patagrammes,* he deliberately chooses ordinary vocabulary and subjects—guinea pigs, anticlericalism, kaleidoscopes, aspirin, and arthropods—and treats them in a humoristic, disparaging and absurdist manner. Later in *Mount Analogue* he addresses such earthly subjects as seamanship and alpinism in both serious and humorous ways. We will see that in the poetry of *Le Contre-Ciel* however, he never broaches such ordinary pursuits as politics, love, sex, or science. He only speaks of life and death, in terms of allegorical animals and the basic elements—fire, earth, water, and stone.

Some examples of Daumal's humor can be found in a short play entitled *"en gggarrde!"* The play's prologue describes the set as the field between the poles of a magnet. Scene I takes place inside a snail's skull. Among the characters all wearing roller skates (Napoléon, Bubu, The Sociologist, The Leech, The Pernod with Sugar, Migraine, and the Toothbrush), a strange dialogue takes place:

NAPOLEON (to Bubu): Don't put your tongue in the yes of my girlfriend, The Toothbrush, or I'll make you eat it, by my old nanny!

BUBU: I won't so there! (He climbs onto The Leech and cries), Gentlemen, you are the object of an abominable machination! There are strawberries in the world, don't forget! . . . Well, then, your duty is clear!

(*They go out in a conga line, to the sound of "La Marseillaise."*)[29]

Ever since the playwrite Eugene Ionesco and the postwar Theater of the Absurd, playgoers have become more accustomed to this kind of nonsequitur, inane dialogue. It hardly appears startling today. But in 1930,

Daumal's work was outrageously avant-garde, and whether it was judged positively or negatively, it was certain to jostle the viewer's mind. Daumal's open abandonment of rational devices and discursive thought was considered extreme even by many of the Surrealists. (André Breton's revolutionary ideas, for example, were still expressed in classical phrasing and traditional rhythms.)

Daumal contributed several pataphysical essays to the *Journal of the College of Pataphysics*. Julien Torma, supposedly a founding member of this institution (still in existence today), with Raymond Queneau and Jacques Prévert, wrote Daumal a friendly chiding letter, expressing his surprise to find that "Pataphysics can be married to mysticism."

> You're right to speak of chaos. But it's obvious that you believe in it as a kind of God. In spite of all your finesse, dear René, you're on a pilgrim's progress. Let me be malicious. You're playing with the absolute. Your Pataphysics laughs too much. And with a laughter much too comic and cosmic. Putting metaphysics behind Pataphysics is like making a belief into a mere façade. When in fact the real nature of Pataphysics is to be a façade which is only a façade, with nothing behind it.[30]

In other letters, Torma kidded Daumal for his metaphysical essays ("orientaloid salads") and felt that true Pataphysics cannot serve any other aim than itself. If Torma represented the majority of pataphysicians who saw no meaning to the universe, Daumal was able to gradually perceive a great plan behind the apparent meaninglessness. (Roger Shattuck reports that he corresponded with Julien Torma in recent years, but Claudio Rugafiori and Helen Maxwell, the late authority on Daumal, claim that the person Julien Torma did not actually exist. Maxwell explained that Daumal himself invented this diatribe which he ascribes to the character Julien Torma. The question remains open.)

Daumal's natural sense of humor was consonant with his dire seriousness: he understood that wit could perforate the solidarity of our concepts and opinions. Many ancient cultures honored the half-wit as a garbled source of wisdom. So he was comfortable working within the tradition of the laughing Buddha, the Medieval court jester, the hallucinating shaman, or the eccentric Jarry. He realized that the Sufi "Wisdom of the Idiots," full of irreverent wit and joyous, iconoclastic wisdom could open up the third ear of true listening.

DREAMS

> Sleep has two gates, they say one is of horn
> And spirits of truth find easy exit there,
> The other is perfectly wrought of glistening ivory
> But from it the shades send false dreams up the world.
> —Virgil, *The Aeneid*

The Surrealists acknowledged the importance of earlier dream explorers, such as Nerval, Rimbaud, Baudelaire, and Lecomte de Lautréamont. They read Baudelaire, who was the first to describe "the absurd dream," in *The Artificial Paradises*, as "a hieroglyph which represents the supernatural aspect of life, and it is specifically because it is absurd that the ancients believed it to be divine."[31] But the Surrealists felt that they, along with Freud, were the first actually to explore scientifically the realm of dreams.

André Breton is given credit for introducing Freud to France. Although Freud published *Humor and Its Relation to the Unconscious* (*der Witz und seine Beziehung zum Unbewussten*) in 1905, and it appeared in an English translation in 1917, it was not published in French until 1930. Breton, a young student of psychiatry and medicine, studied Freud's theory and worked with the mentally ill prior to World War I. He was granted an interview with Freud in 1921. After that he and his confreres gave much publicity to Freud in their two major periodicals, *La Révolution Surréaliste* and *Le Surréalisme au Service de la Révolution* (1924–1933).

Practically every one of the fifty bona fide Surrealists wrote and published accounts of their dreams, as much in the spirit of experimentation and investigation as it was a form of pure creative expression. There were various categories of dreams: the natural dream, the prophetic dream, the experimental dream, and the self-induced dream. Although the Surrealists admired Freud's discoveries and original thinking, he, on the other hand, did not appreciate their activities to the same degree. Balakian writes:

> Upon receiving Breton's *Les Vases Communicants*, Freud had to confess in his letter to the author that it was not at all clear to him what surrealism was. "Perhaps I am not made to understand it," he said, "for I am so far removed from art." The reason he could not understand it was that the Surrealists were launched on

a much more adventurous investigation than he; theirs was not an observation or interpretation of the subconscious world, but a colonization of it.[32]

Breton claimed that Freud drew too great a barrier between the exterior world and the dream experience and ignored their mutual influence on each other. He felt that he and his confreres carried Freud's research further than Freud himself and justified it with a quotation from Freud: "Poets are in the knowledge of the soul, our masters, for they drink at sources not yet made accessible to science. Why has the poet not expressed himself more precisely on the nature of the dream?"[33]

The Surrealists were more than willing to comply. The poet Pierre Reverdy contributed a text on the value of dreams in the first issue of *La Révolution Surréaliste*. He believed that dreams are not contrary to thought, but "a freer, more abandoned form of thought. Dreams and thought are the two sides of the same material, dreams constituting the side whose texture is richer but looser—thought the side whose texture is more restrained, but tighter."[34] It was through their technique of automatic writing that they were able to transpose a spontaneous or provoked dream onto the page and thus liberate the unconscious. Breton felt that dream and waking states were communicating vessels in which events were homologous and equally real in the moment for the individual.

Notes found among Daumal's and Lecomte's lycée philosophy class papers from 1924–1925 testify to their extensive study of the philosopher Henri Bergson's theories about dreams. The same topic heading was found in each boy's handwriting: "The activity of consciousness in the dream state."[35] Daumal and his group placed a tremendous importance on dreams as being a relevant glimpse into another realm of existence. In his letters to Vera and his friends, Daumal often referred to his own dream life. In 1927 he wrote to Lecomte: "Again last night I saw the lost country. It is an unknown region of Auvergne. I already spoke to you of the palace with endless stairways. A group of men in turbans—Hindus, I think—spoke near the top of the stair."[36]

He began a letter of 1928 with a dream description: "I am dead. Francois died at the same moment as I, under the same circumstances which I have forgotten,"[37] and continued the dream for almost four pages. For Daumal, dreams were not merely an intellectual intrigue; he recognized their influence on both his unconscious and conscious endeavors.

Philippe Lavastine revealed one story about the telling effects of Daumal's dream life. At age eighteen, Daumal dreamt that he was deeply in love with a woman whom he had never met before in his life. In the dream, their intense union lasted eight years. This dream experience was so vivid that for eight years thereafter, until he met Vera, his wife-to-be, René had no relationships with any women. This single dream had been so lifelike, and the vision of this relationship so fulfilling and long lasting, that no woman until Vera could compare with the woman of that dream. Lavastine underlined how absolutely serious Daumal was about this dream, and how intent he was to wait for the woman of his dreams.

This kind of poetic single-mindedness seems to contrast with the Surrealist's quest for random occurrences, and with their openness to experiences (André Gide's *disponibilité*) as well as with the total sexual liberation advocated by some of his peers. But, actually, Daumal's passionate love for one mythical woman is in keeping with the Surrealist conviction that devotion to a single woman over a long period of time is the surest means of liberating desire and imagination. Maurice Nadeau explains that the Surrealists' celebration of love for a woman results from their belief that a woman's intuition and accessibility to other states was exactly what they were seeking. In Breton's thoughtful essay "Amour fou, amour unique" he enlists Engels and Freud to substantiate the primacy of monogamy as the best means to transcend the ordinary. Nadeau writes:

> Amazingly enough, that kind of imagination, kindled in the house of love, brought back to poetry the long lost figure of woman as the embodiment of magic powers, a creature of grace and promise, always close in her sensibility and behavior to the two sacred worlds of childhood and madness. . . . The cult of the mythical woman, foreign as it may be to some contemporary readers, lies at the heart of the Surrealist credo.[38]

PARANORMAL EXPERIENCES

> Remember the magic, the poisons and the tenacious dreams;
> you wanted to see, you covered your eyes to see,
> without knowing how to open the other one.
>
> —"Mémorables"

Before they had even invented the name Le Grand Jeu, the young Simplistes were experimenting with extrasensory perception, trying to attain other prenatal states, somewhere between life, dreams, and death. They valued the more accessible states connected to childhood and the animistic mind of primitive man.

Daumal describes some of the various activities of Le Grand Jeu in a scathing letter to André Breton, published in *Le Grand Jeu II*, 1927 in which he contrasts his group with the Surrealists.

> In response to your amusing science, we have the study of all the procedures of depersonalization, telepathy, clairvoyance, mediumism; we have the unlimited field (in every conceivable mental direction) of Hindu yoga, the systematic confrontation of lyrical and oneiric elements with the teachings of the occult tradition (but *to hell with* the picturesque in magic) and those of the so-called primitive mind, and that is not all.
>
> Rolland de Renéville is working on establishing the multiple coordinates of poetic creation. Gilbert-Lecomte is building the architecture of fire of mystical thought and the spirit of participation. He and I have undertaken research into experimental metaphysics. The consequences of our search for the real (which you so poorly name, to the extent that you see it, the surreal) are much more risky and concrete than your dialectic and pseudoprophetic exercises.[39]

Monny de Boully, the Surrealist refugee who came to join Le Grand Jeu, provides several anecdotes about René's psychic tendencies:

> Hendrick Kramer [Vera's first husband] and I accompanied Daumal to the métro. He was not rushed, because he was never rushed, even when he arrived late—which was rare. If he missed the train, he would stay the night in Roger's room where there was a permanent cycle of discussion, sleep, going out for a bite, and occasional opium smoking.
>
> One day an absolutely amazing thing occurred: As we accompanied Daumal to the métro station Vavin, Daumal remarked: "Look at his back," referring to a tall, thin man, walking ahead of us. Daumal said, "It's curious, but I feel that this man is about to descend the subway steps ahead of me, but I sense black clouds around him, leaden clouds that are suffocating him, I sense that

before reaching the stairs he is going to collapse." The next moment we saw the man stop, drop to his knees and lie down on the sidewalk. We continued, Daumal, lymphatic, did not look or stop. He had two minutes until his train. He said "Good-bye Monny, Good-bye Hendrick," as if nothing had occurred.[40]

We can only speculate as to why they did not stop to assist the man; in some ways it seems uncharacteristic of Daumal's caring nature. Perhaps he was too much in a psychic state, or they were simply staying within the bounds of Parisian, noninteractive, big-city behavior. In any case, Daumal devoted much time and energy to developing psychic channels in his brain and he always insisted on being sober when he attempted parapsychic experiments. Among the writings of the group there was often mention of astral travel and actual descriptions of it by participants and witnesses. While a pensioner at the Lycée Henri IV in Paris, Daumal had frequent nocturnal somnambulant encounters with his friend Robert Meyrat. In a letter to Roger Vailland in 1925, Daumal wrote: "Once with la Stryge (Robert Meyrat), one of these angel emanations sent by him brutally bounced off an impenetrable surface and came back at me, overpowering me until the intended receiver finally accepted it."[41] He elaborated further on these experiences in a long essay entitled "Nerval Le Nyctalope," in which he describes his intense affinity for the nineteenth-century poet Gérard de Nerval.

> This is the procedure that I had found for leaving my body (since then I've learned that occult science has known this since antiquity). I went to bed in the evening as usual, and carefully relaxing every muscle, verifying that each one was completely relaxed, I breathed slowly and deeply, with a regular rhythm, until my body was no more than a paralyzed mass unfamiliar to myself. Then I imagined that I was rising and dressing, but—and it is for this essential point that I require extraordinary courage and power of attention from those who would imitate me—I imagined each gesture in its slightest detail and with such exactitude that I had to put on a shoe in the same exact amount of time as I would have spent in my regular corporeal life. I admit furthermore, that sometimes it took me a week of vain efforts each night before I was even able to achieve getting to a sitting position on the edge of the bed, and the fatigue brought on by such exercises often obliged me to discontinue them for long periods of time. If

I had the force to persevere, a moment came, more or less fast, when I was launched. Seen from outside, I was asleep, but in reality, I was wandering effortlessly—and even with the despairing ease that those persons who remember dying know so well—I was walking, and immobile, I saw myself walking, in completely unfamiliar neighborhoods with Meyrat beside me. The next day, in daylight, we met Gilbert-Lecomte and Vailland and told them about our stroll.[42]

In a 1979 interview Robert Meyrat added:

This was a very dangerous period. We spent many long nights without sleeping. Daumal was very suggestible in the alpha sleep state. I could make him say whatever I wanted. He was less receptive and experiments would fail if he had used tetrachloric acid or opiated tobacco. But when he was in a completely normal state we had a technique for communicating without any intermediary. I have nothing to add to what Daumal wrote in "Nerval le Nyctalope." It is the strict truth, but I will not divulge our technique which, in its simplicity, could be dangerous and should not be revealed to the general public. If you need to communicate with someone, use the phone—if you need to enter the adjoining room, use the door; do not try to pass through the wall. That is all I will say about it.[43]

Yvonne Duplessis describes some of their parapsychic activities in her article "La Vision Extrarétinienne," (Non-Retinal Vision) published in the special 1977 issue of the review *L'Originel*, dedicated to Le Grand Jeu. She described how they took part in experiments from 1925 to 1932 with their former lycée professor, René Maublanc. Maublanc had collaborated with the renowned author, Jules Romains, who experimented extensively with hypnosis and clairvoyance and in his 1920 book, *La Vision Extrarétinienne et le Sens paroptique*, proposed the theory that if the eyes were closed, a kind of vision could be developed in the epidermal cells of the fingers. René engaged in frequent trials with this technique. He became particularly adept at determining the identity of objects when his eyes were tightly covered with thick black glasses that adhered to the skin (similar to motorcyclist's glasses). Maublanc would put Daumal into a light state of hypnosis during which Daumal was able to describe objects in a specially covered box, or the images on book covers. He could differentiate colors by the sensation of heat and cold that he absorbed from different hues. The most precise description of Daumal's paraoptic activities is reported by Monny de Boully:

> I was a witness, not just once but many times, to Daumal's vision via his fingertips. It was extraordinary. In Lecomte's room, for example, if you pulled any unexpected object out of your pocket, Daumal could see what it was from twenty to thirty centimeters away, with his two hands, fingers spread apart. It could be an advertisement for a film and he would describe it. "I see a woman and a man, they are embracing," or, "There's a man on a horse, yes, yes, it seems to be a cowboy." And, in effect, it was a cowboy. After these experiments, Daumal would be completely emptied. And yet he was never *completely* emptied, because he was always empty and never empty and this was a characteristic of Daumal, a definite character trait.
>
> We were in a hotel room in Montparnasse; Daumal was very fatigued. He probably hadn't slept the night before and he said, "Well, I feel like I could fall asleep with my eyes open." Then he lit a cigarette, his gaze became frozen, his pupils stiff, the cigarette continued to burn, he held it between his fingers, it continued to burn down to his skin, he did not scream, he did not drop it, and at that moment, the cigarette still burning between his fingers, he closed his eyes. Roger Lecomte turned out the lights and in the darkened room, Daumal identified objects by holding his hands near them at a distance of a few centimeters. He said, "It is a book." Then, near another object he said, "It is a manometer," and of course, there was a manometer on the table. And each time that he named an object, I would then turn on the light, and it was clear that what he had seen with his paraoptic vision was absolutely exact.
>
> He would come near a drawer and say, "In this drawer there are three boxes of matches, a box of cigarettes and a handwritten paper. We opened the drawer and these items were there. Then Daumal came out of his second state, his cigarette still burning and, I remember his statement: "*Zut alors*, my fingers already smell like beefsteak." They were burned.
>
> It goes without saying that all these objects, seen through paraoptic vision, he had not seen before. It was only when the room was totally black that the objects were put in place. Each time they were identified, the lights were turned on.[44]

LE GRAND JEU VERSUS THE SURREALISTS

Although Daumal's group was greatly overshadowed by the Surrealists, it was the former that deliberately kept its distance when courted by the latter. In 1926, André Breton recognized the literary genius of Daumal and Lecomte and formally invited them to join the Surrealist group, which they declined to do. But by 1929, the Surrealists had developed serious reservations about Le Grand Jeu and saw themselves as superior and more far-reaching in scope. Nadeau writes:

> All the same, Le Grand Jeu was not admired by the Surrealists. It seemed (to the Surrealists) that these young men were keeping too easily within the bounds the Surrealists had already left behind. There was too much talk of "mysticism"; too much Plato-Hegel-Buddha-Christ-Balzac-Rimbaud. They were, in short, too close to literature. And if Breton returned, in the *Second Manifesto*, to occultism and the Initiates, it was a long way from his methods to those of these "God-Seekers."[45]

In 1929, Breton, having become politically active in the Communist Party, invited three members of Le Grand Jeu to attend a Surrealist's meeting at the Bar du Chateau to discuss Stalin's recent expulsion of Leon Trotsky. The meeting soon became an inculpation of Le Grand Jeu members for not being sufficiently radical in their politics. Although Breton hinted at a higher, redemptive function of poetry when he wrote, "We now know that poetry must lead somewhere,"[46] he decided that Le Grand Jeu had become too "spiritualist" and referred to God too frequently. Yet, even as he criticized them, he never ceased in wooing certain members of Le Grand Jeu, and attempting to undermine the cohesiveness of the group. Ribemont-Dessaignes wrote:

> Breton had an enormous ambition to keep Surrealism "pure" even though there was nothing pure about it. He always maneuvered, unconsciously perhaps, to create crises whenever his authority was being challenged. He accused Le Grand Jeu of being deists. It is certain that if one judges the subsequent personal conduct of Daumal, who followed a man such as Gurdjieff, it certainly was entirely anti-Surrealist.[47]

The editors of Le Grand Jeu refused to submit to Breton's inquisitorial judgment and withdrew altogether. In a 1930 letter to Renéville, Daumal says: "I am still just as categorical about the necessarily severe measures we should take in order to avoid a fusion with Susurralisme [sic]."[48]

In the first issue of Le Grand Jeu, there appeared an advertisement for Breton's Nadja, and Daumal wrote a very positive review of this novel. But clearly by 1930, relations had cooled. The eminent writer Antonin Artaud did all in his power to effect a reconciliation between Breton and Daumal and his confreres. When word spread that Daumal was about to publish an "open letter" to Breton, Artaud tried to dissuade his friend, while Breton tried to learn its contents in advance. Ignoring Artaud, the intrepid Daumal proceeded with his long "Open Letter to André Breton," published in Le Grand Jeu III, discussing the relationship between the Surrealists and members of Le Grand Jeu. He spared no words in deprecating the Surrealists' activities as being nothing but confusion, trickery, and diversion. First he stated that: "Le Grand Jeu is a sort of initiatic community; each of the members, whatever he may do, does it with the desire to maintain and reinforce the spiritual unity of the group."[49] Then he proceeded to deride the Surrealists for their weak political stand, their lack of cohesion, lack of original research, and their poor understanding of Baudelaire, Swedenborg, and Hegel. He explained that it was impossible to consider joining their ranks, but then meekly invited Breton and his associates to join Le Grand Jeu. Although Daumal admitted that this invitation might seem pretentious (members of neither group ever lacked gall), he claimed to speak from a "disinterested point of view." He finally underlined the basic fraternity of the two groups in the fight against common enemies such as capitalism and fascism, and suggested that a minimum program of collaboration might be possible and even desirable in the future.

> It is too certain that you, André Breton, cannot come toward us. But our respective situations in the world, among the whole crowd of our common enemies, does not permit us to ignore each other; let us therefore observe each other from now on, and we will see which of us goes the furthest toward the goal that you have so clearly glimpsed. Thus, when you write: "Everything leads me to believe that there exists a certain point in the mind where life and death, the real and the imaginary, the past and the future, the communicable and the incommunicable, the higher and the lower, all cease being perceived as contradictory," it is toward this same point that we are directing our efforts, this point

where finally we have invited you to meet us. We reject those persons who, as you say, "continue to worry about their status and position in the public eye." We are certainly the most conscientious of the seekers dedicated for their whole lives to this nameless identity, and we are the most pitiless to those who, by force, by ruse, or by sophistry, are opposed to our progress. Whereas you, to whom we turned for guidance in the past as one of our guides, whose function was to lead men as far as near themselves, you run the definite risk of remaining paralyzed, caught in the traps that you have set for yourself and those that your extraordinary blindness has allowed your enemies, disguised or not, to set for you. Watch out, André Breton, that you don't end up in a survey manual of literary history. Whereas if we solicit any honor, it would be the honor of being inscribed for posterity in the history of cataclysms.

But after all these reservations, which relate only to the possibility and the timeliness of an imminent material collaboration, know well, André Breton, that if, in the absence of an exterior Event, imperious enough to warrant our immediate reconciliation, we are far from being ready to work together, please know we still continue to think of you as one of those rare men who follow, without ever betraying, the only path we allow ourselves to follow. Here and now we declare loudly and publicly that you have men before you who, though keeping their distance from you, and often severely criticizing you, still are not about to vomit their basest insults on you. If we cannot undertake anything definite with you for the moment, if we have reproaches to level at you, it will in no case be your moral person that we attack; that appears to us, from near or from afar, as intact as in the past and it would take more than temporary discord or shifts in mood to destroy the esteem which you inspire in us: you as a man, possessed by the same search for which we, like you, have sacrificed everything.[50]

This letter is quoted at length because of its historical interest and because it shows us many facets of Daumal. In his eagerness to criticize the narrow sectarian attitudes and heavy theorizing of the Surrealists, Daumal himself often sounds overly intellectual and righteously earnest. As a result, his style is somewhat convoluted, a characteristic occasionally seen in his early writing. Daumal's polemics and jousting with the Surrealists were a necessary part of his literary and spiritual adolescence. By outlining the pitfalls of Surrealism that had alienated him, he freed himself to concentrate on his own path.

In the fourth issue of *Le Grand Jeu*, Daumal takes a further swipe at the Surrealists. In an article entitled "Le Surréalisme et *Le Grand Jeu*" (also published in his first volume of essays), he considers automatic writing to be one of their games that quickly becomes "means for thinking, thinking mechanisms, otherwise called procedures for sleeping."[51]

Anne Balakian discusses the implications of the criticism of the Surrealists by Le Grand Jeu in her biography of André Breton:

> The most serious indication of weakness in the Surrealist circle was its alienation of a younger generation of adherents. Those who had gathered around a new magazine, entitled *Le Grand Jeu*, were not in disagreement with the major Surrealist tenets, but in effect, they accused Breton of not having made enough progress in the directions in which his first proclamation had pointed: social rebellion and psychic occultism. It was particularly painful for Breton to lose these young men, including René Daumal, Roger Vailland, and the literary critic, Rolland de Renéville, the last of whom has done much interesting research into the occultism of Rimbaud. In 1928 the first issue of the magazine (*Le Grand Jeu*) had appeared; it greatly resembled Breton's revues in format, in orientation, in tone, in its association with painters. But without attacking Breton's integrity, these young writers were voicing their disappointment in the slow pace with which Surrealism was advancing in the field of reality; however, their own efforts had neither produced earth-shaking results nor induced Breton to change from theorist to activist. In fact, as (Breton's) Second Manifesto demonstrates, he was plunging deeper and deeper into the philosophy of realism, perhaps because the area of greatest possible pragmatism—that is, association with Communism—had so rapidly collapsed.[52]

Monny de Boully paints a different picture of the relative weight of the two groups. He felt Le Grand Jeu was a much more serious group than the Surrealists:

> Le Grand Jeu was in reality a hermetic group that worked in a kind of absolute. We were outside the exigencies and contingencies of time. The very discretion of Le Grand Jeu did it a disser-

vice. Lecomte and Daumal were metaphysicians in the sense that they opened up new pathways of consciousness, conceiving measures infinitely more valuable than automatic writing or the surrealist pseudo-sleep. They remained faithful to the great mystical texts yet without mysticism. There exists a yoga of Le Grand Jeu, as secret as that of the great yogas of India. Le Grand Jeu is an affair of poets just as much as Surrealism is an act of the literati.[53]

Marianne Lams, a Grand Jeu associate and friend at the Sorbonne describes the special qualities of Le Grand Jeu:

I was greatly affected by Le Grand Jeu. We all had big projects. They wanted to create the anti-Sorbonne. Nathaniel (Daumal) gave me my first lessons in Sanskrit and I studied the astral themes of Daumal and Lecomte. Lecomte was the most charismatic. He was very sweet and attentive, he knew how to listen because he wanted to communicate. Daumal was more ascetic and critical, distant, silent . . . but did he have a sense of humor! As to Rolland de Renéville, very "literary," full of university discipline.[54]

She describes how they would sometimes meet with Breton and the Surrealists at Joseph Sima's home, but generally they kept to themselves because their style of life was younger and leaner than that of the Surrealists. She wrote:

Breton was authoritarian and wanted to control everything. But Le Grand Jeu loved their liberty! They were wild and anarchic without taking sides, without contact with the current literary salons. They were not worldly and their revolt was more than theoretical. They incarnated the great knowledge by testifying to the great Tradition of the great spiritual teachings, even while avoiding the reactionary trap of traditionalists. Lecomte called his group "technicians of the essential!" Le Grand Jeu was one of those bursts of energy that touched very deep. They did nothing to make themselves known, and yet today there is such a desire to know about them. Very modestly they pointed out the essential things.[55]

By 1932, the life cycle of Le Grand Jeu was beginning to ebb. The journal itself never attained much commercial success and only meager critical acclaim. They merited five good reviews in such publications as *Les Cahiers du Sud*, *Europe*, and *Les Nouvelles Littéraires* as well as several negative and paternalistic reviews, as in *Mercure de France*. Over time, its members slowly veered off in other directions.

Roger Vailland left the group early on and had a long successful career as a political writer. Rolland de Renéville likewise went off alone to enjoy a long literary career. Roger Gilbert Lecomte continued writing and working under the aegis of the Le Grand Jeu, long after it ceased to exist. He truly believed that living in a state of drug-induced delirium was ultimately his genetic destiny. Several books devoted to his career hail him as a true "poète maudit" (cursed poet), in the tradition of Rimbaud.

Another reason for the general disaffection was that some of the group resented Daumal's dedication to de Salzmann and the Gurdjieff teaching. But it was the political turmoil of the times that would take the biggest toll. Monny de Boully describes his own trauma at seeing Le Grand Jeu dissolve.

> The disintegration of Le Grand Jeu was the major drama of my life. I had felt early on that this search, full of tenacity, activity, perseverance, and mutual support, required that each member carry his part with the totality of his being. Among our group, only Daumal was capable of doing it. Lecomte was the black angel. It was through him that everything started to corrode, to be frittered away in toxicomania, in a kind of hedonism vis-à-vis oneself. For me it was an extraordinary interior suffering, metaphysical in this case. We were the true messengers of this period. Ever since the demise of Le Grand Jeu, the history of this period has been subverted, resulting in an indiscernible mixing of true mystery and mystification. Le Grand Jeu was on one side, Surrealism on the other. The effectiveness of true literary history will be to reverse the values, to show that the true ideas, the truly subversive ideas were born from Le Grand Jeu, only secondarily from Surrealism.[56]

De Boully also had a rather reductionist viewpoint of Daumal's Gurdjieff experience:

> We should examine how the experimental metaphysic was pursued before and after Le Grand Jeu. Daumal apparently broke with Le Grand Jeu in order to follow Gurdjieff; in reality, it is still

another experimental practice that he is addressing. Gurdjieff developed many of the affirmations already contained in Le Grand Jeu, notably in that which concerns Mechanical Man, Sleeping Man, and the structure of multiple states of being. Gurdjieff is yet another practical work, or a theory subjected to practical experience. Exactly as in Le Grand Jeu. There is a deepening, a substantiation; there is not really a divorce.[57]

To this day, literary historians argue the merits and significance of Le Grand Jeu. Was it merely an appendage of Surrealism? Or did they go beyond the Surrealists in their originality? The verdict may never be decided. Undoubtedly however, Le Grand Jeu can be seen as a group of young writers who, while deadly serious about their metaphysical beliefs, were among the first to celebrate the genius and daring of youth.

As we continue to follow Daumal's path, we will see what changed and what remained the same. Although Daumal may have "outgrown" his Surrealistic beginnings, nevertheless it was his surrealistic tendencies that provided him with much of the "stuff" and style of his writing, including the imagery of *The Counter-Heaven,* the Pataphysical humor of *A Night of Serious Drinking,* and the exotic fantasies of *Mount Analogue.* In all his writings, he never lost touch with the satiric and sublime sides of the same higher vision.

5

The Avant-Garde and Party Politics

Marginal Marxism

> War is due to cosmic forces, to planetary influences; if men were not "slaves" and were capable of "doing," they could resist these influences and refrain from killing one another.
>
> —G. I. Gurdjieff,
> *In Search of the Miraculous*

The creation of a harmonious society in which human beings collectively share the world's resources without greed or desire for power is a vision that has motivated people for ages. Many societies, such as the Greek enclave of Pythagoras, the Incas and the Cretans, have achieved this communal harmony. During the early twentieth century, this ideal seemed closer to realization than it had at any time in the recent past. Many right thinking writers and philosophers believed that mankind could give up their self-serving impulses and join together under the banner of Communism, but these tender beliefs butted up against the harshest realities of power lust all over the globe.

For Daumal, philosophy and literature were hollow pasttimes if not linked to the betterment of mankind. His passionate idealism led him through a phase of active political commitment. He and Le Grand Jeu developed a platform of radical anarchism: they opposed most other "isms," including capitalism, colonialism, militarism, scientism, industrialism, materialism, fascism, and later Nazism. We will see however that, although Daumal's interest in politics never waned entirely, it was gradually superseded again by his ever-present interest in metaphysics. We can appreciate his political activities better by placing them in the Surrealist context.

In spite of their idealistic intentions, involvement in politics for both the Surrealists and Le Grand Jeu generally proved to be a disillusioning experience. Amid the postwar polarization between democracy, Communism, and growing fascism, there was a gradual separation of philosophy and politics that occurred toward the end of the 1920s. Soon the lines were drawn and the Communist Party found many recruits, even among uncommitted writers who felt obligated to maintain their integrity, status, and fashionability by joining the proletarian revolution. In *Consciousness and Society*, H. Stuart Hughes writes:

> During the greater part of the 1920s it might still be possible to live and to philosophize as though the times were in some sense "normal." But the war had revealed the fragility of civilized values in the West. As the decade closed, the coming of the Great Depression and Hitlerism rendered all intellectual detachment impossible. Up to about 1920, no sharp division between literature and social science had been drawn, and the intellectual still felt himself as free as Goethe to roam at will throughout the varied domains of human activity.[1]

In the twenties, both the Surrealists and Le Grand Jeu were filled with rage toward bourgeois society and its notions of patriotism and commerciality. Other literary groups had been concerned with political and social issues, but the Surrealists and Le Grand Jeu were the first to try to bridge the gap between the introversion and aesthetic mysticism of much literature of the day and the fanatical devotion to the dissemination of particular political and social ideologies, the so-called proletarian literature.

In the fourth (unpublished) issue of *Le Grand Jeu*, we find Daumal's essay "Le Surréalisme et *Le Grand Jeu*," where he expressed an esprit de corps vis-à-vis their common political purposes:

> In the abstract, the Surrealists occupy the same historical position as Le Grand Jeu. Having arrived at the understanding of the dialectical necessity of the Revolution, they confirm that their

active role is the intellectual aspect of the revolutionary force while the proletariat is the physical aspect.[2]

In *La Révolution Surréaliste*, Louis Aragon, an avid Communist, wrote:

> The idea of patriotism is truly the most bestial concept, the least philosophical.... For the last century human dignity has been debased to the level of a monetary exchange.... We do not accept the slavery of work. We are the revolt of the mind and spirit. We consider the bloody revolution to be the ineluctable vengeance of the mind humiliated by your works.[3]

Although the Surrealists focused primarily on literature and psychology, they did not want to be considered mere *littérateurs*, especially when it came to changing the world through political action. Likewise, Le Grand Jeu often expressed similar sentiments. In *The Declaration of January 27th*, 1925, the Surrealists exclaimed: " First, we have nothing to do with literature; but we are very capable, if the need arises, of making use of it like everyone else."[4]

On the other hand, the Surrealists and Le Grand Jeu agreed in opposing a purely political point of view, and thus tried to maintain their special status, vis-à-vis Moscow, even after several of the Surrealists—Breton, Aragon, Desnos, Eluard, and Tzara joined the Communist Party in 1925. According to Philip Rahv, in his *Literature and the Sixth Sense*,[5] the writers of the 1920s thought that they were allying themselves with the working class. Soon they realized they had merely surrendered themselves to the Communist Party, which for its own convenience had fused the concepts of party and class. In spite of their deep commitment to the cause, there soon developed a mutual disillusionment with Moscow. The Communists considered Surrealism just another symptom of "bourgeois neurosis." The Surrealists considered the Communists to be just as entrenched in the positivist spirit and "vulgar materialism" as the capitalists. In *L'Aventure des Surréalistes*,[6] Jean Jacques Brochier discusses how the Surrealist ideology was incompatible with a bureaucracy. He suggests that the reason Breton was so fascinated with Stalin's arch rival Léon Trotsky over the others was that Trotsky was not a "party man" but rather represented the opposition, and being in opposition was the essence of the Surrealist *weltancshauung*. Brochier claims that Breton and the Surrealists were the first to denounce the Moscow trials, and the heaviness and absurdity of the Party apparatus.

Pierre Naville, one of the staunch party-line poets, wrote a brochure entitled "La Révolution et les intellectuels," in which he is critical of the Surrealists: "If they want to be truly revolutionary, they must abandon their metaphysical doctrines and particularly this reference to the mystical East, so frequently mentioned by Artaud. They must sign up with the party of the working class."[7] Brochier describes Breton's response to Naville's pamphlet and his criticism of the Communists for presuming to monopolize the revolution. The poet Ribemont Dessaignes describes Breton's brief stint in "social action" labor for the Communist Party: "They assigned him to a workers' 'cell' unit of plumbers. He was so revolted by the job that he did not last long."[8] In his own words, Breton refused "to be limited to the political terrain of social action; the surrealists have another terrain, just as revolutionary, to occupy, the moral terrain. We must separate the problems of research and education on the one hand, and immediate action on the other"[9]

In 1929–1930, provoked by the political, social, and economic unrest around them, Le Grand Jeu became more and more politicized. Their concern for the world turmoil caused a gradual polarizition of the members, which led to dissent within the ranks of Le Grand Jeu, just as it had occurred among the Surrealists. For example, Roger Vailland, one of the original four members of the Simplistes and Le Grand Jeu, came under attack by the Surrealists for having written several articles favorable to the Paris prefect of police. By 1930, he had fallen out of favor with his own band as well, and formally resigned from Le Grand Jeu. Years later in 1948, Vailland contributed to a book commissioned by the Communist Party in which he exhorted: "The Revolution does not need Surrealism; it needs coal, steel, probably atomic energy, and especially that virile energy which makes the scientists great, the leaders clearheaded, and the thinkers heroic."[10]

The political tenor of the times was the underlying catalyst for the various ideological rifts between and among the Surrealists and Le Grand Jeu. In an article entitled "René Daumal et Le Grand Jeu," Léon Gabriel Gros writes:

> The end of this movement [Le Grand Jeu] is due to the economic collapse of 1929, which hastened for many people the development of a social conscience. Yet it is worth noting that even if the doctrine of Le Grand Jeu was by its nature "evasionist," they never hesitated in becoming "*engagé*," most notably by taking a definite part against police repression. These collaborators dis-

persed in many directions, but none ever betrayed the beliefs and needs of the group, no matter what was their subsequent evolution. All of them followed through on their chosen path and none ever degenerated into being mere "littérateurs."[11]

Various members had different interpretations of what their public position should be vis-à-vis the Communist Party. Still, the group came to a complete accord in signing a letter (1930) written to Rabindranath Tagore, the Indian poet who translated important Eastern works into English. They took him harshly to task for being so Westernized in his tastes and philosophy, and so uninvolved in his native country's fight for independence.

Today just as the Hindu revolution is beginning, you publicly declare your admiration for the West. While the Indian people are rising up and getting themselves slaughtered, you speak of the beauties of the universe right in the country against which they are revolting and which is slaughtering them. . . ."All of the East will be thankful to the West for the intellectual light which it sends," you say. The West to which you address yourself, Sir, should only merit your distaste, if the worry over your personal security allowed you to embrace a "truth" and a "cause" which were not those of murderers, imbeciles, and bankers.[12]

In the early 1930s the Surrealists began to attack certain members of Le Grand Jeu, notably Rolland de Renéville, for not being sufficiently involved in the united front against fascism and imperialism. From the vast correspondence between Daumal and Renéville it is clear that the latter's interests were strictly in the domain of poetics and mysticism. By highlighting some of the correspondence concerning the issue of art versus politics, we can get a glimpse of Daumal the political activist. This involvement in current issues is evidence of Daumal's social conscience and interest in the real world. Renéville, on the other hand, did not wish to be distracted by political events and ideologies, and remained convinced of the power of poetry to change men's hearts. This had been Daumal's original position as well and one that he never truly abandoned, even as he engaged in social action. Yet for a while, this issue provoked an emotional debate between the two friends. In 1930, three months after the letter to Tagore, Daumal wrote to Renéville:

We must manifest all the subversive consequences of our thinking in the social realm. Here, we could collaborate on a much larger scale: it is a question of doing what the Communist party does so poorly: to demonstrate, by an analysis of the facts of the current situation, the intimate contradictions of capitalist society. For example, prove by precise calculations, that the fact of buying a share of X francs of "Royal Dutch" is the equivalent of shooting a bullet through the head of a Palestinian Arab.[13]

In 1932, Daumal, in response to accusations from others that Renéville was counter-revolutionary, tried to explain, defend, and chastise Renéville for his lack of social and political awareness. He wrote to André Delon and Pierre Audard, the attackers: "I also do not approve of Renéville's article, nor in general, the lack of clarity in his social attitude when he presumes to speak publicly. I believe Renéville to still be very maladroit and uninformed in the political domain of literature."[14] Daumal maintained a staunch Marxist stand in his letter to Renéville:

> Now you talk of "regurgitating Marxist theories." Truly, have you tried that hard? Does classic political economy seem more exalting to you? To my mind, declaring oneself anti-Marxist is the same as calling oneself anti-Euclidean (in practical geometry), or anti-Copernican in astronomy, etc.; Marxism is the only true science of economic facts that I know.[15]

Renéville responded by chastising René for having abandoned his belief in the omnipotence of art:

> I come from the point of view of poetry in order to consider Communism, and you, you come from the point of view of Communism to consider poetry. This is, in effect, a change of position for you, which has been going on for two years (while I, on the other hand, have maintained the initial position of Le Grand Jeu). This has resulted in a gap between us. The fact that you could regret that in an article on Aragon, I told the Truth, even though it was not a good Communist tactic, is enough to show me how much separates us. For me, the social revolution is a little accident to encourage, from which I expect practically nothing in terms of any kind of revelation. Communism is the son of capitalism. It is its sanction. To confuse its future with that of poetry appears to

me to be confusion of the same order as the error of confusing the loss of personality in a mystical experience with that of the individual submitting to communal living.[16]

It would be a while before Daumal gravitated back to Renéville's attitude. Even in 1934, several years after the dissolution of Le Grand Jeu, Daumal continued to be concerned about the political activities of his day. At this point he had had three years' involvement with Gurdjieff's philosophy, which considers political and social phenomena to be the mechanical result of the workings of much greater cosmic laws. In "Lettre de Paris" (which was included in volume I of his collected essays entitled *L'Evidence Absurde*), Daumal relates the events of a national workers' strike in 1934. He discusses various aspects of the political situation, refers to Hitler as an "Ubu Sanglant" (a bloodthirsty Ubu), and ponders the history and future of his nation: "Here we affirmed a dominant and sometimes irritating trait of French intellectuals: the distrust of extreme doctrines, the taste for individual nuance, to maintain a doctrine within the specific limits of a personality."[17]

By this time, however, Daumal was becoming generally disenchanted with the meager outcome of political action. In a letter to Emile Dermenghen, he seems to reiterate the stance taken by Renéville.

> I am not Marxist (if it isn't a badge, combat banner, that is, I am not anti-anti-Marxist) in the sense that I do not believe the economic revolution will suffice to "create a new man" (as Aragon said, for example); but . . . each time I speak of social realities, I think Marxist.
>
> I am not a philosopher in the sense that I do not believe this individual revolution can be accomplished by pure speculation.
>
> There is a profound sickness in Western civilization which the proletarian revolution will not be inadequate to cure (but which will not be cured without it).[18]

Daumal never joined a political party, but for one year he belonged to the AEAR, the Association of Revolutionary Writers and Artists. (L'Association des écrivains et artistes révolutionnaires). As his political fervor waned, he explained his position in a letter to Julien Benda:

> A certain atmosphere of poorly digested Marxism and catechism alienated me. After a year of fumbling around, I finally saw what

my role was as an intellectual vis-à-vis the revolution. In an exclusively political group I would only have committed blunders and neglected the work for which I am irreplaceable, as meager as that might be. This work, for the moment, is the critique of the culture [society].[19]

In 1936 in a letter to Jean Fiolle, he discussed the problems of the Russian proletariat and its glorification of science and industrial progress. According to Jack Daumal, René seemed to return more and more to Renéville's position, and spoke less and less often of current events. In 1940 Daumal suggested to Max-Pol Fouchet some principles for a "Décalogue de l'Ecrivain" (a Ten Commandments for the Writer): "Have them work in common to serve these principles and under the control of these rules. The most urgent themes to treat would be: What matters most above everything else in human life? To put back in their royal place the great values: Goodness, Beauty, Truth."[20]

In the forty-one pages of the chapter "La Mort du Grand Jeu" (facts and letters compiled by Jack Daumal chronicling the demise of Le Grand Jeu, included only in the French edition of *You Were Always Wrong*), the younger Daumal brother makes an important point: René did succeed in finding a teacher and his meeting with de Salzmann did create a distinct inner change in him, as clearly conveyed in the poem "Mémorables":

> Remember the beautiful mirage of concepts, and of moving words, a palace of mirrors built in a cave; and remember the man who came, who broke everything, who took you by his rough hand, pulled you out of your dreams, and made you sit down on the pine needles of broad daylight, and remember that you do not know how to remember.[21]

Nevertheless, this meeting did not mark a sudden change in the outward process of his life. Daumal's political and philosophical leanings were not suddenly altered. Gurdjieff's teaching had no relation to political or ordinary philosophical beliefs; it went above and beyond such things. Like the *Bhagavad Gita* and other Eastern spiritual teachings, Gurdjieff urged the individual to be active in the world but not of the world. It is not what you choose to do but how actively conscious you remain while doing it. Jack Daumal reports a story about Madame de Salzmann. When one of her students insisted, "I am a communist and I want to remain a communist. So what could this teaching possibly do for me?" She replied, "You would become a better communist!"[22]

In his final years during the war, René often referred to world events in his letters, comparing "the howling dog" Hitler to the "breathable," honest Roosevelt. He appreciated the special circumstances that he had been given in his life—to live through two wars. From the Gurdjieff Work he learned to transform the encircling madness into usable energy. In 1917, during the Russian Revolution, P. D. Ouspensky complained to Gurdjieff: "Events are against us. It is by now clear that it is not possible to do anything in the midst of this mass madness." Gurdjieff replied: "It is only now that it is possible, and events are not against us at all."[23] While Daumal spoke of the "convulsing planet," he felt that one lives in the era that one chooses: "Whether one lives in the time of Hitler or Attila or Napoléon, there always exits concurrently a Golden Age that is maintained by certain rare individuals. The challenge is to acquire the power and ability to find them."[24]

Although the meeting with de Salzmann did not constitute a sudden transmutation, it did mark the end of Daumal's first growth cycle. The embryonic stage of Daumal's thought was seeded by the synergistic energy of his own coterie, influenced by Alfred Jarry, Freud, and the parallel research of the Surrealists. These Western strains together with Eastern mystical thought enabled Daumal eventually to plunge deeply into the teachings of Gurdjieff.

III
EASTERN STUDIES

6

The Influence of Hindu Thought

Renunciation and Transformation

> The essential weft of my thought, of our thought, is inscribed—I've known it for years—in the sacred books of India. Each of my discoveries, I always find, shortly after making it, in such and such a verse in one of the Upanishads or in the Bhagavad Gita, that I hadn't noticed before. This necessarily leads me to put my confidence in these Words, in the unique Word from which they proceed, and in the mystical tradition which flows from these Words.
>
> —René Daumal, "Encore sur les livres de René Guénon"

Daumal's interest in the idea of self-transformation through nonattachment or renunciation drove him to investigate many religious traditions. From the very first issue of *Le Grand Jeu* in 1928, there were frequent discussions of religion, theology, and especially Hindu theories of nonduality and renunciation. The second essay of this first issue by Roger Gilbert-Lecomte, was entitled, "The Force of Renouncements." In the second issue in 1929, Rolland de Renéville wrote an essay in which he correlated the theories of Arthur Rimbaud concerning nonduality with those of the Vedas and the *Bhagavad Gita*. Renéville wrote: "*Vedism and Brahmanism* teach that the human soul is merely a spark from the universal fire, a reflection of God at the heart of its physical mass."[1] He traced Rimbaud's study of Oriental metaphysics that led the Symbolist poet to replace Western individualism with nondualism. But no one among the Surrealists, and modern writers in general, was as obsessed with the concept of renunciation as Le Grand Jeu. The youthful fanaticism of their quest for rigor and purity brought them (and especially Daumal) to seek affirmation of its importance in these ancient texts.

The concept of nonattachment and renunciation is present in varying forms throughout the centuries of Hindu thought. In fact, it appears in all traditional religions to varying degrees, yet emphasized in different ways at different periods. Whether linked with individual denial or institutional monasticism, it is one of the most fundamental traits of the Indian religious spirit.

In the *Rig Veda*, written 1200–900 B.C.—the earliest collection of hymns and prayers to a group of nature gods (Brahma, Vishnu, Shiva, gods of sun, wind, and fire, all contained in the One God)—renunciation means a "giving up to the gods" by performing sacrificial and magical rites. In the Aryan household a sacred fire was kindled at the marriage ceremony and continually fueled throughout the life of the family. At this fire the household would make offerings to the gods, three times daily. The sacrificer could transcend the limitations of the phenomenal world through a successful sacrifice (that is, a giving up of himself through his gift). The sacrifice was both appeasement and communion with the primordial energy that bathes the planet.

The Hindu tradition of sacrifice by fire was more than mere ritual; it was a symbol of the nature of all life—spiritual and physical. According to early Hindu thought, everything lives and grows by heat; as the combustion of our food creates muscular energy, so spiritual energy, as well, must come from fire. A parallel in Christian theology is the central story of Calvary, where Christ sacrificed his life and then overcame death. Even the Hindu Prime Mover is born out of sacrifice: "That, which possessing life-force, was enclosed by the vacuum, the One, was born through the power of heat from its austerity."[2] Thus austerity can create heat—the power to give birth to and transform life. Through austerity, man can accumulate substantial life-force to control the environment, and give birth to a new etheric spiritual body; hence the Sanskrit term *dvija* (*twice born*). The term *etheric body*, or *astral body*, refers to the concept found in several religions—Hinduism, Taoism, and Buddhism in the East, Sufism in the

Middle East, theosophy in the West—as well as in the Gurdjieff philosophy. It is the belief that human beings, through efforts at self-transformation, can create another "body" of a finer vibratory frequency that exists simultaneously with the corporal body. Evidence of this spiritual body is sometimes visible as an "aura" or "halo," depicted in the religious art of many cultures.

Even though they speak of austerities, the early Vedas reflect a joyous, positive attitude toward life. There is very little consideration of a dualism or separation between the material world and the spiritual world. Everything is holy, in the Blakean sense:

> To see a world in a grain of sand
> And heaven in a wild flower;
> Hold infinity in the palm of your hand
> And eternity in an hour.
> —William Blake (1757–1827)[3]

The conjugal union of the divine parents, Heaven and Earth, symbolized the vastness, brightness, and bounty of nature. Hymns of praise express the desire for a sharing in the bounty on the material plane:

> May Heaven and Earth, honey dripping, honey dispensing with honeyed courses, shower down honey for us, bring unto the gods sacrifice and wealth, and for us great glory, reward, and heroic strength.[4]

This celebration of abundance and desire for abundance, contrasts sharply with later Hindu thought about austerity, in which the very existence of the material universe would be considered an illusion (*maya*). These early hymns were anthropomorphic and personal: "O Agni, be easy of access to us as a father to his son. Join us for our own well-being."[5]

The Vedas also included much cosmological speculation. During this period, the various gods were accorded much veneration. Yet there was, even at this early stage, a movement toward monotheism, a tentative understanding that there existed some mysterious, all-powerful force behind all the gods. Predating the Gospel of St. John by 1200 years, the *Nasadiya* or Creation Hymn of the *Rig Veda* describes the beginning of the world in a nontheistic manner similar to John's gospel ("In the beginning was the Word," expressing so humanly our wonderment before the vast universe):

> Neither nonbeing nor being was there at that time;
> There was no air-filled space nor was there the sky beyond it.
> "That One" breathed without air in its own special manner.
> Other than It, there did not exist anything whatsoever.
> Wherefrom this creation has issued, whether he had made it
>   or whether he has not—
> He who is the Over-Eye of this world in the highest heaven—
> He alone knows, *or, perhaps, even he does not know.* [Italics mine][6]

The experiencing of this Oneness that creates multiplicity, not just once and for all, but continually, is the aim of Hindu teaching and its techniques of austerity.

In addition to sacrifice by fire, renunciation took a particular form in each of the prescribed life stages of the individual. *The Arthava Veda* outlines these four stages of Aryan life. The first is the *brahmachari*, the celibate "student of the Veda" who studies under a competent teacher (*guru*), an authority on the Vedic texts. This stage is followed by that of the *grhastha*, the householder, husband and father or wife and mother; the third stage, is the *vatarasana*, or the ascetic who withdraws into the forest in later life to meditate and live in harmony with nature (*vatarasana* stands for nakedness, "one having only the wind of air for one's waist girdle").[7] The final stage (*sannyasin*) is the ascetic who returns to society as a mendicant to teach and help those around him. The following description of the liberation of the fourth stage (*sannyasin*) echoes the words of Liselle Raymond as she described Daumal's lack of interest in the material world. To quote Alexandra David Neel in her book, *Buddhism*:

> The renunciation of the *Sannyasin* differs greatly from that of the Christian monk who gives up worldly benefits in order to earn heavenly merits, or that of the mystic who burns with a desire to unite with God and believes that he can achieve this by rejecting the world. The monk's renunciation has more the character of "sacrifice," but the *Sannyasin* rejects the world because he feels an aversion or repugnance for what most men consider to be the good things and the "joys of life." *Sannyasa* is not a "means" to attain an end, *Sannyasa* is the end itself, a joyous deliverance. Furthermore, the *Sannyasin* functions above all social and reli-

gious laws. He is liberated from all ties, and walks on his own path. He is "on the outside."[8]

Daumal felt himself to be at the level of a *brahmachari*, a student of the Veda, who must work with a teacher. By studying the tradition of this crucial teacher-student relationship, Daumal was later quick to recognize his own teacher. Once a Vedic teacher accepts the *brahmachari* as a disciple, he treats him like an embryo within his own body. The *Arthava Veda* gives a lengthy description of the *brahmachari*:

> He carries him for three nights in his belly; when he is born,
> the gods assemble to see him.
> The Brahmachari goes forth, kindled by sacred fire sticks,
> clothing himself with black antelope skin, consecrated,
>   long bearded.
> Within one single day he goes from the eastern
>   to the northern ocean,
> having gathered together the worlds,
>   he fashions them repeatedly.[9]

The student is glorified in a cosmological sense. He is "clothed in heat and with a long beard,"[10] symbolic of the many rays of the sun, the primeval principle of the universe. This radiating light formed Christian halos as well as the flames rising from Mohamned's head in Islamic art. When Moses attained a certain level of enlightenment, he was described as having *carnayim* or rays of light emanating from his head. This word also translates as "horns," hence Michaelangelo's depiction of Moses with sculpted horns on his head. Likewise, Gurdjieff also describes at length the initiation and ascension of the student-initiate in his book *All and Everything*. In the final chapter the main character attains the perfection of his reason and is honored by the archangels of the universe, transfigured with a majestic appearance and crowned with horns, a special sign of worthiness.

In *Sources of Indian Tradition*, Theodore de Barry points out that the heat of the sun and the fervor generated by austerities are the building blocks of creation—whether it is the creation of organic life on earth or the building of an etheric body: "The *Brahmachari* fashioned animals of earth on the back of the waters. He stood in the sea performing austerities. When he had performed ritual ablution, he would shine extensively over the earth, brown and ruddy."[12]

Around 500 B.C., the Upanishads, speculative treatises that probed for a new interpretation of the earlier Vedic concepts, further developed the concept of self-denial. Gradually there was a deemphasis of the ritual sacrifice and an emphasis on a more contemplative aspect of self-denial. De Barry writes: "Here the link between man and cosmos is no longer the ritual act, but a knowledge of forces symbolically represented in the ritual."[13] The Upanishadic writers criticize those who look only to the rituals: "The fools who delight in this sacrificial ritual as the highest spiritual good go again and again through the cycle of old age and death."[14]

In *Dimension of Renunciation in Advaita Vedanta*, Kapil Tiwari writes:

> The *Brhadaranyaka Upanishad* attaches a very positively interior orientation to what has been described as outward in the *Veda*. "Having become calm, subdued, quiet, patiently enduring and collected, one should see the Self in the Self." Commenting on the same passage, Paul Deussen remarks that such activities as *Vedic* study, sacrifice, alms, penance, and fasting are the more outward means (*vahya*), but tranquillity, self-restraint, renunciation, patience, and concentration, are the inward means to knowledge.[15]

Formerly, the *brahmachari* was asked, as a student ascetic, to exercise physical control; now in addition to that, more subtle forms of mental and emotional restraint are emphasized such as systematic self-analysis, breath control, and the psychological disciplines of yoga. The *Manusmriti* states:

> But when one among all the organs slips away from control,
> thereby a man's wisdom slips away from him,
>   even as water flows
> through a single tear in a water carrier's hide bag.[16]

Thus, Upanishadic philosophy came to be more concerned with the internal realization of Godhood through a struggle with one's ordinary manifestations (which Daumal would list as bodily and egoistic desires and cravings in the essay "Freedom without Hope"). According to the precepts of sacred knowledge (*jnana*), struggling this way would result in a transformation: renunciation as linked with the uncovering of *jnana* results in turning the concern of man away from external things and toward his essential inner nature, by accomplishing that by which everything else is accomplished.

> The Golden God, the Self, the immortal Swan
> leaves the small nest of the body, goes where He wants,
> He moves through the realms of dreams;
> > makes numberless forms;
> delights in sex; eats, drinks, laughs with his friends
> frightens himself with scenes of heart-chilling terror.
> But he is not attached to anything that he sees;
> and after He has wandered in the realms
> > of dream and awakeness,
> has tasted pleasures and experienced good and evil,
> He returns to the blissful state from which He began.[17]

Jnana and renunciation take place simultaneously as one of the Upanishad says: "Verily, after they have found this soul, the *Brahmanas* cease from desiring children, from desiring possessions, from desiring the world, and wander about as beggars" (*Brihadaranyaka Upanishad*).[18]

Thus, over the centuries Upanishadic doctrine was the expression of a great quietistic movement characterized by a deep disillusionment with life. No longer merely an outward ritualistic sacrifice, renunciation came to mean an elaborate abstention from the objects of sense and, finally, an attempt to remain active in life yet disinterested and neutral to the rewards of action.

The *Bhagavad Gita* (500 B.C.), purportedly written by the poet Vyasa, extends the idea of renunciation into even subtler areas. The *Gita*, considered to be the New Testament of the Hindu tradition, presents an avenue of renunciation to the layman who chooses not to become a mendicant monk. It goes as far as to oppose the quietistic life suggested in the Upanishads. It advises active participation in life, though always with an unselfish spirit: "Who so performs actions that should be performed, without interest in the fruits of the action, he is the possessor of renunciation, he is the disciplined man, and not he who (merely) abstains from (building the sacrificial) fires and from (ritual) acts."[19]

The *Gita* warns against insincerity, emphasizing the importance of the right mental attitude, over that of the physical act: "Who so restrains his organs of action and sits pondering on the objects of sense with his mind, his soul is deluded; he is called a hypocrite." Harsh penance and torture, as practiced by some extreme sects of Hindu ascetics, is discouraged in the *Gita* as doing violence to God who is within man's person, starving within the body: "The conglomerate of the elements, the fools, and (starving) me myself, who am within the body, know that they have demonic resolve."[20]

At present, the dominant Hindu philosophic school is the *Advaita Vedanta*, established by Shankara (850 B.C.). It elaborates on a still more mystical and subtle interpretation of the Vedas, the Upanishads, and the *Bhagavad Gita*. Shankara believed there are two levels of knowledge: the ordinary level of mere reasoning, and the higher level of introspective realization of the absolute unity of the individual soul and *Brahman* (God). He continued the concept of *karma-sannyasa* (action-renunciation), for he believed selfless action and self-abnegation could be transformed into knowledge (*jnana*) resulting in the complete transformation of man.

In the 1977 issue of a literary review entitled *Port-des-Singes* ("Port o' Monkeys"), named after the port at the base of Mount Analogue, there is a Daumal translation of a poem by Shankara called "The Hammer of Stupidity" (*Mohamudgara*). In verse after verse, this poem questions the value of pursuing worldly pleasures and offers the suggestion, reminiscent of Buddhism, that we seek the happiness that comes from the cessation of desire.

> Do not join the hunt after things, people, and youth,
> In the blinking of an eye, time carries everything off.
> All of this is made up of illusion: reject it.
> Enter quickly into the dwelling of the sacred,
>   as soon as you find it.
> A drop of water trembling on a lotus leaf:
> How unstable our life is
> Only for a moment, the encounter
>   of a few real beings down here
> offers us the only vessel to guide us across
>   the ocean of existence.[21]

In a public lecture delivered in San Francisco in 1973 in the series "Sacred Tradition and Present Need," Philippe Lavastine distinguished between the ancient genuine Vedantic tradition and what he called the recent spurious Vedanta. He felt that the latter always claims the unreality of the world, calling it sheer *maya*, illusion. Lavastine views the earthly plane as a symbol or reflection of a higher one. We are meant to interact with the material forms of the world as symbols, not just as objects of attachment to be avoided. But the later Vedanta turned its back on the objects of the senses, claiming that the things of the world are imbued with poison. According to Lavastine, "the Vedantists feel that God exists for the individual alone. He has nothing to do with social order or collective life. Religion is a private affair as in the words of Whitehead: "God is what a man does with his own solitude."[22] In his early years Daumal had these same Vedantic tendencies, often viewing the material world as poison.

It might seem that each succeeding period of Hinduism: the Vedic, the Upanishadic, the era of the Gita, and finally the Vedandic period attempted to improve upon or purify the concepts and sacrificial practices of the preceding period. My interpretation of this phenomenon—the cyclical variation in religious practice—is that in the beginning of each period there was a renewal or deepening of understanding, a realization that the techniques for self-transformation were to be carried out, not only to the letter but to the heart of the law. Over a period of time, there inevitably occurred a degeneration in commitment and understanding among the general mass of participants. Subsequently, a more subtle reading of the ancient texts, in the form of new holy writings, would then revitalize the rituals that had become empty and stale. And so there occurred a cyclic purification and revitalization of Hindu philosophy while the essential law and sacrificial practices, both external and internal, were retained. Eventually, at least a small core group of seekers would always remember that the ultimate aim of personal or liturgical sacrifice was self-transformation.

In his early years, Daumal held a much more cynical, radically political vision of the cycles of history. In his long essay of 1928 entitled "The Metaphysical Intuition in History," he outlines the concept of religion, down through the ages, from Hinduism to Christ. From his Marxist viewpoint, the causes of modification in religious forms are due entirely to the struggle for power between the clergy and the secular institutions:

> At the origin of every religion there is a doubt, a negation of a faith in a preexisting dogma. This constitutes some revitalized thinking as in the case of Jesus against the Jewish theocracy, Shakya Morim against Brahmanism, or Mohammed against idolatry. In every society where man exploits man, the doubter is a dangerous revolutionary. The greatest cleverness of a reigning class is to co-opt the words of a doubter and make them the core of a new doctrine. The more elevated and violent the original

doubt, the more oppressive the religion. As long as there exists a class of exploiters, all real thought will risk becoming a dogma, an instrument of oppression.[23]

He felt that the clearest expression of metaphysical experiences occurs in religions at their embryonic stage—in heresies, in eruptions of mysticism, or in any struggle against the roots of established religions, instituted as systems of social repression.

Throughout their histories, India and Tibet have experienced more than any other land a tremendous abundance of attempts to think, and more than any other land, the priesthood has always found ways to appropriate all these manifestations of thought and turn them into vehicles for theocratic power.... An example of this degeneration of true insight was the Brahman religions, a product of perhaps the brightest spark of consciousness which has ever flashed in the course of history, and which became the underpinning of a caste system and an abhorrent theocratic tyranny.[24]

Since the book *The Laws of Manu* only concerns the spiritual growth of the Brahmin caste, he feels that the wonderful revelation of the initial mystical occurrence was perverted. "Nearly the entire *Laws of Manu* is devoted to glorifying the power, privileges, and the sacredness of the Brahman. Again, religion is playing its double role of enslaving the people and nipping real thought in the bud."[25] He then explains how, in the cases of the Jain followers of Mahavira and Buddhist followers of Shakyamuni, the caste of warriors and princes used the revolutionary force of these discontented factions of society against theocratic authority. Then, once in power, they perverted it by turning it into a new dogma able to uphold *their* domination. A few pages later, he proposes a guiding principle put forth by Heraclitus and Hegel that explains evolution from the economic, political, and religious points of view: "the dialectical law according to which consciousness, as it manifests itself, constructs the mechanism of its own death, the law of evolution."[26]

Some of Daumal's urgency to uncover a pure form of religious experience is expressed in a poem entitled "Poem to God and Man," a shockingly vehement diatribe against organized religion in general and the Judeo-Christian tradition in particular. The following excerpts from the lengthy poem give evidence as to why it was always refused publication until 1970, when Jack Daumal included it in the publication *Tu tes toujours trompé* (*You Were Always Wrong*):

> Poor damn old nothing God!
> it's not your fault you've got that dirty hairy face
> white and pink and harmlessly senile,
> it's that bastard that slapped on the paint,
> that padre who stuck you up in heaven
> with his Desire to Enlighten the Universe
>   with Stupidity [D.E.U.S.]
> he's the one that smeared paint on that senile face
> in his image, that sneaky old bastard,
>
> As for me, priest, I spit in your face in the name of God
> it's for my own health,
> and it's a ritual gesture.
>
> The sail of throbbing flesh cruises on,
> my good old brother's Corpse, deaf and blind
> still hauling the Ship
> the Good Ship Christendom through the ages.
>
> He hadn't planned on that. . . . But
> even though I love you from the depths of despair,
> man my good old Brother, you're just a piece of carrion.
>
> Your tortured body, which you threw to us as fodder,
> stinks just like my human corpse will stink,
> it's chewed up by millions of worms: by
> Roman Catholic worms, by
> Orthodox worms, by
> Protestant worms,
> the Christian pestilence, the great Lamist pestilence
> the great Brahman pestilence, the great Buddhist pestilence.[27]

The overstatement of this poem is evidence that Daumal could never have gravitated toward the local Christian church of his community, or any organized world religion. He saw only the oppressive, bourgeois aspects of these institutions. It is certainly true that in the Western Judeo-Christian tradition, followers are not encouraged as much as they are in

Eastern religions to meditate and *internalize* higher spiritual energies. In *Lost Christianity*,[28] Jacob Needleman describes the contemplative tradition as "apaphatic": etymologically "not expressing," that is, withdrawing from thoughts, images, and emotions, leading to an inner attention and a contemplative attitude of nonattachment. This kind of "mindfulness" is a minor stream in Christianity, exemplified by the writings of Meister Eckhart. Many Christian sects such as the twelfth-century Cathars (who engaged in yogalike somatic practices to induce internal mystical states) were deemed heretics and ruthlessly put down by the church in an organized genocide known as the Albigensian crusade.

More dominant in the Christian traditon, according to Needleman, is the "cataphatic" phenomenon: the outward expression of religious insight, focusing on stories and events in the life of Christ. Christians are encouraged to venerate Christ rather than copy his visionary trance states or what St. Paul called his "self-emptying." Jesus said, "The kingdom of God is within you," but since then, the emphasis has been on following moral precepts and participating in the community of the church, admirable activities that also conveniently suit the needs of the state, more brahmanic than yogic. This narrow focus limits the "followers" to set much smaller metaphysical goals for themselves. Christian theology sees the pre-Christian world as totally *un*spiritual, dark and foreboding, *pagan*. In the Christian tradition the followers see God as a person: a father figure, or the painterly version of a young or infant blue-eyed Christ. It is less common to really think of God as the universal consciousness penetrating all things. More commonly they achieve an intellectual understanding of God as an abstract concept, or a powerful personal ally in times of crisis.

All these Christian details of historicity and dogma did not interest Daumal in the least. For him, the only thing that held any meaning was the single inexpressible reality behind all science and religion. For this, one needed the practice of "gnosticism," which is the attempt to understand the laws of the universe by experiencing them in yourself.

Nevertheless, many years later in 1941, while living in Marseilles, René developed a friendship with two priests and the Christian writer Raymond Christoflour. Through them he came to a better understanding and appreciation of Christianity. He saw that it could be a true path, but he excluded all "pseudo Christian" sects—those based on human reason, or superstition, including Theosophism and some forms of Protestantism. In a letter to Christoflour, René described the parallels between Catholicism and Vedantism and underlined the importance for all religions to cut through illusion, and dissolve what he called the "me-I." If, in his early writings, he spoke of religion as an "instrument of oppression" used by a "class of exploiters," now he discussed it in more conservative terms:

> In any country or in any century, I believe that a certain exclusivism (almost a trace of intolerance) is necessary, on the part of the true religion that reigns there. A religion becomes a system of reference which should not be mixed up with others; for most minds, that would only engender confusion.[29]

Moving from the antidogmatic position of his youth, he now felt that every path should have a guide to direct the seekers and help them stay on the path.

Fig. 9. René and Vera Daumal. Born in Siberia, of Russian Jewish parents, Vera was a naturalized American citizen who, with her first husband, the poet Hendrik Cramer, became associated with Le Grand Jeu in 1927. In 1931, after a year-long transatlantic correspondence, she became René's lifelong companion.

Fig. 10. Jack Daumal, René's only brother, showed the same precocious intellect and interest in metaphysics as René. For many years, a student of Gurdjieff and Madame de Salzmann, he eventually embraced the Muslim faith while continuing to include Gurdjieff's teaching. He lived for thirty years in Egypt where he taught classical languages. He now resides in the south of France.

Fig. 11. Philippe Lavastine in the 1950s. Very close to René and the de Salzmann family, Lavastine shared Daumal's interest in Hinduism and the Gurdjieff Work. His lively accounts in 1977 and 1983 brought the young Daumal to life.

Fig. 12. Rarely did René take on any of the outer trappings of Hindu culture. As a Frenchman and Westerner, he felt that the inner teaching alone is universally accessible to all who genuinely seek it. Nevertheless, in this photo, he agreed to demonstrate the proper method of *Padmasana* yoga, complete with traditional garb.

Fig. 13. Uday Shankar, a master of classical Hindu dance, performed in the capitals of Europe with his younger brother and dancer, Ravi Shankar. Daumal accompanied them to the United States as their press agent. He felt that Uday Shankar's movements embodied the essence of Hindu spirituality.

Fig. 14. René Guénon

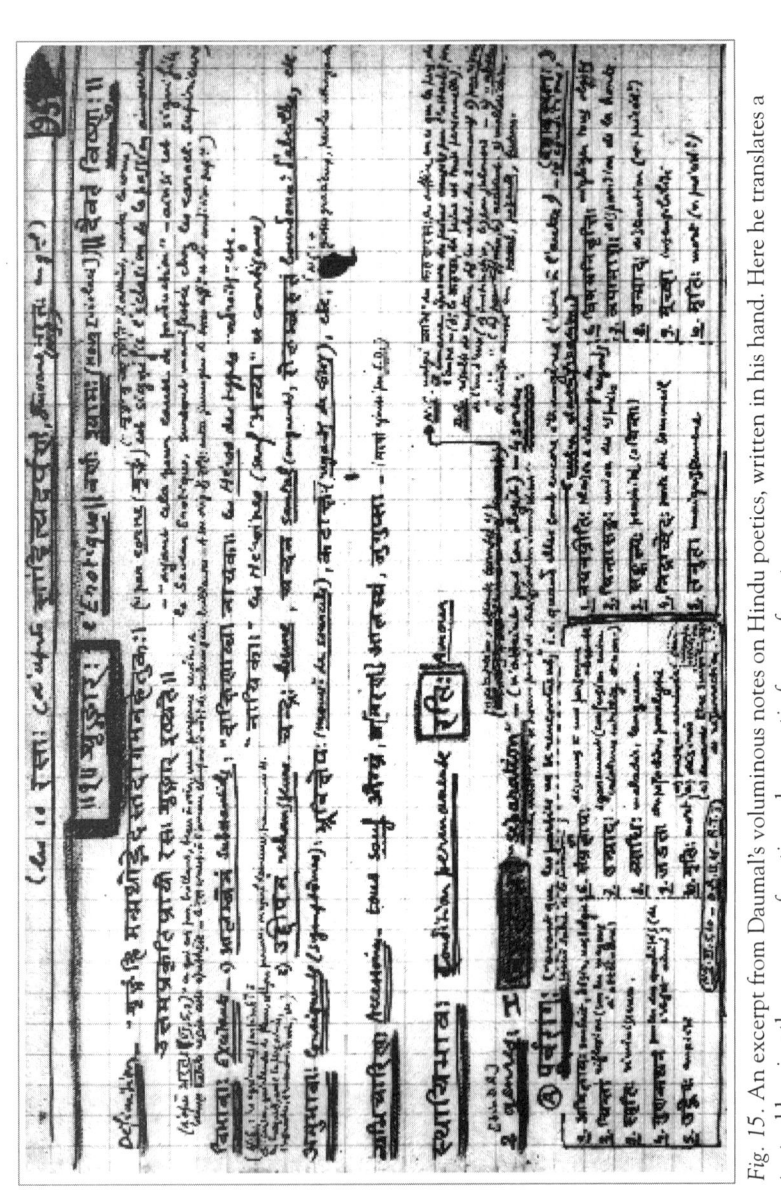

Fig. 15. An excerpt from Daumal's voluminous notes on Hindu poetics, written in his hand. Here he translates a text addressing the essence of erotic and romantic forms of poetry.

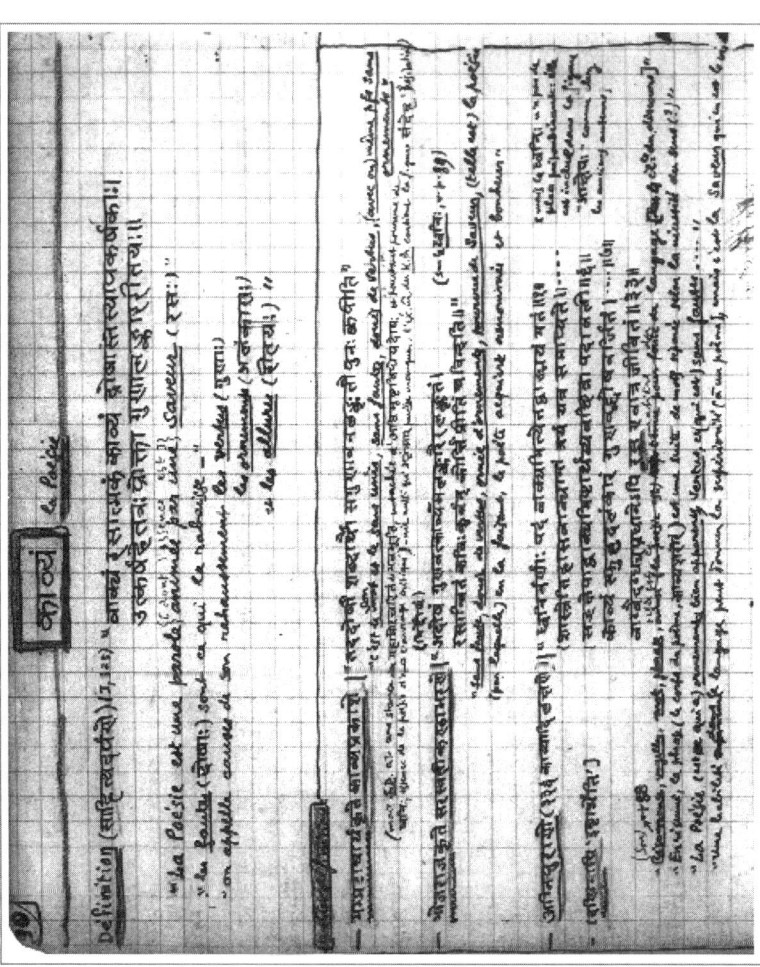

Fig. 16. A transcription and translation of Visvanatha's definition of poetry. Daumal's translations were so subtle and thorough that often he would list four French words to correspond to one Sanskrit word.

7

Daumal in the Labyrinth of Pathways

The Influence of René Guénon

> *Om Ganasya Namah!*
> Om, homage to Ganesh!
>
> The elephant god Ganesh is invoked at the beginning of any enterprise, especially a literary one, because he helps to overcome obstacles.*

René Daumal came from a long line of European writers who were drawn to the mysticism of the East. The nineteenth-century Romantics, though essentially rationalistic and naturalistic, attempted to grapple with the occult through the works of Swedenborg, Mesmer, and Eliphas Levi. In her book *The Literary Origins of Surrealism*, Anna Balakian writes:

> About 1830 it can be noticed that this increasing interest in Illuminism [the claim to a special enlightenment not accessible to mankind in general] is beginning to modify the earlier pantheism of the Romanticists [the doctrine that God and the laws and forces of Nature are one]. Both Lamartine and Balzac, and of course, Nerval later on, find in the mysticism of the Orient a more complex process of ascension toward the infinite, than that of the Christian resurrection after death. What the Romantic visionaries took from Oriental Illuminism was primarily the idea

of metempsychosis—a gradual transmutation from one form of life to another, a series of expiations leading to infinite existence. It is as if terrestrial existence moved along a road to the Absolute; the beginning of the road seems almost completely paved with material substance. Gradually matter is mingled with spiritual essence, and as physical existence finds its way toward the infinite, the ratio between the material and the spiritual changes until matter at last completely disappears.[1]

This movement toward Spirit was an idea that would grow in the midst of overwhelming materialism. Gurdjieff describes the potential of a similar trajectory of matter toward spirit in his cosmology, as described in his Table of Hydrogens.

Toward the end of the century, the Symbolists brought about an upsurge of interest in Christianity and Oriental religious and metaphysical thought, much of it stemming from the publication of Edouard Schure's *Les Grands Initiés* (*The Great Initiates*) in 1889. Simultaneously, there was a renewed interest in such subjects as theosophy and occultism. Many Symbolists believed in Swedenborg's theory of "universal analogy"—a belief in the existence of a mysterious relationship between the material and spiritual worlds, as celebrated in Baudelaire's sonnet "Correspondences":[2]

> Nature is a temple from whose living pillars
> Comingling voices emerge at times;
> Here man wanders through forests of symbols
> which observe him with knowing eyes.
>
> *La Nature est un temple où de vivants piliers*
> *Laissent parfois sortir de confuses paroles;*
> *L'homme y passe à travers des forêts de symboles*
> *Qui l'observent avec des regards familiers.*

Daumal differed from these predecessors who were often elitists at heart. They saw their mystical search as an enhancement of the self that set them above the mob (*la foule*). While Symbolists borrowed from Eastern thought to enhance their expression of individualism in art, their anarchism was essentially aristocratic. Symbolist idealism was a liberating, ecstatic excuse to turn away from the problematic contingencies of the world toward a contemplation of one's own "self." Daumal, on the other hand, did not try to elaborate the "self"; rather, he sought to submerge his self in the totality of the Absolute, while not neglecting his public duty to rectify the injustices of the social order.

As mentioned in chapter 3, Daumal and the Grand Jeu were driven to study in depth at least one Western philosopher who catalyzed their young philosophies: the great German idealist Hegel (1770–1831). Countering the Aristotelian belief that reality had to be separated into discrete parts, Hegel saw the world as a dynamic process, a giant organism in which nothing was unrelated. What connects the threefold realities of Absolute Spirit, Nature, and man's mind is a threefold movement of thought itself—the dialectic. This was a process of logic by which our experience could lead us to the Absolute Idea—"thought thinking itself," or God. This Absolute Idea or Spirit is in movement and has unfolded through the ages. The notion of *zeitgeist* (literally Time-Spirit)—the interconnections between individuals, society, art, and religion—is in a dialectical becoming. For Hegel, all history was the working out of Spirit and the embodiment of mind moving through time. Hegel felt that the individual is unaware that reality is a construction of the mind. Through the movement of reason, the mind eventually recognizes reality as its own creation.

Hegel's philosophy resonates well with Eastern nondualistic thought. In fact, much of India's Hindu renaissance of 1850 was influenced by the British interest in Hegel. This world view appealed to the young idealists of Le Grand Jeu, who wanted to reconcile all contradictions and wake up the spirit of hardened materialists. René often referred to Hegel in his letters and essays. In a 1927 letter he wrote: "Francois and I are drunk on Hegel."[3]

As Daumal began to study the Hindu tradition, it is a fact that many of its esoteric truths were expressed by him before he was ever exposed to its great works or teachers. He believed that there exists in every human being an *intimation of immortality* and the greater possibilities of higher consciousness.

By age fourteen, Daumal began to sense this God-energy directly. He understood that the real confrontation with truth had to take place within himself. He went from engaging in vague reveries stimulated by exotic notions of the mysterious East, to becoming a serious seeker. Later, in 1940, while preparing an article for a special Hinduism issue of *Cahiers du Sud*, Daumal outlined the development of his own personal interest in India. Initially, India represented for him the land of mystery evoked by his childhood readings of Kipling's *Kim* and other adventure novels; later, from his reading of Schopenhauer, the Theosophists, and René Guénon, India became a land of wisdom. As he continued to explore, however, he found that many orientalist writings were unsatisfactory. In 1931 he wrote:

> But Western hands turn gold into lead. Hindu metaphysical thought turns to crumbs in those big red fingers; it turns into a mere curiosity for mythology and exoticism, or into very consoling research for a particular paradise, or into little salutary counsels that no clergyman could disagree with.[4]

As much as Daumal was a devotee of Oriental metaphysics, he was not at all an orientalist. He was photographed sitting in a lotus position with a Hindu turban and clothing, yet he avoided all pretense of attempting to immerse himself in a culture that was not his own. His brother Jack reports that he felt strongly about the inappropriateness of this conduct; he was not into "le folklore." He felt that the Hindu customs and dietary prescriptions were part of that culture and was not something to dabble with. When Uday and Ravi Shankar visited the Daumal family home, they stayed late into the evening talking with Jack and René, who made no attempt to invite them to stay for dinner. It was clear that this would make them feel awkward by compromising their obligations of caste and culture.

Likewise, with guidance, he succeeded in avoiding the same pitfalls of facile exoticism in the realm of Eastern philosophy. Neither did he seek a strictly academic education or a career opportunity when he began to study Sanskrit. Instead it was a pure quest for knowledge and understanding—*gnosis*. He was fortunate to come upon the writings of René Guénon [pronounced gay-noh], a metaphysician in the true sense of the word. Guénon was Daumal's first teacher in an area that was to become a major focus in his life, although the two men never met in person. Guénon's interpretation of esoteric knowledge contrasted sharply with that of the Surrealists, and it is just at the conjunction of these two strains that we find Daumal's developing position.

As a young man, Guénon had been actively involved with various occult societies in Paris. Gradually, as he read more of the original Hindu and Islamic texts, he began to write voluminous, scathing exposés of theosophism and spiritualism. Although he lectured at the Sorbonne, he lived the rest of his life in relative seclusion, fearful of reprisal from his previous associations. After the death of his first wife, Guénon became an Egyptian citizen and took the name Sheikh Abdel Wahel Yahia. He lived in Egypt with his Egyptian wife and children until his death in 1952. After his death, his wife told Jack Daumal that Guénon gave her instructions on how to deal with occasional pilgrims. When his admirers arrived, seeking to pray in Guénon's place of worship, she would simply send them, with their beliefs intact, to any mosque in town.

René Guénon was one of the first Western scholars to make an in-depth study of Oriental philosophy. He had an uncanny understanding of Eastern doctrines and was determined to rid them of all the exotic trappings that served to blind the Western seeker. By 1911, he had written the *Symbolism of the Cross* and *Man and His Becoming According to Vedanta*. It was his 1921 work, however, that first influenced Daumal: *An Introduction to the Study of Hindu Doctrines*. Here, Guénon began the comparison of Eastern and Western civilizations that was to continue through all his works. In this book he argues that the Greek, Roman, and Judaic origins of Western philosophy, society, and religion are all offshoots of a much more ancient Oriental heritage. "The West is like a branch that has broken off from the Eastern trunk."[5]

Guénon criticizes the Greeks for having started "the individualization of concepts and the substitution of reason for pure intellect."[6] He traces the degeneration of Western thought, which he considers the ransom we have paid for our dubious material progress. He regards the Middle Ages as the last period in Western civilization that had any intellectual intuition of other realms beyond the purely material and measurable. Guénon believed that this intuition was possible then, because all society flourished intact under a unifying principle, "a traditional bond of a religious nature."[7] This kind of *tradition* ("that which transmits"), could be found until recently in Hinduism, Islam, Buddhism, and Taoism. It was destroyed in Europe, according to Guénon, during the Renaissance and the Reformation because Christianity was fragmented into secondary units, that is, nationalities. This loss doomed Europe to an "irremediable intellectual decline."[8]

> Traditional sciences began to degenerate into profane sciences, art lost its signifying power and its raison d'être, by according more and more importance to esthetics, even to propaganda, and the Reformation completed this general deviation in the domain of religion by introducing the notion of free conscience, that is, the absence in the doctrinal order of any principle superior to individual opinions.[9]

One of the logical results of this absence of religious principle would be Marxism, the very philosophy that impassioned Daumal for a while. The Great War had destroyed any remaining respect for traditional society and thought, or any belief in the idea that traditional lawmaking bodies (such as governments and churches) could maintain order on the planet. At first glance, it might appear that Guénon's concept of tradition that holds and molds all aspects of a society together would be difficult for the young Daumal to accept. He was an anarchist, a scorner of traditional society and thought. In the opening remarks of the second issue of *Le Grand Jeu*, in the spring of 1929, Daumal and Lecomte announced their iconoclastic point of view:

> If we are dogmatic, our only dogma is THE BREAK-DOGMA. Note therefore: DEFINITION: "*Le Grand Jeu* is entirely and systematically destructive. If dogmas are forms of thought, then universal thought, which is the truth of all dogmas, is the negation of all dogmas.[10]

But in reality, what they wished to destroy were the same sclerotic structures that Guénon despised. Daumal writes:

> We are resolved . . . to pillage, spoil, disparage or blow up the social edifice, to shatter all moral gibberish, to break down this colossus with a cretin's head that represents Western science, accumulated for thirty centuries of experiments in nothingness: probably because this discursive and antimythic thought prepares its fruits only to go rotten.[11]

So Le Grand Jeu found in Guénon confirmation of their own disdain for the established scientific and rationalist thinking of the West, and then added their own strident iconoclasm to the opinions held in common. Guénon, as a more mature thinker, was able to discuss and criticize in a more detached manner, eschewing the emotional element of the young iconoclasts.

Guénon took Descartes to task for having reinstated forever after the irreducible duality of mind and matter, "an error which weighs heavily on all of modern philosophy."[12] These are the issues of duality that the Pataphysicians found so absurd in Western thinking, from the "individualization of concepts" of the Greeks to the mind-body duality of Descartes. Guénon felt that the traditions of science, art, and medicine are more intact and alive in the Orient because they have emerged from the main tradition of pure metaphysical thought. "In India there is a tradition, purely metaphysical in its essence, to which were added diverse applications."[13]

Daumal understood and valued this integration of purpose among the Hindu arts and sciences. In *Bharata*, he wrote: "From metaphysics and dance to the training of elephants and mechanics, for the Hindu, all doctrinal bodies are linked by a common goal, call it deliverance, consciousness, or unification; in learning archery or grammar, one learns to know oneself."[14]

Guénon makes a distinction between Hindu metaphysics and religion, stating that the latter, especially in its more exoteric forms, comprises such contingencies as dogma and morals, ritual and cult. He feels these aspects are to be encouraged as part of the general cultural tradition, but that they dilute the singular tradition of esoteric metaphysical thought found at the heart of Hinduism.

> The religious point of view implies, as a fundamental characteristic, the presence of an emotional element which influences the doctrine itself, and which prevents it from conserving an attitude of purely disinterested speculation. Emotion is, on the contrary, only relative and contingent, and this can be observed particularly with regard to the need for consolations to which the religious point of view relates, for the most part. Truth in itself does not have to be consoling.[15]

If the esoteric teaching remains even for a small number of people, free of moralistic, rationalistic and practical considerations, then these individuals can focus on the struggle toward transformation and the attainment of *Tad Atman*. This was most likely Daumal's first literary introduction to the concept of *Tad Atman*. (His first subjective encounter was his drug-induced *Expérience fondamentale* described previously.) Guénon's description of this union parallels Daumal's own understanding of this principle, his Jarryesque Pataphysical reaction to the absurdity of dualism.

Guénon systematically rejected various concepts considered to be important in the West, such as rational, dualistic thought, and the moral, social, and emotional aspects of ordinary religion. He saw them as totally irrelevant to the attainment of higher knowledge. They only reinforce the sense of the individual and his or her needs, whereas the true esoteric initiation raised the initiate above his individuality, into a state of nonself.

Guénon is quite extreme in his views. He felt that contemporary religions consider the human being only in the individual human state and do not aim at having him rise above this state. Modern religion provides methods for the individual to achieve a favorable condition in this limited state, whereas the true spiritual initiation has as its essential aim "the superseding of possibilities of the individual state in order to make possible the passage to superior states, and even, finally, to lead the person beyond any and all conditioned states."[16] This same emphasis on the universal, the group over the individual, was mirrored in the fraternity of Le Grand Jeu and will arise again in our discussion of Daumal's poetry and fiction. Daumal and Le Grand Jeu joined Guénon in putting very little importance on the individual psyche and great importance on its attainment of higher consciousness.

In contrast, André Gide, an early influence in Daumal's life, deprecated Guénon's deemphasis of multiplicity and individuality. In a 1951 interview, he said:

> I find nothing, absolutely nothing, to object to in what Guénon has written. It is irrefutable. But I passionately love life, multiple life. I do not consent to deprive my life of the pleasure that it takes in the marvelous diversity of the world. And what for? to sacrifice to an abstraction: to Unity, to undefinable Unity![17]

In *Les Nourritures terrestres* Gide's outlook, as Daumal's, was to be essentially a spiritual one, but it is pantheistic: Gide sees God in the multiplicity of things: "The infinite variety of landscapes ceaselessly shows us that we have not yet known all the forms of happiness, of meditation, of sadness that they can envelope . . . perpetual novelty."[18] On the other hand, his opening lines seem to indicate that salvation is found in the all and not the particular: He is proposing the same quest for God, and in a manner closer to Daumal's than Guénon's. Gide feels that the particular is a trap and sees multiplicity as the many reflections of the One: "Never hope, Nathaniel, to find God anywhere except everywhere. Each creature indicates God, no single one reveals him. As soon as our glance stops on one creature, it turns us away from God."[19]

Guénon's particular understanding of the way to this attainment also eschews mysticism. He writes: "The mystic state is just another vague indefinite extension of mere individual possibilities,[20] while the metaphysical initiation is strictly "supraindividual," that is, it encompasses the individual. Philippe Lavastine echoed this thought in a 1973 lecture given in San Francisco. He felt that in our unevolved state we are not true individuals, rather we are "dividuals"—divisible, divided within ourselves; we are a multiplicity, in conflict and suffering. Lavastine had little respect for the solitary yogi who remains alone and does not integrate himself again into the community of his fellow men after he learns to achieve oneness with God.

> The yogi is fundamentally anarchic, individualistic. He cares only for ecstasy, for personal liberation, freedom from every collective discipline. By contrast, the Brahmin is the spiritual man who returns from the forest, lives in a larger reality, well-ordered, well defined, well-horizoned.[21]

According to Guénon, the mystic is too passive and thus open to any and all kinds of influences, some of which may not be from higher and beneficial sources. He points out that the word *mysticism* does not even exist in India or Islam. He feels that the mystic is primarily interested in entering an altered state of exaltation and ecstasy. The word *ecstasy* is etymologically (*ex-stasis*) "a leaving of oneself," while the spiritual striving of the initiate is to be more inside oneself. It is possible that this idea influenced Daumal to follow the Gurdjieff teaching. Gurdjieff accentuated the importance of being more in oneself as one is, and not to try to achieve an instant state of ecstasy, outside oneself.

It was largely due to Guénon's influence that Le Grand Jeu gradually steered away from the facile psychic experimentation and occultism of the Surrealists and other spiritualists, toward a more serious study of metaphysics. Later we will see that Daumal frequently parodied various sects and cults that grew up around the Theosophists, for instance, and certain fanatical followers of Krishnamurti, as depicted in *A Night of Serious Drinking* and the essay "La Bête noire," reprinted in *Les Cahiers Daumal*.

This brings us to a discussion of Guénon vis-à-vis the Surrealists, crucial because it involves a major convergence of influences in Daumal's life. All the elements of Surrealism (including the politics, the literary experiments, and the explorations of the subconscious) were combined with Hindu metaphysics and finally the Gurdjieff philosophy (after 1931). This crossroads is fascinating in that the Surrealists presumed these influences to be parallel, while Guénon saw them as diametrically opposed. For Daumal, all of these strands were woven together in the course of his lifetime.

First, let us examine how Guénon and his contemporaries, the Surrealists, viewed each other at the time. Although Guénon rarely commented on the Surrealists, André Breton wrote an article entitled "René Guénon Judged by Surrealism" that was published in 1953, following the death of Guénon.

> Always soliciting the mind, never the heart, René Guénon receives our very great deference and nothing else. Surrealism, while associating itself with what is essential in his criticism of the modern world, basing itself as he does on supra-rational intuition (also found through other avenues), even submitting to the attraction of this so-called traditional thought, which he has rid of its parasites with a master's hand, Surrealism does avoid him, just as much for the reactionary that he is on the social plane as for the blind deprecator of Freud that he is proving to be. Surrealism honors nonetheless this great solitary adventurer who rejects faith for knowledge, opposes deliverance to salvation, and salvages metaphysical thought from the ruins of religion that cover it over.[22]

In these few concise lines Breton delineates well his understanding of the divergence between Guénon and the Surrealists. Guénon would place them even further apart. He considered the basic aims of Surrealism—the study of Freud, the subconscious, and dreams, as totally irrelevant to metaphysical initiation. He believed that the dream state is merely another state of illusion, neither superior nor inferior to that of the waking state. In his book *Man and His Becoming According to Vedanta,* he devoted a chapter to "The State of Dreaming or the Condition of Taipasa," a commentary on a text from the *Mandukya Upanishad.* He agrees with the Surrealists that some attention to the dream state helps to destroy some of the barriers that are erected by the waking state since our mind gives the waking state such unjustifiable exclusivity on the interpretation and perception of reality.

The Indian theorists gave more status to dreams. According to Wendy Doniger O'Flaherty, in her article "Hard and Soft Reality," the earliest Indian references to the dream state in the *Prasna Upanishad* considered it to be closer to Godhead than the waking state, and as such, more real. The text says that in dreams, one sees both the real (*sat*) and the unreal (*asat*), a liminal state that is the key to the material power of dreams in later Indian texts. Both the *Chandogya Upanishad* and *Brhadaranyaka Upanishad* relate the content of a dream to the objective world. "The dreamer takes apart the elements of the outside world and rebuilds them into an inside world of dreams, without affecting their reality status."[23] In *A New Model of the Universe*, P. D. Ouspensky expressed the idea that sleep and the waking state are not two distinct, successive states; rather, sleep and dreaming are a constant underlying state to which is overlaid the waking state, "which muffles the voices of dreams and makes dream images invisible."[24] He then describes how, if we achieve a short period of consciousness without thought, a strange world of shadows, moods, pictures—the dream world—intrudes easily into our "awake" state.

Guénon has even less regard for the concept of the subconscious— "the ensemble of lower extensions of the unconscious." He distinguishes it from the supraconscious: that part of the mind which, by its very nature, is completely above the area that psychologists can investigate and which relates to "everything of a traditional order." The confusion arises because "the subconscious, thanks to its contact with psychic influences of a lower order, apes the supraconscience: a spirituality reversed."[25] Psychoanalysis is for him an element of subversion, possibly even a form of Satanism, especially when substituted for traditional practices. In his *Studies on Hinduism*, he quotes the Indian philosopher, Sri Aurobindo:

> Freudian psychoanalysis is the last thing that one should associate with Yoga. It takes a certain part of the mind, the most obscure and the most dangerous—the lower vital subconscious—isolates a few of its most morbid phenomena, and attributes to them an action completely out of proportion to their true role in nature.[26]

In his article on the writer Jean Prevost, Daumal reproaches the so-called introspective psychologists for trying to "impose silence on the soul in order to better observe its movements."[27] Likewise, Gurdjieff found psychoanalysis to be useless on "mechanical men.... Psychology refers to human beings. What psychology can there be in relation to machines? Mechanics, not psychology, is necessary for the study of machines."[28]

Guénon calls the attraction toward exploring the subconscious "a sort of reverse development which not only contributes nothing of value, but actually delays further spiritual realization, to the point where the individual is definitively led astray in these lower protractions of his individuality."[29] Breton, on the other hand, was very interested in the many avenues into the subconscious—mediumism, automatic writing, occultism, telepathy—all areas considered dangerous by Guénon. In his *Second Manifesto*, Breton writes:

> The idea of Surrealism aims at the total recovery of our psychic force by a means which is none other than the vertiginous descent into oneself, the systematic illumination of the hidden places and the gradual darkening of other places, a perpetual stroll through forbidden zones. . . . The devil preserves, I say, the Surrealist idea to begin to get along without avatars.[30]

Breton takes pride in seeking out "the forbidden zone," while Guénon finds this endeavor countereffective and harmful. Breton's point of view is that of the young revolutionary, eager to pursue anything prohibited as a reaction against the centuries of mass mental slavery to traditional religious thought. Breton and the Surrealists could not understand how Guénon could be so blind to this dimension of the psyche and to the important roles of imagination and emotion in the development of the human being. This is not surprising, considering that Surrealism was born out of an emotion—that of despair and revolt against all established values. This, in turn, gave rise to a new interest in the imagination as a product of the unconscious mind.

For Guénon, higher consciousness could not be attained through more active imagination, but only through the directed efforts of the conscious mind, and the intuition and inspiration of the "supraconsciousness." He does allow the possibility of what he calls "supports" to help raise one's consciousness to a higher level. This includes magic, which he considers to be a legitimate but very secondary and contingent traditional science, as well as geomancy and divination. But he warns against the danger of deviation from one's true aim in the face of the ever-increasing materialization of these supports. He also counsels against cultivating magic as an end in itself, imprisoning ourselves deeper in illusion rather than seeing beyond it.

We can contrast Breton's eclectic metaphysics with Guénon's analysis of the pure metaphysical tradition in Hinduism, and observe Daumal's gravitation toward the latter. Guénon and Daumal considered Breton and his associates to be metaphysical dilettantes. Nevertheless, the Surrealists must be given credit from the point of view of ordinary psychology, for historically they were the earnest vanguard of a movement that opened up new frontiers in human consciousness. These goals were in concert with their global aims to revolutionize all aspects of human existence—political, cultural, aesthetic, and metaphysical. Breton's beginnings as a student of medicine and psychology influenced all his subsequent theoretical writing. For him, a primary goal of Surrealism was to change men's hearts and minds on a spiritual level. The Surrealists were committed to erasing social and economical inequalities, and they believed they were heralding a new age. Their forays into the occult, psychicism, and what they considered esoteric thought, were part of a long tradition going back to Hugo and Nerval, seeking the *l'au-delà* ("the beyond").

Yet seen from Guénon's point of view (and Daumal's of the 1930s), they were as misguided as the majority of humanity in failing to comprehend the purpose of human existence. Both Guénon and Daumal rejected the Surrealists because of their inability to accept the idea of a transcendent law, greater than that created by the mind and imagination of men. They were prepared to conquer the Absolute; they were not prepared for the Absolute to dictate its laws to them. It is very likely that the Surrealists served as a model for the second ship of seekers in Daumal's novel, *Mount Analogue*. They too were looking for the magic mountain, but were caught in a whirlpool and doomed to turn endlessly in a circle. The narrator tells us: "Condemned to turn round and round in slow circles, they could still bombard the coast, but all their shells came back at them like boomerangs. It was a ludicrous fate."[31]

Guénon believed that the lack of serious study of true metaphysics in the nineteenth century predisposed individuals to pick and choose arbitrarily among the more exotic elements of Eastern thought. He felt this approach tended to satiate the individual's thirst for something higher without truly feeding the soul. In his books *The Crisis of the Modern World* and *The Reign of Quantity and the Sign of the Times*, Guénon attacked the "intuitionism" of Henri Bergson and the "voluntarism" of William James as being even more insidious than rationalism, positivism, or materialism, the limitations of which are more easily detected. The concept of intuition, mixed with imagination, instinct, and emotion, he argued, is more dangerous in subtle ways, particularly to sensitive individuals choked by modern materialism. This kind of thinking seduces one into believing that the feeling of consolation and well-being or the encountering of expanded imagination and psychic phenomena are themselves the stuff of higher consciousness and not just its secondary characteristics.

Guénon did not take the Surrealists seriously when they professed an interest in Eastern religion and higher consciousness. In 1932 he described them as "a little group of young men who amuse themselves with jokes of dubious taste," and considered Surrealism to be inspired by what he called "counter initiation."[32] Only on two occasions did he give praise to two individuals connected with Surrealism: one was Antonin Artaud and the other Daumal. Guénon found "interesting" the stage directions and metaphysics of Artaud and he praised Daumal's 1945 essay "To Approach Hindu Poetic Art."[33]

Daumal and his Grand Jeu colleagues had been reading Guénon for only four years, but his influence can be seen throughout the four issues of Le Grand Jeu. A comparison of their positions reveals a wholehearted agreement on almost every major point. In the first issue of Le Grand Jeu in 1928, Roger Gilbert-Lecomte gave a brief critique of Guénon's The Crisis of the Modern World: "To Mr. René Guénon we declare: First, that his theoretical thinking is in essence the same as ours; and that the tradition he believes in is the only one we recognize.[34]

Although Daumal praised Guénon in the fourth issue of Le Grand Jeu (1931), he gradually detached himself from Guénon as a middleman, learned Sanskrit, and went directly to the original texts themselves. Daumal continued to hold his teacher and "initiator" in high esteem and exchanged letters with him through the years. In a letter to Geneviève Lieff, he wrote:

> I have great esteem for Guénon and I like his vituperations.... He knows the impotence of books—of philosophical prose—which is why he has recourse to symbolism. There one has to proceed with prudence in order not to make it into an intellectual game, but to read in the way one would listen to myths and symbols, by letting them evoke in oneself the interior resonance based on real experience.[35]

However, in a 1938 letter to Jean Paulhan, Daumal wrote: "If one limits oneself to following Guénon or Thomism [St. Thomas Aquinas] or any other dogmatic system, one ends up either a scholastic or in despair."[36]

In the 1967 issue of Hermés devoted to Daumal, Jacques Masui wrote a chapter entitled "The Experience of Daumal and India" and quoted a remark Daumal had made to him: "Yes, when Guénon is not being 'guénonist,' he is strong and certain."[37] The following passage from Masui explains what Daumal meant by "guénonist":

> To my mind, Daumal even surpassed Guénon in the comprehension of this tradition, because, if he had the innate taste for metaphysical thought, he was also a poet. What was most lacking in Guénon, by contrast, was a certain taste for art, emotions, and

the senses. He remained a rationalist for whom symbols could only vibrate in one part of his being, the most cerebral part. Nevertheless, he rendered an immense service to many by awakening in them a metaphysical faith long asleep and his scholastic rigor was successful in definitely burying an occultism made of very poor alloys. He was a sort of Vedantist Thomas Aquinas.[38]

Daumal's working definition of *guénonist* was "an excess of theory and too much fanaticism and sectarianism." However, Jack Daumal, who lived in an Islamic milieu in Cairo, as did Guénon, finds the judgment of Masui unacceptable. "If Guénon remained rigorously intellectual in his published writings, it was for very definite reasons—his own sense of mission or perhaps a task given him by his Muslim superiors. But in his private life he was not insensitive to art or to the sensual beauty of nature."[39]

Guénon was instrumental in pointing Daumal in the right direction: Eastward. In *Mount Analogue*, Daumal acknowledged his debt to the East. He has Father Sogol explain that the ship must approach the island from the west at sundown and not from the east at sunrise due to the offshore breezes.

> Furthermore, the result was symbolically predictable. Civilizations, in their natural process of degeneration move from East to West. To return to the source of things, one has to travel in the opposite direction.[40]

8

Daumal and Hindu Poetics

The Rasa of the Word

> Self is everywhere, shining forth from all things,
> unreachable, yet nearer than breath, than heartbeat.
> Only in deep absorption can the mind,
> grown pure and silent, merge with formless truth.
> As soon as you find it, you are free.
>
> —*Mundakya Upanishad* 3.5

In the 1920s, when Daumal was reading both Guénon and the original Sanskrit texts, he was able to recognize the wealth of knowledge at his fingertips. He believed that the Sanskrit language "was intimately linked to a whole architecture of life," and in its esoteric usage was the poet's mirror and the mirror of the gods. Yet he felt that Hindu concepts of poetics could not translate directly into poetry, which can only be born from a direct experience of life and from the poet's congruency of mind and heart.

For Daumal, the questions were: How to express in language the inklings of truth he had glimpsed in the deeper reaches of his soul, without resorting to abstract concepts? How to create a poetic formula that would open up the reader's layers of selves and reveal his own innermost nature? These were difficult questions for the young poet. He felt that poetry potentially offered the greatest possibility of meaningful communication, and yet living in a war-torn country, he could also see that philosophy and religion were in an impoverished condition, as were the

European nations around him. His own thoughts about this were underscored when he read Guénon's observations about modern culture.

Guénon gave little or no attention to the value of poetry as a tool, while for Daumal, it was the one concrete mode of understanding and knowledge still accessible to modern man. In the Hindu texts, Daumal found confirmation of his belief in the importance of poetry as a means of transmitting higher Truths that were otherwise incommunicable. These ancient writings confirmed his innate understanding of how the clarity of the poet's internal state determined the effectiveness of his writing.

In 1928, at the age of nineteen, the basic premises of Daumal's life were established, couched in a blend of youthful revolt and piety, outrage and understatement. These were the very qualities of fire and water (ardor and fluidity) that the Hindu poets deemed essential to poetry. His first literary undertaking, *Le Grand Jeu*, did not emphasize the pursuit of an absolute truth, but stressed the experience of a lived truth. At a time when many traditional concepts were being questioned, *Le Grand Jeu* pursued the theme of a "métaphysique expérimentale" that translated as both an "experimental" and an "experiential" metaphysic. This theme manifested itself as a return to the idea of a primitive Revelation—the original "Word" as expressed in the Vedas and in the Bible. Here we find an intense belief in the immediate presence of God in the world, accessible to man if he could break through the blinding layers of *maya* (illusion). The following is Daumal's translation of "Knowledge of the Self," an extract from the *Brihadaranyaka Upanishad* (IV, 4, 10–21):

> If he knew himself,
> if man could say: this is I,
> by which desire, for which goal
> would his body be inflamed?
>
> He who has found himself, in whom being
> buried in the depth of this death has awakened,
> He is all active, he is the author of all,
> for him the world—he is, himself, the world.[1]

Daumal elucidates the religious origins of this poetic revelation. He grasped the sacramental nature of poetry and the sacerdotal role of the poet/priest (*kavi*). The written or spoken word is a basic form of communication that could achieve incantatory, magical levels. According to one's level of being, one might rise above the lower levels of discursive thought and ordinary language to achieve the level of language called *pashyanti vak*—by which one could experience the noumen of a word, its transcendent truth. At this level, a spoken word was understood to have a mysterious, supernatural power; it contained within itself the essence of the thing denoted. To "know the name" of anything was to control the thing. "The word" means wisdom, knowledge (*gnosis* in Greek), and knowledge was magical power. So Brahman (the "holy word") soon came to mean mystical power inherent in the holy word. Sound (*Vac*, whence "vocal," "vocation") was considered a female deity, the equivalent of Brahman ("the Holy Word") and, according to Hindu cosmological theory, sound held a primordial place among the sensory qualities. Above the human level the *para vak* is the unspoken Word, the Absolute that vibrates in its own silence. Daumal also describes "mots-germes" (*sphota*), which translates as "seed words" or "embryo words" that are contained in this rarefied dimension of eternal peace, words that are manifestation of the eternal Verb.

The Veda itself is considered to be "Sacred Utterance" (Mantra), of nonhuman origin, and was largely transmitted orally. In the first hymn of the *Atharva Veda*, the "Lord of Holy Utterance" (*vaca-pati*) is invoked to come and abide in the practitioner and endow him with mystical knowledge. Edwin Gerow in his *History of Indian Literature*,[2] suggests that the Vedas may have served as a model for subsequent poetry, so that even when the Hindu theorists began to approach the poetic phenomenon as belletristic literature (i.e., literature as fine art [*kavya*]), they were still more concerned with it as sacred utterance.

In his chapter "Pour approcher l'art poétique hindou" (1940), Daumal describes how the writing of poetry is a kind of yoga for the poet to discipline himself, in order to become a better instrument for "supranatural" functions: "By the play of sound, meaning and resonance, his whole internal world is set in motion. And, as he is a reflected glimmer of the universal Atman, his poetic act participates in the cosmic movement."[3] Daumal wrote: "Art is not a natural activity of man."[4] He uses the word *natural* in an unusual manner; here the word connotes the idea of "automatic," that is, ordinary or undeveloped behavior. In a footnote he explained that the Sanskrit word for natural (*prakrita*) describes a person who has not created a "self": he is as nature and environment have made him, with no personal effort at development. *Prakritia* is contrasted with *Sanskritia*, which refers to one who has created an interior being, i.e., who is twice born. (Language is also divided into *prakrit* [ordinary language] and *Sanskrit* [sacred language].)

In ages past when knowledge of the Real was the most important goal in life, even the ordinary natural activities were at the same time analogies, signs and tests for interior searching. Then when the age of darkness came, the Kali-Yuga (we are in the midst of it now), men began to engage in these activities for their external rewards only. The couple "like-dislike" led the cortege of passions and became the main motivator of behavior.[5]

From this point of view, art can never be a natural activity. True art can only be created by someone who has given birth to an interior being, who is born again. Such art requires a special attention and effort from its creator and its audience. This higher state is not achieved automatically. Daumal believed that these qualities of true art can potentially emerge from poetry through a deliberate attempt to achieve *Tad Atman*, the communion between the Universe and the deepest self. This is Daumal's definition of the poetic act. For Daumal and the Hindus, it was not a case of "Art for art's sake." Art is not an end in itself but a means for understanding sacred laws. "Thus art was launched into the world by superior beings with the purpose of enrobing Truth in order to attract to it our spirits, which have become incapable of loving Truth all naked."[6]

Daumal was intrigued with the compact yet multidimensional concept of Hindu poetics called *rasa*, the means by which Art puts us in contact with Truth. *Rasa* (savor or taste) signifies the establishment of an emotional contact between an individual and a work of art, through which the direct apprehension of sacred knowledge is possible.

Daumal translated into French two ancient texts written by Bharata and Visvanatha, respectively, that discuss and exemplify this concept. Bharata's *Treatise on the Theater [Natya Shastra]* and Visvanatha's *Mirror of Composition [Sahitya Darpana]* are both dedicated to the elucidation of the notion of *rasa* and its preeminence over any of the other contributing literary elements. Daumal emphasized these two works and discussed the theory of *rasa* in four different essays on Hindu poetics, collected in *Bharata*, a compilation of essays and translations of ancient texts into French.

Daumal relates that Bharata's *Treatise on the Theater* is the most ancient text written about Hindu dramatic art, dating from the fifth century B.C. It is a compendium of theater and dance-containing elements that indicate an even more ancient, pre-Aryan theatrical tradition.

Krishna Chaitanya, in his book *Sanskrit Poetics*, likens Bharata to Richard Wagner, who, centuries later, saw drama as a *gesamtkunstwerk* or synthesis of all the arts. No existing Hindu epic poems (*kavya*) predate this treatise. It is the first work to discuss *rasa* as a definable aesthetic principle and the critical principle of drama. Much later, the term would include a universal and psychological principle as well, both central and specific to Indian art.

Gerow describes *rasa* as "delectation" in its original context of theater: *rasa* is a mood, an emotional consciousness wherein all the disparate elements of the play (language, gesture, imitations, and scenery), coincide and are understood after all not to be disparate. It serves as an organic principle in terms of which the integrity of the drama can be understood. It is also the result of the drama, its "end," understood as a state of awareness peculiar to the drama—distinct from normal worldly consciousness.

In Daumal's essay "L'Origine du théâtre de Bharata" (which is listed as a bibliographical reference in Gerow's work), he discusses the sacred origins of *The Treatise on the Theater* and its respected status as the "Fifth Veda." He includes his translation of the first chapter of the treatise which consists of 127 verses in which Bharata speaks to his 100 sons explaining the origins of theater. The goal of Art is revealed by Brahma himself: "I created the Theater, as a metaphor for the movement of the universe. It will provide the audience with Sacred Knowledge, science and myths, as well as a distraction for the crowd: such will be the Theater." Bharata says to his sons:

> In the past, when the Age of Perfection and the reign of the Son-of-the-Being-born-of-himself had past.... Then came in its turn the profane law of the village (as opposed to the "law of the forest"). Falling under the slavery of cupidity and desire, misled by jealousy, anger, and other madness, the world was subject to pleasure and pain.
>
> The gods, the titans, the celestial musicians, specters, giants, and dragons ... through the mouth of their prince Indra, all proclaimed to Grandfather (Brahma): "We want something to make us rejoice, something to see and listen to. The servile generations cannot understand the sacred oral tradition of Knowledge. Think up a new and fifth science of Knowledge for people of all castes."
>
> "So be it," said the king of the gods, he who sees all things as they are. "The substance of all sciences, the depiction of all trades and skills, and in addition to that, the Myths (fables and epics),

I do create the Fifth Science which will be called Theater."
(verses 8–13)[8]

In one of his 126 footnotes, Daumal explains that the oral circulation of the Veda was reserved to the three higher castes (priests, warriors, and peasants). Heretofore women and servants had not taken part, but now the theater would be a spiritual enlightenment for them as well.

In verse 14 Brahma goes on to explain that this new science will consist of the four major goals of human beings: justice, wealth, glory, and deliverance, the last of which is "the renunciation of the fruits of the first three desires while considering what they are worth." Theater would also include "the representation, for the world to come, of all forms of activity." "To intelligent beings, having the fire of understanding, walking with audacity, and conquerors of fatigue . . ." (verse 20).[9] Daumal describes the performing gods and other celestial beings:

> . . . using Verbal, Heroic, Fantastic, and Gracious expressions, the suave movement of the limbs of the dancing god Shiva, the tenderness produced by the erotic *rasa*, as well as the Nymphs of the celestial waters, the Fulgurant Celestial Army, the Clairvoyant, the Juggler, the Wigged Players.[10]

Daumal explains that each divinity, each *rasa* or taste has its preferred rhythms, which are translated prosodically by combinations of certain meters. When observed, these correspondences can impart the right tone to the audience.

> Then Brahma and other gods, overcome with delight by the spectacle, their spirits radiating, all came forth to offer us their services.
> The Sun offered a parasol, Shiva the magic Vehicle, the Wind a fan, Vishnu a lion's throne and the celestial River—Word (Brahma's wife) gave the sonorous substance of the spectacle.
> And all the others, gods, celestial musicians, giants and dragons transported with joy by this seance, according to the diverse attributes of their natures, came to offer their particular talents, and one by one they gave to my sons Dialects, Moods, Tastes, Forms, Forces and joyous ornaments. (verses 57–61)[11]

The rest of the text is encyclopedic in character, dealing with every fine detail of dramaturgy: the construction of the theater, all aspects of music, singing, and dancing, the one hundred or so positions of the hands, chest, waist, abdomen, legs, feet, and so on, and exhaustive treatment of meters and modes of delivery. Above all it insists on a high and noble purpose for the drama and holds out great merit to the actors who can dedicate themselves to their work as a service to society.

Daumal expressed enthusiasm for this ancient treatise heretofore completely unknown in the West. He fully appreciated the aspects that the author Bharata emphasized: not theater as representation, but theater as action, exercise, and ritual. All the elaborate instructions included in the treatise are conducive to systematically creating the correct ambiance and the appropriate *rasa*. The resulting inspiration brings about the desired magical transformation of both the players and audience. This sacramental nature of art was Daumal's ideal for all poetic undertakings, and Bharata's text validated Daumal's own striving to create a transformative kind of poetry. Upon reading this text, he understood that these goals had been accomplished before and could be again. Daumal's works *A Night of Serious Drinking* and *Mount Analogue* are both built upon this kind of mythic, ritual structure.

According to Gerow, Visvanatha's *Sahityadarpana* (*The Mirror of Composition*) was written in the first half of the fourteenth century, and is probably the second best known Indian text on poetics. It is considered by subsequent tradition to be the culmination of efforts to widen and systematize the scope of poetics. In it we find a further expansion of the concept of *rasa*, which Daumal summarizes:

> *Rasa* connotes the immediate perception of a moment or of a particular state of existence, provoked by the display of certain methods of artistic expression. It is neither the object, nor a feeling, nor a concept; it is the immediate evidence, a tasting of life itself, a pure joy of tasting one's own substance, all while communing with the other, the author or the actor.[12]

Ananda Coomaraswamy, the reknowned philosopher and commentator on Indian poetics, frequently refers to the *Sahitya Darpana*, paraphrasing its definition of *rasavadana* or aesthetic experience.

> Pure aesthetic experience is theirs in whom the knowledge of ideal beauty is innate. It is known intuitively, in intellectual

ecstasy without accompaniment of ideation, at the highest level of conscious being; born of one mother with the vision of God, its life is as it were, a flash of blinding light of transmundane origin, impossible to analyze . . . and yet in the image of our very being.[13]

Rasa is the supernatural essence (*Atman* or soul) of poetry; it is never seen as an emotion connected with one's personal life, nor can it be identified with any of the constituent factors of the work of art. Daumal writes: "In order for *rasa* to be actively present, one must experience an emotion while at the same time distinguishing oneself from it."[14] If the reader becomes obsessed with the particularities of a work, the ability to appreciate and relish the whole of the work will be blocked. Coomeraswamy further discusses the theory of *rasa*:

> The idea of an aesthetic beauty to be tasted, and knowable only in the activity of tasting, is to be clearly distinguished from the relative beauties or loveliness of the separate parts of the work, or of the work itself considered merely as a surface, the appreciation of which is a matter of predilection or taste (*ruci*) not *rasa*.[15]

In *Sanskrit Poetics as a Study of Aesthetics*, S. K. De describes the proper aesthetic enjoyment (*rasa*) as closer to pure intuition than an empirical feeling. To achieve this requires

> a process of idealization by which the reader passes from his troubled personal emotion to the serenity of contemplation of a poetic moment. Put another way, an ordinary emotion (*bhava*) may be pleasurable or painful, but a poetic sentiment (*rasa*), transcending the limitation of the personal attitude, is lifted above pleasure and pain into pure joy, the essence of which is its relish itself.[16]

To quote *The Mirror of Composition*, "Rasa can only be grasped by a person capable of judgment (sometimes the result of merits earned in a previous existence); it also requires the power of 'representation' and an act of communion. One only knows it by eating it. He who is able to perceive it tastes it, not as a separate thing, but as a part of his own essence."[17]

The three "virtues," or *gunas*, of *rasa* are: (1) suavity, the water quality that liquefies or softens the emotions; (2) ardor, the fire quality that inflames and expands the spirit; (3) clarity (*buddhi*), illumination or total comprehension. Visvanatha describes *rasas* according to the emotion that colors them: comic, erotic, furious, pathetic, heroic, marvelous, repugnant, terrific, quiet (religious), and parental. These *rasas* are realized through "manifestations of being." There are eight "permanent manifestations" (which he believes can sustain an entire work) and thirty-three "temporary manifestations"—that is, tears, sweat, doubt, regret, shame, drunkenness, elation, anticipation. He describes four ways to bring these into play: verbal, grandiose, charming, and violent. Each of these is subdivided again to determine whether its order is psychic, physiological, rhythmical, melodical, pictorial, or grammatical. Each of these qualities has a spiritual aim. Daumal quotes Visvanatha: "By serving the musical sound, one is serving the gods Brahma, Vishnu and Shiva, because they are made from it."[18]

In a letter to Renéville, Daumal highlights some Hindu concepts of poetics, explaining how this elaborate effort at establishing the appropriate savor and the appropriate "manifestation of being" culminates in creating the right tone and final effect on the reader. He felt the Sanskrit theorists had revealed extreme aesthetic acumen by emphasizing the purely spiritual character of poetic creation, which in its essence is autonomous, independent of ordinary emotion, intellectuality, utility, or morality. They never regarded poetry as merely an amusement or frivolity, although spontaneous songs of enlightenment have always been song by India's transcendental humorists, such as the poet Kabir. The grace and humor of these parables and poems opened the mind and heart more effectively than mere instructions or moral maxims. These teachers saw poetry as an activity belonging to the intuitive sphere of a free mind.

Visvanatha considered other schools of thought that proffered different definitions of poetry, that is, that resonance (*dvani*), the derived or suggested sense of a word, is the essence of poetry. But he finally concluded that "Poetry is a word of which the essence is savor" (*vakyam rasatmakam kavyam*) and described how all the elements of poetry fit together:

> Words and sense are the body of poetry; *rasa* is its essence; the Virtues are as heroism and other qualities of the soul; the faults are comparable to having one eye or other infirmities, styles are like particular attitudes of the body; ornaments are like bracelets and other decorations.[19]

Visvanatha described in depth all these various elements, always preferring the image phrase to the literal phrase. An example he cites is: "'The startled young girl felt shame when her lover kissed her'—it would have been better to describe the feeling of shame by one of its physical effects, such as 'she lowered her eyes.'"[20] This image is representative of the overall subtlety that the Hindu authors tried to convey. Visvanatha exhorted the writer not to "teach," but rather to make the reader actively experience something. Writers could deliberately obscure an image with elliptical phrasing, double meanings, or semantic superimposition in order to shake the reader's preconditioned mental process, allowing in finer shades of meaning. In *Vedic Literature*, Jan Gonda writes: "For the Vedic authors, the effectiveness of poetry does not depend upon the power of description releasing clear mental images, but upon the energy with which words and combinations of words arouse emotions."[21]

Daumal viewed the role of poetic imagery in the same way—as a vehicle to describe the unknown and the unknowable, and to open the doors of perception. Daumal began his literary career with a tendency toward obscurity, but then gradually evolved toward a supreme clarity. From beginning to end, he continually sought means of expression that would shake the reader and create a *rasa* to arouse a heightened response.

※

Daumal was interested in many aspects of religion and wrote essays on Judaism, Indian Buddhism, and Tibetan Buddhism. Among his essays collected in *Bharata* and in the more recent English version entitled *Rasa*, is Daumal's 1934 review of a translation of *The Tibetan Book of the Dead*, originally published in *Les Cahiers du Sud*. His writing is scholarly in the best sense of the word: elucidating the original meanings of words, while avoiding what he called the "metaphysical sauce" or the "theosophistic sacristy" of the intellectualizing "sweet sirs" and "filthy poisoners."[22] Again, the goal is to bring the reader back "to the confrontation of reality in each instant of time, millions and millions of instants, each of which is an open door to consciousness, completely unnoticed by us."[23]

The theoretical concept of union between one's internal self with the greater Self can be better understood by the concrete examples offered us in Daumal's two illuminating essays, "*A propos d'Uday Shankar*" ("Concerning Uday Shankar") (1931), and "*Sur la Musique Hindoue*" ("On Indian Music") (1940). In these essays Daumal analyzes the difference between the Hindu experience of music with that of the Western experience. He isolates what he considers to be the key element differentiating the two: the attitude toward the passage of time. Occidental man seeks to "kill time" and as such prefers music that impassions, soothes, and generally distracts: "a sonorous procession that will clothe and conceal duration."[24] Oriental music, on the other hand, does not mask time but rather incessantly recalls the gnawing obsession and insists on intensifying the sorrowful consciousness of time: "The Oriental musician aspires, above all, to sculpt in the duration a sequence of silent moments; and the listener realizes each of these moments as the substance of his own life, and his own consciousness."[25] This music facilitates the experience of consciousness and communion with God, an art form that forces one to meet oneself in one's own eternal solitude. "A given *raga* (musical composition) must allow the listener to grasp the naked reality of his immediate existence."[26]

This internal experience is not necessarily painful. In fact, Hindu poetry is often aimed specifically at alerting the reader to the positive relish or *rasa* of his or her own experience. The communion is in itself the source of savor. According to the Upanishads:

> Savor can be found in every breath—if it is sought:
> who indeed would inhale,
> who exhale, if this ether were not Joy.
> Joy here is the Deity himself, the Essential Excitant
>   of the Savor (*rasa*).
>
> *Taittiriya Upanishad*[27]

The overall effect of Hindu aesthetics on Daumal's work comes through in the essay "Dialogue du style par René Daumal et Lanza del Vasto," a joint effort of the two metaphysical poets, undated but most likely written in the late 1930s. Here Daumal elucidates the "divine origin of style" and the importance of a tradition that honors laws of style.

> Style is the imprint of what one *is* on what one *does*. One can only BE to the extent that one renounces that which one *believes* oneself to be. One of the virtues of style is that it makes the artist's intention communicable and integrates his work into the ensemble of living traditions. I live in an epoque without style.[28]

In conclusion, we can refer again to Daumal's article in *Cahiers du Sud* where he details the history of his interest in India:

> These readings in Hinduism led me to believe that there exists a science and a technique for the transformation of the self, but the texts left me unsatisfied: no practical techniques were given, and the contradictory texts of the vulgarizers made clear to me the danger of attempting things without a real guide.[29]

He then relates that when he went to the Sanskrit texts themselves, the exalted ideas thrilled him and yet he still felt that the "what to do" (*quoi faire*) and the "how to do" (*comment faire*) were lacking. He finally went through a fourth stage he refers to as "The Return":

> Just when I was about to fabricate for myself a philosophy to appease my needs, the "quoi faire" and "comment faire" were indicated to me—completely independently from India and by a path that I do not need to discuss here.
>
> The error that I committed was this: I investigated these texts as if I myself were a Brahman, a sannyasin or a yogi. Theoretically I recognized the necessity for a teacher, but in truth I thought that perhaps I was above the law of acshama that specifies the need for a guru, that I could learn this sacred science by using my own intelligence. Now, having changed the direction of my research and my life, I have recognized that the Upanishads are not offered to just anyone (and I am still "just anyone"). Rather, they are a shining light that I can only see after long and painful efforts to open my eyes, and under the direction of someone who already has eyes.[30]

He was, of course, speaking of his contact with the teachings of G. I. Gurdjieff.

IV
GURDJIEFF AND THE DE SALZMANNS

9

Daumal
with
Gurdjieff
and the
de Salzmanns

Finding a Path ⎯⎯⎯⎯⎯⎯⎯⎯⎯⎯⎯⎯⎯⎯⎯⎯⎯⎯⎯⎯⎯⎯⎯⎯⎯⎯

> A Man will renounce any pleasure you
> like but he will not give up his suffering.
> —G. I. Gurdjieff

In October of 1930, René Daumal and his friends began to notice a tall, solitary man who had recently begun to frequent their haunt, the Café Figon on the Boulevard St. Germain, where they convened every Thursday following their meeting at Joseph Sima's studio. This gentleman would always sit in a corner of the terrace, drinking many glasses of calvados and endlessly drawing curious Arab and Chinese characters. Finally, in early November, Joseph Sima recognized Alexandre de Salzmann from an earlier collaboration at the publishers Pégase in 1923. He presented the legendary artist to his young friends. According to Georgette Camille, a contributor to *Le Grand Jeu*, de Salzmann approached them on another occasion. After conversing a while, he asked those at the table to try something: to hold their arms straight out to the side for as long as they could. Minutes later, Daumal was the only one with arms still outstretched, and de Salzmann said, "You interest me!"[1] As it turned out de Salzmann was a pupil of G. I. Gurdjieff, and these encounters were one of those fated "coincidences" dear to the Surrealists. It was a major turning point in the twenty-one-year-old Daumal's life. Jacques Masui writes in his article

"René Daumal et l'expérience Gurdjieff" that "Daumal was not content merely to accept the Gurdjieff teaching; he gave himself over to it."[2]

Who was Gurdjieff the man and and what was the teaching that so intrigued Daumal? According to those who knew him, he was a powerfully spiritual, enigmatic, unpredictable scientist of the soul. The late P. L. Travers, author of Mary Poppins, described the effect Gurdjieff had on his followers:

> His mere presence gave out energy. To receive his glance was to receive a moment of truth that was often very hard to bear. A master like Gurdjieff is not someone who teaches this or that idea. He embodies it himself.... I think I saw in him what every true master has: a certain sacrificial quality as though he clearly had come for others.[3]

In this chapter, we will give a brief overview of the history and teaching of Gurdjieff directly, and then examine the same concepts through the public and private writings of Daumal. In addition, we will open the door a second time to Daumal's last fourteen years of life, viewing them through this new lens—his association with the Gurdjieff phenomenon.

George Ivanovich Gurdjieff (1867–1949) was born in Alexandropol in Armenia and spent his boyhood in Kars in northeastern Turkey. Sources indicate that he was a child of exceptional capabilities, greatly influenced by his father, a bard or storyteller, who could recite from memory long stories dating from antiquity. Even as a youth Gurdjieff wished to understand the significance and purpose of man's life on Earth. In this pursuit, he spent many years traveling in the Middle East, India, and Tibet. It seems that he visited monasteries of the Essenes, the Sufis, the Yasavis, the Kwajagan, and the Sarman Brotherhoods. These were esoteric communities connected with both Islamic and Christian traditions—what the Sufis call the "Inner Circle of Humanity."

The Kwajagans, for example, emphasize the practice of spiritual discipline without retiring from the world. These are practical people, often craftsmen, who live in society but remain "invisible" to the uninitiated. The Kwajagans value the *Khalka* or group, the companionship of Master and disciple, and spiritual exercise (Zikr). They believe in the necessity for constant vigilance, in the *Mujahede*, the holy war, otherwise known as the struggle with one's own weaknesses. Similarly, the Gurdjieff Work is a way "in life," a "work on oneself" in the midst of the usual conditions of life. Gurdjieff seemed to have the ability to synthesize and incarnate in himself the essence of the ancient traditions he encountered. His mission as a teacher was to make them known in the West.

Gurdjieff attempted to bring his students to an awareness of the automatic nature of their behavior, to clarify the ways in which the undeveloped individual constantly reacts according to the notions of "like and dislike," a slave to the conditions in which he finds himself. Gurdjieff drew upon an allegory originating from Central Asia, also found in both the Vedas and Plato wherein the human being is likened to a carriage with a horse and a driver, these aspects corresponding to the physical, emotional, and mental natures of the individual respectively. However, in the average man there is no passenger or master whose presence can unify and give direction. This is the condition Gurdjieff refers to as being "asleep," that is, less than fully conscious, and thus incapable of "remembering ourselves." There is no master because the master is asleep. P. D. Ouspensky, one of Gurdjieff's foremost pupils, reports:

> In ordinary conditions of life we do not remember ourselves, that is, we do not feel ourselves, are not aware of ourselves in the moment of a perception, an emotion, a thought or action. . . . In an ordinary psychic state I simply look at a street. But if I remember myself I do not simply look at the street. I feel that I am looking, as though saying to myself: "I am looking."[4]

The teaching of Gurdjieff, known to his followers as the Work, speaks of the possibility of awakening to a higher level of consciousness. The first step in the search for greater awareness involves seeing oneself more objectively and developing an impartial moment-to-moment attentiveness toward impressions of the body and senses. In Buddhist practice this is also known as *Dharmakaya*, or mindfulness of the body/mind. "Self-observation" brings body (the carriage) and mind (the driver) into a new relationship, one that can attract feelings (the horse) as well. It is this awareness, this remembering, that can bring together all three parts (carriage, horse and driver) in a more conscious state of integration, "self-remembering"—being present in this moment. "Remembering oneself" is the key to reestablishing the directive of the passenger (master). Dr. Michel de Salzmann, (the de Salzmanns' son who also worked with Gurdjieff), describes this experience in *Seeing: The Endless Source of Inner Freedom*:

> In the progressive process of seeing, one should first learn certain difficult things: not to interfere, not to prefer one aspect to

another. . . . As one begins to realize that the fundamental aim is to become aware of the whole of oneself, then the sacred quality of "seeing" becomes as important as what is seen, and a balance begins to appear. . . . An attitude of seeing begins to prevail. . . . One is no longer taken by the forces interacting in oneself. We are speaking of a long, patient work—staying present to oneself and feeling the need to come back. . . . In the Gurdjieff teaching this is sometimes called "self-observation," finding a sensitive place where one can receive impressions, and letting things be as they are.[5]

These higher states of being depend on continued attentiveness to the inner experience of being present. Through such efforts the capacity for conscious attention (mindfulness) grows, as does one's capacity to inhabit the body consciously and to open to finer perceptions of oneself and the universe. Gurdjieff utilized many approaches to assist his students in developing this capacity for consciousness, including meditative exercises, tasks requiring inner attention, sacred music, dances, and movements from the East, as well as the cornerstone of the teaching, the group work. The music and movements were not simply recycled from ancient traditions, they were *reactualized,* based as well on Gurdjieff's own understanding of human energies. One anonymous French student of Gurdjieff, interviewed in 1977, said that "each dance seemed neither like something newly invented nor a literal reproduction of an ancient dance. When you were in front of him, each movement seemed like a creation, not an improvisation but a creation."[6]

In 1922, in Fontainebleau, France, Gurdjieff established the Institute for Harmonious Development, a community of seekers who lived together under "conditions in which man could be continually reminded of the sense and aim of his existence by an unavoidable friction between his consciousness and the automatic manifestations of his nature."[7] Within this community Gurdjieff himself provided the friction by creating difficult conditions for his students, exercises and tasks requiring concentrated effort and self-awareness, unexpected events, and hard physical labor. He tried to galvanize his students to a sense of the urgency, a sense of the inevitability of their own death, of the need to awaken now.

According to Gurdjieff, one of the main purposes for disciplinary exercises was to distinguish in oneself the place of origin of one's reactions. He felt that man had to study his "machine"—his body and his instincts—in order to begin to understand the mechanisms and the accidental external influences that drive him to move, now in one direction, now in another. We have seen that in Hindu tradition, disciplinary exercises were similarly encouraged. The special postures and breathing techniques that Gurdjieff demonstrated are similar to some yogic *asanas* (positions) and *pranayama* (breathing techniques). His exercises for focusing attention recall the Hindu *dhyana* (mental exercises).

Gurdjieff came to the realization of man's state of sleep by observing his own psyche. He, like Daumal, had a tremendous interest in psychic and occult powers and developed them to a heightened degree. Nevertheless, he found that these powers did not help to maintain simple self-awareness. He then reasoned that he needed a "reminding factor," a deliberately chosen difficulty or renunciation to keep himself awake. This "reminding factor" or resistance could be some permanent source of "voluntary suffering," or any difficulty that was deliberately met. Consequently, Gurdjieff renounced his psychic powers, thus denying himself something he valued greatly.

Among Gurdjieff's main sources was his early training in the Armenian Christian Church. According to its doctrinal teaching, renunciation or *abashkharel* is similar to the Greek concept of *metanoia* (religious conversion), literally, "to renounce the world, to carry punishment, or to deprive oneself of food." It is similar to *kavoutioun*, another Armenian term meaning "suffering as expiation in order to straighten wrongs, to purify with blessing, or to heal by changing the flow of blood."[8] Thus we see that the elements of renunciation and nonattachment pertinent to the Armenian church doctrine, and to Sufi and Indian traditions, became themes in the Gurdjieff teaching.

As in Hindu philosophy and in Daumal's personal beliefs, here renunciation and nonattachment can be understood on several levels. The word *deliberate* is a key to understanding what Gurdjieff called "conscious labors and intentional suffering." Just as the friction of rubbing two rocks together can spark a fire, so the friction of deliberate renunciation can create the energy to see ourselves and change our "mechanical" thinking. On the other hand, Gurdjieff considers passive suffering and negativity to be one of the greatest blights on the psyche of humankind. Our basic outlook, he said, is so habitually negative and our emotional life so generally empty that the emotions most frequently available to us are negative. Our lives are grand melodramas as he explained:

> I have already said before that sacrifice is necessary. Without sacrifice nothing can be attained. But if there is anything in the

world that people do not understand it is the idea of sacrifice. They think they have to sacrifice something that they have. For example, I once said that they must sacrifice "faith," "tranquillity," or "health." All these words must be taken in quotation marks. In actual fact, they have to sacrifice only what they imagine they have, and which in reality they do not have. They must sacrifice their fantasies. This is difficult for them, very difficult. It is much easier to sacrifice real things.[9]

This quotation touches upon Gurdjieff's belief that human beings are deluded. We think we are at peace, that we love, that we are Christians (or whatever), and that we are awake. Gurdjieff then discusses the prevalence of accidental, unconscious, or mechanical suffering, the kind that makes us feel dramatic, self-righteous—the hero or heroine of our personal novel. He points out the shocking fact that we refuse to admit our attachment to being a victim and he reiterates the crucial distinction between deliberate and mechanical suffering.

Another thing that people must give up is their suffering. It is very difficult also to sacrifice one's suffering. A man will renounce any pleasure you like but he will not give up his suffering. Man is made in such a way that he is never so attached to anything as he is to his suffering. And it is necessary to be free from suffering. No one who is not free from suffering, who has not sacrificed his suffering, can work. Nothing can be attained without suffering but at the same time, one must begin by sacrificing suffering. Now, decipher what this means.[10]

In 1934, Daumal included this theory about suffering into his essay "The Non-Dualism of Spinoza." He classifies under the heading of "sorrow" all suffering and pleasure that are passively undergone, and, under the heading of "joy," all suffering and pleasure deliberately experienced: "the joy of a being creating himself and knowing himself as real."[11] In a 1937 letter to his wife, Daumal relates Jeanne de Salzmann's discussion of negative emotions—how practically all of our daily feelings and emotions are negative in quality and passively felt. In fact, they are imaginary emotions that we take for real ones. Daumal writes:

I remember well the moment in childhood when I began to let myself be invaded by these illusory sufferings; and little by little it became nearly impossible to free myself because it would have left a terrible void. You cannot chase them or overcome them; it would be like trying to remove a hole in the carpet by cutting around it. You make a bigger hole. These sufferings are not real—they are absences, lacks that come from our identification with things and people. Their imaginary nature is actually quite obvious.[12]

Daumal goes on to describe how elders inculcate in children even more reasons to feel bad: the acquired shame of not living up to certain imposed codes.

> At first as children, we feel abnormal and ashamed if we see that these inculcated sufferings are only imaginary and do not really touch us. Then eventually, we succumb. Finally one day we realize that we must re-learn how to see the emptiness of these negative emotions with which we are so identified. Sometimes it seems easy until we realize that we have only drowned one imaginary suffering in another more subtle one. Negative emotions can take on very subtle even sublime forms, such as we see exhibited in artists.[13]

It is difficult to assess the effect on Daumal of Gurdjieff's concept of awakening. This is complicated by the fact that Daumal's most elaborate discussion of awakening took place at least two years before his 1931 encounter with de Salzmann. In "Nerval the Nyctalope," written in 1929, he wrote, "Man goes to sleep when he stops distinguishing himself from his sensations."[14] Independently, he intuited how much of our so-called waking consciousness is a kind of hypnotized sleep—that we rarely do distinguish ourselves from our vision, taste, feelings, likes, and dislikes.

In 1970, Daumal's brother Jack published a fifty-five-page manuscript that Daumal wrote in the years 1926–1928. Jack notes its "intransigent juvenile Marxism" but also, its "perception of truths in the forest of authentic traditions of the East."[15] In it, Daumal exhibits his own innate understanding of the concept of awakening, years before he encountered Gurdjieff or de Salzmann. "Stay awake!" he exclaimed and then describes the subtleties involved in the process. He lists various daily activities of a human being, and notes that the body carries out most of them automatically:

In order to awaken you have to think: "all this agitation is external to me." You need an act of reflection. But if this act sets off in you new automatisms, in one's memory and one's reasoning process, your voice could continue to maintain that you were still reflecting: but instead you would have again fallen asleep. Thus you can spend entire days without awakening for a single instant. *Waking is not a state but an act.*[16]

Similarly, in "Provocations to Asceticism" ("Les Provocations à l'ascèse"), he asks, "Why this perpetual race after awakening, why try to be more conscious—why desire to leave the condition of ordinary man?" He answers his own questions: "The vision of the intolerable is enough to create the necessity for human consciousness to transform itself. And [it is a] provocation to asceticism: a summons to man saying, 'pull yourself up by an ever new awakening, or sleep in a spiritual death.'"[17]

Thus we can see that in Daumal's earliest metaphysical searching, his vision of the absurd and his belief in asceticism led him to the same realization confirmed in Hinduism and later in Gurdjieff: that we must evolve and awaken. Using arithmetical equations, Daumal compares the consciousness of the average man getting on a bus (which he designates by the number 3), with the idealistic artist believing in art for art's sake (#8), and the charitable old lady giving to the poor (#17): "If we agree to designate 'lack of being' by zero, (#0) then all these somnambulants differ among themselves as the equations (0×3), (0×8), (0×17), etc., differ among themselves. There is an infinite number of ways of not being."[18]

Gurdjieff's emphasis on nonattachment, inner freedom, and discipline was readily accepted by Daumal since effort and hard work came naturally to him. For years he had focused on the need to tame and quiet the body and deny the ego. As useful and necessary as this tack might be, Gurdjieff also emphasized the importance of relinquishing tension and generating deep relaxation in the body, in order to achieve an integration of the many parts of one's being.

There is brief mention of working with breath and sensation in Ouspensky's writings. He recalls Gurdjieff's group work in Essentuki just following the Russian Revolution. Gurdjieff gave an exercise that created a "circular sensation" when the attention was focused on different parts of the body. Ouspensky himself concluded that physical states, which are connected with new psychological experiences, begin with *feeling the pulse throughout the whole body*, as one stroke, which is what we do not feel in ordinary conditions. There remains with me a deep conviction that control over the body begins with acquiring control over the pulse.[19]

He then describes various muscle relaxation exercises organized by Gurdjieff that always began with relaxing the muscles of the face. There were noticeable effects on heart beat, neuralgias, and sleep patterns among the group.

Madame de Salzmann reported that, particularly in the last decade of his life, Gurdjieff focused more and more on the importance of connecting with the body through sensation. In his groups, he discussed various techniques to awaken to one's inner vibration through breathing exercises. It is also confirmed by Jack Daumal and Maurice Desselle that Gurdjieff often spoke about training the mind to sense the body by "following" the breath down through the trunk and limbs while exhaling the carbon dioxide. Since we realize today that the atoms of the body are primarily made up of space, then the bioelectric energy contained in the air that we breathe is the major component that fills the vast atomic spaces in our bodies. If we breathe with attention, we pull in the finer energies from the earth's atmosphere into this vibrating physical mixture of air, water, and carbon molecules. Gradually this provides an immediate physical experience of the integration of mind, body, and emotions.

In a lecture given in New York as early as 1930 Gurdjieff explained the importance of sensing the reverberation of energy in one's solar plexus, especially while pronouncing the words *I am*. Later that year, Gurdjieff demonstrated a breathing exercise to the same group of pupils. His "Third Series" of writings, not published until 1975, gives his first-person account as he sat in front of them. He describes how at that moment he was directing his attention to the part of the breathed air that settles in his lungs and gradually penetrates inward spreading through his whole organism. He states:

> Now I direct the second half of my attention to my head brain for the purpose of serving and possibly constating any process proceeding in it. And already I am beginning to feel in it, from the totality of automatically flowing associations, the arising of something very fine, almost imperceptible to me. . . . I now consciously

direct this second half of my attention and, uninterruptedly "remembering the whole of myself," I aid this something arising in my head brain to flow directly into my solar plexus. I feel how it flows. I no longer notice any automatic associations.[20]

This is one of the rare descriptions in the public record of Gurdjieff's actual techniques. Most of his teaching was transmitted orally.

Daumal explains the Gurdjieff movements as a means of integrating the mind and body. In the essay "Le Mouvement dans l'éducation intégrale de l'homme," he describes the subtleties involved in trying to "wake up." First he proposes that all real searches require exterior help to indicate the correct route. He then compares modern pedagogic theories with this "other method" by which the pupil is taught "to center himself with all his organs and faculties, from his head to his toes, passing through the heart."[21] We are shown how the trained teacher can supervise the pupil's attempts to carry out simple physical and mental exercises that lead to an acute awareness of one's condition:

> The teacher suggests that you try a simple movement or gesture, but your body no longer obeys as soon as you stop depending on your old habitual ways of moving. He asks you to express a simple emotion, but you remain speechless or choose inappropriate words as soon as you are stripped of your learned attitudes and your conventional masks. He asks you to do a simple exercise of memory, calculation, or reflection, but your associative mechanisms for discursive thinking, your formulas and your clichés all fall like cold cinders into your brain and onto your tongue. Life is very stingy with experiences like these, but here they are offered to you every instant. Every minute you see more clearly all that is mechanism, dead sleep, laziness, posturing, vanity, and chatter in the various functions of your being. But you will not be crushed with despair because you will see an open door . . . to the kingdom of which you are the king.[22]

If Gurdjieff confirmed for Daumal the importance of nonattachment and working with bodily sensation, he also reiterated the Hindu belief in the high purpose of art. Art should help the upward flow of consciousness in man, struggling against the current of mechanical life. Gurdjieff had very definite views on art and literature, finding value only in what he called "conscious" or "objective" art. For Gurdjieff, real art had a functional purpose: "In real art there is nothing accidental . . . the artist knows and understands what he wants to convey, and his work cannot produce one impression on one man and one impression on another, presuming of course, people are the same level."[23] Therefore the consciousness of the creation depends on the relative degree of spiritual development of the artist. Most art, however, is merely "subjective" art, a soulless mechanical reproduction or the elusive depiction of an isolated individual temperament. Gurdjieff explained further:

> You say an artist creates, I say this only in relation to objective art. In relation to subjective art I say that with him "it is created. . . ." This means that he is in the power of ideas, thoughts and moods which he himself does not understand and over which he has no control. They rule him and they express themselves in one form or another.[24]

In Gurdjieff's works *All and Everything* and *Meetings with Remarkable Men*, and in excerpts from his lectures, he frequently alludes to this degenerated quality of art produced during the last few centuries, particularly in the West.

> For us art is not an aim but a means. Ancient art has a certain inner content. In the past, art served the same purpose as is served today by books—the purpose of preserving and transmitting certain knowledge. . . .
>
> I found nothing in the West to compare with Eastern art. Western art has much that is external, sometimes a great deal of philosophy; but Eastern art is precise, mathematical, without manipulations.[25]

Many critics and writers feel that Gurdjieff's own work, *All and Everything*, as well as the body of music and dances he produced, were examples of conscious art. In the words of one of his close admirers, Frank Lloyd Wright, "we have for the first time a philosopher distinguished from all others . . . Gurdjieff was not only an original philosopher; he was a great artist." Referring to the music that Gurdjieff composed with Thomas de Hartmann, the architect wrote: "I often hear his music. It is from another world."[26] The exotic comedic flair of Gurdjieff's writing found favor in an unlikely corner: André Breton admired his oblique sense of humor and included *Beelzebub's Tales to His Grandson* in his *Anthologie d'humour noir* (*Anthology of Black Humor*).

If Daumal was such a student of the ancient Hindu tradition, why did he not choose a living Hindu master? Certainly Guénon, his early mentor, felt that the ancient tradition was the only safe path. Guénon abhorred modern forms of religion and apparently, in the beginning particularly disapproved of what he had heard about Gurdjieff. James Moore writes in *Gurdjieff: The Anatomy of a Myth*:

> To envisage two characters or indeed two authors more preposterously contrasted than Gurdjieff and Guénon exasperates the mind. Guénon's exquisite prose style was smooth as a mill pond, but, gliding just beneath the surface like a cruel pike, his spiritual paranoia snapped at the anti-traditional counter-initiatic forces, which a trick of parallax caused him to detect in virtually every modern renewal. Gurdjieff (so near, so practical, so full of being) attracted Guénon's special anathema: "This man of Greek extraction is not purely and simply a charlatan, but this makes him the more dangerous.... The truth is that... Gurdjieff exercises on those who go to him a kind of grip of psychic order which is quite astonishing and from which few have the strength to escape."[27]

It is possible that Guénon was deceived by both Gurdjieff's chameleon-like quality as he adapted to the level and needs of the person he was addressing, and the veneer of charlatanism and chicanery Gurdjieff frequently employed as a smoke screen to ward off pseudo seekers. In actuality, Gurdjieff may have been exactly what Guénon revered, his only crime being to appear in this century, instead of millenniums past.

In the fourth issue of *Cahier Daumal* and in a recent personal letter, Jack Daumal described Jeanne de Salzmann's decision to meet with René Guénon in order to explain certain essential aspects of Gurdjieff's teaching, of which he was unaware. According to Jack Daumal, the result of their meeting was an acknowledgment on Guénon's part of the validity of the ideas and teaching of Gurdjieff. Yet, there exists a third party who prefers to remain anonymous, who was present at this meeting at the pyramids in Egypt, and who at first feigned to be Guénon so as to screen this foreign visitor. In a transatlantic telephone conversation in June 1997, he claimed that Guénon had still continued to hold serious reservations about Gurdjieff. This close associate of Guénon felt that "Gurdjieff did not make adequate accommodation for the performance of religious rituals and sacraments for purification and setting the soul in order." It seems clear to me that Guénon could not accept the concept of what Gurdjieff called "the Fourth Way," a spiritual path in life, which did not in itself focus solely on liturgical and ritual forms but which could serve as crucial adjuncts to them. Notwithstanding, Guénon's work has been studied, translated, and held in great esteem by subsequent followers of Gurdjieff.

In contrast to Guénon's opinion, many scholars feel that Gurdjieff succeeded in breathing life into ancient traditions. A recent author, Ravi Ravindra, discusses Gurdjieff in the context of the *Bhagavad Gita*. His viewpoint sheds light on Gurdjieff's potential to clarify traditional beliefs. As a professor of physics and comparative religion, Ravindra feels that both Easterners and Westerners have been cut off from the pure source of true religions, menaced by the twin scourges of sentimentality and scholasticism. The holy texts and rituals are rich with meaning and knowledge, but we have become inured to them. Revindra writes:

> The old traditions take on meaning when they come into contact with the Gurdjieff work. He provides a fresh intuition as an access to the ancient formulations and thus a practical method to reconnect us to both the depth of our being and the depth of the tradition.... In our day, Gurdjieff brings to the traditions this revitalizing challenge, not to destroy them but to search for and reveal again their essential core, released from the rigidities of dogma, from exclusivism and mechanical repetition.[28]

According to Ravindra, Gurdjieff had the greatest respect for traditional religions and felt that the core of truth they revealed long ago could be recovered through the fragments of hidden meaning preserved in sacred texts and in religious rites.

It is difficult to guage the impact of the Gurdjieff teaching on Daumal's life because he had always approached everything with extreme intensity. It is hard to imagine any endeavor more intense than his early years spent writing his dark poetry and promoting his mystical and political idealism through Le Grand Jeu. He plunged into Sanskrit with a true passion. All of these pursuits were equally important, but being mainly intellectual endeavors, they did not offer the integration of mind, body, and heart that was provided by the Gurdjieff Work. Furthermore, Daumal had no personal guidance from an established mentor in any of these early endeavors. The members of Le Grand Jeu had bravely charted new waters and naively attempted positive action. For Daumal, this was a perfect initiation for eventually realizing the limitations of action in the ordinary world.

Within just a few years Daumal had tasted a vast number of experiences and philosophies. William Blake's observation "The road of excess leads to wisdom" seems particularly apropos. As a youth Daumal exploited that belief, not as a hedonist but as a psychic experimentalist, until his physical body could take no more. In a letter, he wrote:

> Thinking to break with my past excesses, I am falling into a sort of inconsequential asceticism, vegetarian diet, no more wine, etc, but my life remains irregular. . . . Very tired by this life. Demineralization—I'm beginning to lose my teeth. Violent headaches and anemia. I hesitate between despair and philosophy.[29]

In the late 1920s, he seemed to be drifting even while involved in Le Grand Jeu. He wandered from political meetings to literary debates, realizing that agitation was not action, and that "without a direct contact with someone more advanced on this path, man cannot even take the first steps."[30] In 1930, Daumal told Vera of his intention to leave the intellectual world and go to Africa (she remarks that he was probably thinking of Rimbaud, whom he admired, who also went there). Instead, he met de Salzmann, whom he described as "a former dervish, former Benedictine, former jiu-jitsu master, healer . . . an incredible man."[31] In "Mémorables," he writes:

> And remember the days that followed when you walked like you've been eaten by infinity, rendered null and void by the single existing Absurdity. And above all remember the day when you wanted to throw everything away, not caring how, but a guardian watched over you in your night, he watched while you dreamed, he made you touch your flesh, he made you remember your own, he made you gather up your tatters—remember your guardian.[32]

In 1931, de Salzmann took an apartment in Daumal's neighborhood in the Convention quarter of Paris, and they both frequented the nearby Café de la Convention. One night, speaking about Gurdjieff's teaching, de Salzmann stated:

> I will die soon, and I will receive nothing of what I would have liked to have. And yet, this nothing is enough to keep me living. If this *nothing* is sufficient to keep me living, then what finally, is the *thing* itself?[33]

There are several ways to translate "me faire vivre": "to make me live," "to keep me alive," or "to give me life." Given his ill state, he may have meant that this teaching gave him not only a renewed spiritual life but also helped to prolong his life.

In a letter to Rolland de Renéville, Daumal chided his friend for taking offense at de Salzmann's remarks about Renéville's "occultism."

> I am full of gratitude toward the man who—through truly efficacious goodness—attacks and challenges my dearest beliefs because they are precisely the most dangerous ones. And more so if he judges you worthy of the same provocation. I remember several conversations with de Salzmann and you: several times you answered in occultist terms, and the sarcasm of our Socrates cut through your words so that you could see the obscurity that they were masking. Seeing that you were attached to this "occultist" point of view, he went right for it. Once he has taught you to put your thought process through torture, you will be able to do it yourself systematically. It is in this way that I have learned a few little things, which no Bible and no Upanishad could ever have taught me.[34]

All reports seem to concur that Daumal was inexorably drawn to Alexandre de Salzmann. He felt a sense of fulfillment in the Gurdjieff teaching and a certainty that this was *the* Teacher for him. We might also consider other ordinary explanations as to why this path would suit him more than any other that he had investigated. Recalling his early Marxist indoctrination, he had too many complaints against the hierarchical structure of the Hindu caste system and the priestly hegemony of Brahminism. Gurdjieff was offering the pure essences of these ancient stratified religions, without promoting any allegiance to a large governing body. Although Gurdjieff wielded a certain autocratic power over his followers, the teacher-pupil relationship was clearly evident without a hidden agenda of a power structure. In 1935, Daumal alluded to de Salzmann in a letter: "I have met a human being. I would not have thought it possible. And nevertheless, I had to give up lots of convenient feelings of despair. It is hope that is heavier to carry."[35]

Gurdjieff himself is conspicuously absent throughout the early years of René's involvement with the Work. Although Gurdjieff was often in Paris in the 1930s, he was then involved primarily with writing; after twenty-five years of direct teaching he was working with only a small number of students.

In a 1932 letter written in English, Daumal mentions that de Salzmann gave him some excerpts from Gurdjieff's forthcoming book, which contained discussions about art, recently translated into French. He noted, "Yes, there are words there very heavy!" When shown photographs of de Salzmann performing Dervish dances, Daumal remarked, "Even after passing through the mechanical eye [of the camera], something expressing inexpressible things was cast onto the paper."[36] Then de Salzmann brought him to the Café de la Paix where Gurdjieff often sat writing all day. While Daumal watched from another table, de Salzmann went over to have a few words with Gurdjieff. Describing this scene in English, Daumal remarked: "Till he has raised up his head, one could think he is only a great scientist, or something like that. But when he looks at you, you can no more see his face, neither know if he has great or little eyes: you see only two immense wells of black light—you can say: supernatural."[37]

Both René and Vera worked closely with de Salzmann until his death in 1933. Very soon they became students of Alexandre's wife, Jeanne de Salzmann, the pupil to whom Gurdjieff later entrusted leadership of the Work after his death. The Daumals lived a total of five years with Madame de Salzmann at Evian and Sèvres in France, then later in Geneva, Switzerland. Gurdjieff met with this fledgling group in their small communal setting in Sèvres, but it was not until 1938 that he would work with them on a regular basis.

It is during these years in the mid-thirties that Daumal wrote his brilliant essays on Hindu philosophy, poetics, and music, availing himself of the Geneva and Paris libraries. Far from abandoning his interest in Hinduism and Sanskrit, his understanding of it was nurtured by his years in the

Gurdjieff Work. In a letter from 1936, Daumal contrasts his life before and after encountering the Gurdjieff teachings:

> I searched a long time . . . for this non-verbal method toward an active knowledge of oneself. I stuck my nose into mysticism, esotericism, etc.—words, words, results (or at least experiences) had by others. Finally, I found someone with whom I work, who has consecrated his whole life to this problem and who can help others to seek out a solution. It is a question of a work in each moment in which the human being, with his body, his instincts, his feelings, and his intelligence, experiments on himself and fully actualizes himself.[38]

Indeed, as Jean Biès writes in his article "René Daumal et l'expérience Gurdjieff," Daumal's fateful meeting with de Salzmann divided Daumal's life into two very different periods. At the very least, it "made him renounce his anarchic tendencies as well as revise his excessively intellectual conception of esoterism."[39] Similarly, Lavastine describes how Daumal found "an axis" in Gurdjieff, a point at which all his previous knowledge could converge and from which he could begin to understand in a new way the great abstract concepts of Hinduism concerning how to know God in the moment. Shortly before his death, Daumal wrote to Raymond Cristoflour: "I had the good fortune to find a teaching (apostolic in the universal sense of the word), in a language disconnected from any particular theology and with a practical apparatus which teaches the mother truths of all authentic religions."[40]

In 1977 Jeanne de Salzmann provided several letters that Daumal had written to her in which he describes his attempts at inner work. They show a keen sense of self-scrutiny. In discussing the source of laziness in himself, he writes:

> As soon as a difficulty presents itself which I cannot immediately overcome (i.e., the difficulty I spoke of—trying to write without "becoming a writer"), this becomes a pretext for laziness, which gradually invades all other activities. . . . Certainly I am lazy on a very deep level. I had believed at first that I had become lazy. But if this laziness manifests more easily today, it is because the forces that stymied it in the past have begun to weaken: namely, my vanity and intellectual curiosity.[41]

Several reports attest to Daumal's spirituality, and his steadfast commitment to the Gurdjieff Work. Madame de Salzmann confirmed this in three personal interviews in 1977 and 1983 in her Paris home. As a young woman she too had traveled through the East looking for spiritual masters: Of all those that she met, none could compare to Gurdjieff. She said that she felt Daumal was an extraordinary man, second only to Gurdjieff himself. She too felt Daumal had an innate understanding of Gurdjieff's ideas, even before he encountered her husband, Alexandre de Salzmann. Yet she noted a qualitative change in him through the years. Although he had always had a certain physical agility, his focus had been primarily on intellectual pursuits. As a result, his body was neglected and underdeveloped. Several years of performing Gurdjieff's sacred movements had a salutary effect on his body and helped to integrate his three centers. He was also given a special exercise program tailored to his needs and was encouraged by his teachers to take part occasionally in strenuous work activities. As a result, Madame de Salzmann reported that he became more muscular and robust even while his body was slowly deteriorating from tuberculosis. Finally, she spoke at length of Daumal's commitment to the difficult path of spiritual growth, of his infinite subtlety, humanity, and reverence for life, and finally his immense intellectual power.

Lavastine feels that the very struggle to build physical strength was a measure of René's ever increasing inner strength. Lavastine was constantly amazed by his perseverance. He recalls a task that was suggested to a group, to each demonstrate their most desired, comfortable walking gait. Daumal walked in long, fast strides across the room. This was not his own normal gait but his ideal speed. He was now very interested in observing and understanding his own physical machinery.

Dr. Michel de Salzmann reports that his earliest recollection of René is at the age of eight, before he went off to English boarding school. Whenever he returned to France to visit his family, he would see René. They became fast friends early on. Looking back, he realizes that he himself was subject to a common tendency of youth to judge by appearances, such that he was put off by the serious, somber faces of his mother's students. René and Luc Dietrich were the only two that he found to be spontaneous and interesting. During his years in medical school, he would meet René every Wednesday for lunch. De Salzmann attests to Daumal's profound *interiority*. He was affected by Daumal's ability to be open to everyone around him and still attend to a vast interior life within.

When Daumal first became involved with Alexandre de Salzmann and the Gurdjieff ideas, he made attempts to explain his experience to his friends who wondered how he could put all his faith in one man. Daumal wrote to Renéville:

> A master will never think for you; he will provide opportunities to think, which you may or may not take advantage of. Finally, little by little, you will learn (and I will learn) to consider every man, every thing, every fact, as an occasion to think, and as a master to learn from. In the meantime, since a man has appeared who, consciously, by an act of veritable charity, wants to play this role for our benefit, it would be crazy to allow this opportunity to go by and not recognize him as a master.[42]

Daumal discussed the effects of his encounter with de Salzmann in a letter to Jean Paulhan. He wrote that even before the dissolution of Le Grand Jeu, he had the feeling that he was on the wrong course. "The angel and the devil were using the same mouth to speak through simultaneously,"[43] that is, like the many modern seekers that Guénon describes, Daumal had, with good intentions, confused higher and lesser aims. Political aims, psychic research, and the development of inner consciousness were all mixed together. For someone who had always disdained any form of dualism, his words here are rather strong: "no longer any conciliation possible between the angel and the devil." His colleagues who decided not to follow de Salzmann, "withdrew, inventing the most stupid pretexts, and becoming, for the most part, partisans, mystics, fanatics, suicides and maniacs."[44] In a letter to Emile Dermenghen, Daumal wrote:

> Old "friends," seeing me leave the world of café chats, metaphysical coquetries, and mysteries, have started all sorts of perverse rumors about me. I risked upsetting their repose (some have found this repose in a pretended "Marxism" which only engages the body, and often yet the bodies of others; others have found it in psychological researches which are based on the results of other people's thinking).[45]

His old friend André Rolland de Renéville had witnessed most of René's evolving dedication to poetry, to politics, and then to the Gurdjieff philosophy. He highlighted what in his mind were the reasons for Daumal's lack of stature and fame in the literary world:

René Daumal showed all the promise of becoming the best poet of his generation. He could have been without doubt if the circumstances of his brief life had been less tormented and provided him with the minimum of leisure and relaxation that is indispensable to the writing of verse; also if his thinking had not moved in a direction that distanced him from the specifically literary field.[46]

Renéville described Daumal's return to creative writing after a long hiatus in the 1930s:

Little by little I saw him return to literature in proportion to the extent to which it could serve him as a vehicle for a teaching. He struggled to create works, in the form of fables or imaginary recits, that would comport a secret meaning, sufficiently clear to reveal itself to any sincere reader.[47]

In a letter to Renéville, Daumal spoke of the difficulty of describing on paper his work activities: "You ask me for a long letter on the teachings of Madame de Salzmann. You won't be getting it. It is impossible. It is not a case of didactic teaching that one can put in writing. She gives us something that no writing could ever give."[48]

Indeed, as Dr. Michel de Salzmann points out in "Footnote to the Gurdjieff Literature," the word *teaching* "should refer strictly to a direct relational experience that takes place in the presence of a teacher, in particular, through oral transmission."[49]

In many of his letters, Daumal underlined the importance of having a teacher, someone farther along the road. He described the teaching as a reeducation, a breaking down of self-serving beliefs. He felt this can best occur when working with a master teacher, and preferably in a communal living arrangement. He never attempted to give a personal description of his three teachers nor did he transcribe their words verbatim. But he often urged his friends to come and experience an exchange first hand. He tried to relate his overall experience to his friend Paulhan, describing a typical day's activities with Jeanne de Salzmann in Geneva.

After an eight-hour day spent working on an unidentified translation, Madame de Salzmann came for the solfeggio [music study]. Vera and the others knew something about music; Lavastine was as ignorant as I in this field. But I did my best to assimilate this sonorous nourishment for which I had hungered so many years, and which no one but Madame de Salzmann could give me intelligently. We study less the external sounds than the structure of our human machine under the spotlight of sound (because it is opaque to light.) We attempt to erect or to legislate this structure, according to perceptible tones and harmonies, measures and rhythms. What chaos and how the machine functions poorly! How difficult for it and the luminous, foggy consciousness. But here at least there is the possibility for learning more than cleverness and esthetics: to take the sounding harmonies as instruments of edification.

At six P.M. we begin movements (active immobility included) using the physical, emotional and intellectual machine. It is another hour of full integral work, simultaneously, from the feet to the head. There is no way to describe what we do here; one must take part in it. But it is a discovery and full of constant miracles. Everything is put into question, from the simplest physical action like walking to the real functioning of the intelligence; one is forced to make tabla rasa (as much as each one can), to be alone with oneself and to begin again consciously (but how the flame flickers), to put one foot in front of the other, to raise a hand, to look for a word in one's memory, to feel a rhythm, a regime of essence bearing. Alone with your most personal chaos. All of us reduced to the same level under the direction of someone who, through her knowledge, knows how to position each of us each minute in positions of critical attention, each according to the path which is his own. But this is all chatter: you really should come some day to see. That something like this should exist in the West in the twentieth century is already quite remarkable. It comes from this superior logic which we have called . . . a miracle.

In the evening we continue our translation. Sometimes we go to Philippe Lavastine's home on a lake outside the city. We canoe, swim, eat, and talk of Hasidism. We also talk about Alexandre de Salzmann; we try to reconstruct things that he said, which sometimes only now become clear. [There follows a long discussion about Lavastine translating the works of Martin Buber on Hasidism and Daumal's interest in starting a series of books about the great cross-cultural myths: Genesis, the Fall, the Flood, etc.]

I am looking for a means of support in Geneva. Madame de Salzmann is going to stay here and start classes in September. She wants to consolidate the small core of Geneva students that she has already and develop a group that could come from time to time for short stays in Paris, and London, etc.

[Then he jokes at length about Geneva—the slow, hygienic, overprotective, humorless atmosphere.] In Dadaist fashion I tried to hold in my head two antithetical images at once: "humor" and "Swiss." Here there are several interesting animals: "homo mercantilis urinopathicus pyjamescus" and "homo helveticus constipatus seriossimus calvissimus." But you understand why I want to live in Geneva.[50]

Never again would René be that detailed and specific in describing his Work experience. Much later, in a 1942 letter to his pupil Geneviève Lief, he displayed a deeper understanding of the futility of talking about one's path. Even in his public writing, he would now resort more and more to inference and allegory.

A moment comes when the voice that says "I" must jump from the intellect to a more interior, more real life, and this new life sees that it is different from the intellect. Then it must put the intellect into its service. But there is a period of transition between the two, when one feels a disgust at the emptiness of ordinary discussions (those that one has with oneself and with others, and I include the most brilliant philosophical ones). They will no longer do, but one has yet to find a new language at one's disposition. That is why it is suggested that during this intermediary period of maturation, one should not talk about one's work with "strangers." You would like to be open and useful to them and they will want to pull you in. But it is like pouring a drink for someone who has no glass in his hand; your water spills to the ground and only creates mud.[51]

The year 1938 was a pivotal one for Daumal. As the winds of war began to blow harder, he finally began to work with Gurdjieff himself for the first time. As Gurdjieff was again open to working personally with pupils, Jeanne de Salzmann brought to him interested students, many from among the French medical profession, intelligentsia, and artistic elite. With war approaching, Gurdjieff decided to remain in Paris, right in the midst of dangerous activity, and to meet regularly with a group of Jeanne de Salzmann's longtime pupils.

Unfortunately, at this point Daumal's health began to decline most noticeably. It was Jeanne de Salzmann who finally convinced him to see a doctor. She arranged a special meeting at the Café de l'Olympia to include Daumal, Vera, Jack, and Emily Langherhans. When she had their attention, she announced to Daumal, with the others as witnesses, that she was ordering him to go consult her pulmonary specialist, Dr. Jacques Chauveau. If he refused, she swore to him that she would never have anything further to do with him. He went.

Advanced tuberculosis was revealed in both lungs, but he refused to go to a sanitarium. Although René had the discipline to follow the strict guidelines of Madame de Salzmann, he could not stomach the thought of life in a hospital setting, any more than he could have stood being in the army. In any case, Jack Daumal reports in a letter to the author that during World War II, even physicians generally advised against entering a sanitarium because the food and medical supplies were often greatly lacking. It was preferable to find lodging in a healthy mountain area outside the war zone and follow a personal health regime under a doctor's care. This was the plan that René strove to follow.

Two months before the German invasion of Paris, in August, 1940, Michel de Salzmann relates how he left Paris with his mother and family, then returned to Paris in the autumn. Gurdjieff also left Paris for two months then quickly returned. During the war, Daumal and Vera lived under severe conditions; by 1943, they had changed residence six times in two years, yet they returned to occupied Paris to spend as much time as possible with Gurdjieff and Jeanne de Salzmann.

During this period Daumal, Vera, Lavastine, Jack, Luc Dietrich, Henri Tracol, and a few others met with Gurdjieff several times a week. Philippe Lavastine describes episodes of their weekly group encounters. First, Gurdjieff would prepare an elaborate lunch, always managing to procure plenty of war rations and Middle Eastern delicacies, even while living in occupied Paris. Although many writers have exaggerated the exotic excess of Gurdjieff's feasts, Jack Daumal insists that there was nothing bizarre about his largesse in feeding homeless people as well as his students. This was the accepted Middle Eastern custom. Henri Tracol described these meals as a veritable potlatch, a hallowed communion, and Gurdjieff's patriarchal welcome to large groups was a true nourishment for all involved.

After the meal the disciples would usually be castigated for not doing the week's suggested task or exercise. Invariably, Daumal would be the only one to have completed the assignment, according to Lavastine. Gurdjieff would ask them, "Why do you come here? There are plenty of cars, women and distractions out there!" He often told Daumal to "get out of his head." "No more philosophy! *Faire! Faire! Faire!* ("Act! Act! Act!")[52]

During the war years, when René traversed France, shielding his Jewish wife from the Germans and seeking shelter and sunshine for his lungs, he was often separated from Gurdjieff or Jeanne de Salzmann. The recent publication of his final corresondence allows us to intrude on his personal discussions with Madame de Salzmann. We hear a voice that is not meant for others, not a writer writing for the public nor even to interest a friend. The following are translations of some of his most fascinating self-exposés—his own examination of the convolutions and meanderings of his inner struggle. In July 1943, he asked:

> What to do this summer to keep from falling asleep? As I told you, I have even thought of some "violent means"—those that I had tried in the past, before I met you, such as picturing my death: effective if done just right, but dangerous if one deviates from the main aim.
>
> While Vera was in Paris, and I was left to work alone, your letter confirmed and illuminated something that has been ripening in me for a year. I see now that what I used to call "activity" was, on the contrary, "passive agitation." I've learned recently that to become active in thought, one must make this agitation passive, pacify it and remove the yeast. The yeast is the illusion of a personal will. My thought is only active when I renounce my "personal" thinking, an act which gives the external appearance of passivity or submission.
>
> This was tested recently when I was called upon to resolve a delicate situation between people with whom I work [the Liefs], and I found myself "personally" incapable of doing so. I pictured to myself what you would do in the circumstance (not specifically your actions but trying to feel how you would be). Suddenly my conduct was quite clear, as if it had been dictated to me; the details, the words to say, arranged themselves—passively. The interior active "me," compared to the other "me's" has something markedly impersonal.

When I tried the new exercise that you gave me, I had a strong impression of entering into a world that was still forbidden to me. Not having paid in advance to enter, I would have to pay heavily later, but I felt strong enough to assume the debt.

But the next day, thanks to what Vera brought me, I saw the other side of the medallion and I found myself plunged into darkness and confusion. Again I was faced with the dictum that is a terrible enigma for me—what your husband had said to me, word for word, at our third or fourth meeting—that "I pay for the things that I should not pay for, and I don't pay for the things that I should pay for." I can understand the second part, but the first part remains an enigma, although I sense in it a terrible truth. The enigma is: What is it that doesn't function deep inside of me, what creates the obstacles and what is it that I hinder? I sense that one must liquify that which is hard, and harden that which is liquid.... Au revoir, Madame, and thank you for the life that you send me.[53]

If, in later years, Jeanne de Salzmann expressed having been deeply inspired by her pupil, in return it seems that René was especially devoted to her. In frequent letters, he spoke of being truly in contact with her, no matter how great the distance between them. In a 1943 letter to her, he reviewed the past three years often spent away from her, and saw this period as one moment, or one average day, with its little awakenings and little neglects, not all negative but so lukewarm:

Yet never in these three years did I ever feel deprived of assistance, of your assistance. I do not mean merely the memory of your words, but a substantive help in all those moments when I could no longer find any help in myself, those moments when I seemed to see more clearly but still could only see emptiness. How could I have held on at those times, and how could those moments have turned out to be the most fertile, if there had not been help?[54]

Their active correspondence was intensely serious. In August 1943, as his health declined, he answered her specific questions:

"Has the sensation of 'I am' changed?" I have had some moments, short and rare, when "I am" had a new taste—new, yet recovering something very old and buried.... Concerning my "concentration of thought," there is also a change in the sense that, if the battle is harder and more frequent, it seems to be a sign that I have a bit more force myself. A taste and a need for battle is developing. An answer from M.G. [Monsieur Gurdjieff] on the necessity of thwarting one's body in all that it likes or doesn't like has recently made this clearer to me. In my case, I can no longer follow this rule to the letter (regretably indeed, for when I did in the past, it gave me so much.)

Yes, I will try to do the exercises better and better as you requested: "as one learns a trade." The Work is becoming more and more a work "on me" rather than "for me."[55]

He mentions receiving copies of talks given by Gurdjieff or Madame herself, and remarks, "It makes me feel as if I were in Paris (I say 'Paris' the way others say Mecca)."[56] A week later, he thanks her for a care package sent via his brother Jack.

Thank you—a big polyphonic thank you. I will not eat the eggs or the spice bread without recalling, as if you were telling it, a certain Zen master's sermon: he called the monks together and said, "Monks, you are gathered together in this monastery, and every day you partake of vegetables. But if you refer to them as merely vegetables, you are going to Hell straight as an arrow!" And he went away.[57]

During this period, Daumal took on his own students. Geneviève Lief was his student from 1941 to 1944. Although he was already ailing, he instructed her and several other pupils in the theories and practice of the Gurdjieff teaching. She would stay near him and Vera for a month at a time in Allauch in the southern unoccupied zone. He also went to stay with her on the plateau d'Assy to instruct her husband Louis as well. Daumal often brought Geneviève to Paris where they would meet regularly with Gurdjieff for two to three months at a time. In two interviews in 1977 and 1983, she underlined Daumal's strong sense of service toward his pupils and colleagues alike. In a recent telephone conversation, shortly before she died, she reaffirmed how crucial René's instruction had been for her Work.

In his extensive correspondence with the Liefs, one sees how personal and penetrating Daumal's influence was on their inner development and even on their mutual relationship. In one letter written to both of them,

René described a daily Work ritual that he and Vera did together in the evenings, where they would share their innermost thoughts and feelings about their inner Work, including any observations and reflections concerning each other. This kept their inner struggle alive and in front of them. René urged the Liefs to consider the necessity of this practice, even if sometimes they had to wait a day and allow some "fragile words to ripen inside" before expressing them.

Vera also worked with them and wrote to them. A letter to Geneviève reveals her efforts for the well-being of her husband:

> You and I, Geneviève, we have a suffering in our lives which is real though negative: the illnesses of our husbands. I have told you that I have taken it as a task to try to help him heal, not only physically but also interiorly, so that I do not impede his spiritual growth. For this, I needed to heal myself interiorly as well. This task has helped me to pay in advance through voluntary suffering, and to deepen our relationship on a more stable and real basis. This task obliged me to clarify my aims, and to regard myself without pity. I see a being for whom self-love was the very substance of her false personality. I am now learning to carry this self-love like a nail stuck in my heart, so that I never forget it and so I can better pay for it.[58]

René wrote another poignant letter to Madame de Salzmann in August, 1943, where he exposed his private failings:

> Ever since Vera's return to Paris, thanks to all that she brought me, I received a new impetus. I felt that until now, I "worked" too much with the thought of "achieving something," of acquiring powers,—or to be more honestly to the point—of being more happy. Perhaps that was legitimate, but now something else is needed. Everything that you have sent me, particularly the exercises, by confronting me with a superior reality, has helped me to enter a new path. I saw that in the better moments, I could accept being a "nothing special"—or I could forget all thought of "succeeding" or "not succeeding," because I saw a distant possibility of being able to serve a higher reality.
>
> But then the old poison mixes in again with my new revelations: the pride, the vanity, in all their most subtle forms, making me proud of this new stage. I needed help to fight this enemy.

First of all the exercises, and Vera, who with much patience helps me to see more clearly. Since last Sunday, I have focused on a complete and unflattering picture of all that is René Daumal: what he is in his relations as son, brother, husband, friend, student, what he is in his essence: nothing healthy or normal in his thinking, his feelings, nor in his instincts, and then what he pretends to be. With all that, how could I pretend to serve? Yet the path of discouragement and abandon has been definitively closed off to me for around two years (ever since the day I heard the word "despair" pronounced near me—it sounded like such a blasphemy that for the first time, I felt the taste of what *hope* must be, and I cried with joy).

Thus there is no one tenable position. And the worst (or the best!), the last straw is that, even now, as I write to you, the liar and the poseur try to impose themselves at every line. Even in front of you!

At this moment, I understand the necessity of asking for pity and help from higher forces, for without this help, this generosity, I am in Hell. But I feel that I am on the right path. The old poses are worn out and repugnant, yet there is always another to fall into. I must find my right position, my "middle path." If there were no exercises to prove to me that I can find it, I would become mad; or simply, I would remain mad.[59]

The practice of the Gurdjieff ideas provided a much needed adjustment in Daumal's focus that may account for the ever growing serenity of his later years. When interviewed in 1986, Henri Tracol attested to Daumal's ever present sense of humor, still sharp even when discussing serious issues. Tracol mentioned that some Gurdjieff followers reproached him for his "verbal dance" (*sa danse verbale*). And such it was that René never let go of his humorous sense of the seriousness of life. The same individual who had been reckless with his physical body now understood the medical imperatives of good nutrition, rest, and serious inner relaxation. He wrote in 1939, that his greatest relaxation now came from playing the flute: a Rumanian flute for Hindu and Andalusian melodies, and a Mongolian Annamese flute for Chinese airs. He became even more sensitive to the rhythms of the mountains as his rhythm slowed down. He continued to hone his persona and seek out his essence.

In another letter to Jeanne de Salzmann, he discusses that relationship between his health and his inner work, then refers back to the dangerous out-of-body experiences of his youth, realizing how reckless he had been.

> A sign that forces are returning to me is that I feel stronger in the face of nature: wind, water, the sun, plants, etc. While gathering wood, I was able to do my exercises on the edge of a rushing stream, without being distracted by the wind, the sounds of the water, the smells of the earth or the insects. This would not have been possible a few months ago.
>
> I remain suspicious of imagination and its ruses while doing the exercises. What helps is the memory of certain experiments that I attempted in the past, at age eighteen—having read something on the astral body and the etheric double. Based on curiosity, arrogance, and without a real aim, it was all diabolical. The proof is that, having tried these experiments in a particularly toxic state, I was caught several times in a very unpleasant, agonizing situation where, from the outside, I could see and feel my body becoming frozen from my feet to the diaphragm, yet I lacked the ability to re-enter it in order to reanimate it. *I had no control over it*—and that makes all the difference.[60]

From 1941 onward, René developed a tubercular arthritis in his left foot. In October 1943, a painful synovial tumor erupted from it. As in the case of his Ardennais idol Rimbaud, this leg infection caused acute suffering during his last six months and he was never able to walk again. In July of 1943, he seemed to feel better. A letter to Dessaignes describes his state:

> Be reassured. My new and residual lesions are on their way to clearing up. I believe the main cause was last winter's poor nutrition. I haven't felt this well in three years. More and more often—for seconds or even minutes—I feel my body the way normal people do—as something other than a bag of wet laundry.[61]

In unpublished letters to Louis Lief, who likewise suffered from tuberculosis, Daumal often discussed the relationship between health and spiritual work—how in the past, he would deliberately fast and overwork his body as a help in overcoming his incessant laziness:

But now we no longer have the right. We must, for the moment, deal with this carcass to get it back in shape so that it can serve us. We can still be hard on its imaginary desires, its caprices and routines, but we must pay attention to its real needs. While nursing the body, we can be pitiless on that huge mass of intellectual and emotional mechanicalness. Let us not inflict *our* sufferings on the body; let it remain at ease, smiling, even if we are burning inside. But our intellectual tics, flatteries, and self pity, all this we can forbid ourselves. [62]

Writing to Geneviève Lief, he discussed the fact that a minimum of physiological equilibrium is necessary for work.

For the chronically ill like Louis and me, this point is not lost. We cannot wait until our health improves on its own in order to begin to work—otherwise we would never begin. It is a *reversal* that we must effectuate: in order to cure the body, we must subjugate it, give it everything that it needs so that its health improves but not permit it to take things easy. Just as one handles a horse.

[He advised her how to understand this illness and its effect on her husband's interior life.] To know one's self better, one should try to put oneself in someone else's place. And this is only possible if one recognizes the same material in oneself. A healthy person cannot "understand" a sick person. But there is no one with absolute health. If you remember your past moments of illness and how they affected your psyche, then imagine them as a permanent condition. We are all diseased, because disease means a domination of the body over the psyche. One is just as much a slave to good health and sometimes even more so, than one is to ill health.[63]

Mark Polizzatti, the translator of *Le Contre-Ciel*, reports Daumal's remark to Ribemont-Dessaignes: "I often suffered from not knowing, when I didn't want to accomplish some action, whether it was cowardly laziness or legitimate fatigue. . . . Now I simply need a thermometer; up to 99.5 it's laziness; above, it's illness.[64] He wrote to his brother: "This illness and fatigue have forced me to conserve my energy; I limit my activities and discussions with people, retaining only the most essential. Yet this conserved energy acts as a magnet, drawing still more people to me."[65]

Finally the frequent relocations, war deprivation, and lack of treatment caused a severe deterioration in Daumal's lungs. A month before he died, he wrote again to Louis, describing the pessimistic responses of the doctors to his x-rays.... "The worse it gets clinically, the better I feel interiorly; I feel as though I am secretly reassembling forces for an unexpected counteroffensive."[66]

Jack Daumal was separated from his brother during the last year of René's life. Jack was ill from the effects of war privations and went to live in La Mayenne near Bretagne where he took care of displaced and orphaned children. Since it was a region rich in food and dairy production, he sent supplies to René every two weeks via a friend. Jack reports that in his letters, René still expressed hope for recovery. He seemed to believe in the possibility of a miracle. Jack feels that if René could have survived a few months longer, until after the Liberation, he would then have been able to procure the newly developed Streptomycin, recently produced by the war industry. Then he might have survived another ten years or more. He feels that René died when he did for two reasons: lack of proper nourishment and excessive smoking of [Gaulois] cigarettes. This was his one vice; in those years no one realized that it was perhaps the deadliest vice of all.[67]

Gurdjieff came to visit Daumal when he was bedridden during those last months. There is no record of their conversations, but it seems Daumal was mentally active up to the very last days of his life. He was working on a major project that he had been planning for four years: to produce a new literary review based on the noblest, most ethical principles, one which would involve the readers in a dialogue with the writers. In a letter written four months before his death, Daumal discussed how this review would draw from the writer's total being, not just from his mind. Until the end, Daumal was putting into practice the teachings he had embraced all his life.

His years spent living and working with Jeanne de Salzmann aided him in avoiding the blind alleys, surrealist eccentricities, and intellectual baggage of his early years. She acted as a catalyst to help channel the painful fire of his emotions into a serene balance with his mind and body. He came to realize on a deeper level the truth he had always known: that one must maintain a position at the threshold between the material world and the Beyond. At this liminal position, one can include the lower and the higher, allowing them to interact just as yin leads to yang. If one does not maintain a state of awakeness and balance, one can drown in psychic exploration, Surrealism, or Pataphysics; the Hegelian system would lead to Prussian/German imperialism, and Marxism would lead to the destruction of the shrines of the very Eastern traditions that he extolled. The real battle is neither with bourgeois capitalism nor with dictators such as Hitler, but with the forces of "sleep" inside himself.

Thus the effects of the Gurdjieff work on Daumal's life and writings are manifold. As a youth, Daumal had intuited that there existed a larger meaning of life on Earth. The ancient Hindu writings reinforced this feeling, but his moments of vision were often obscured by days of despair and discouragement. All this changed when he began an inner work along the lines suggested by Gurdjieff. Hindu writings may have described a reality behind the veil of ordinary perception, but Gurdjieff provided the practical means to experience *both* worlds, by remaining at the threshold and looking both ways. While Gurdjieff's assertion that man is a machine may have silenced Daumal's orphic lyre for a period of time, he was compelled to become aware of his own "machine" and to see what was necessary to move from being a machine to being a man. When Daumal finally wrote again, it was with less self-pity and more serenity, less panic and more conviction. He came to understand that the "elsewhere" that for so long he had been seeking is *here* in the immediacy of real life.

Whatever the quality of Daumal's experience, he expresses the gratitude that one might feel in just such moments of freedom. Writing about *Mount Analogue*, he seems to be describing his own experience working with Gurdjieff and his pupils, deeply grateful for all he has received:

> And now we have landed on the unknown continent, this kernel of higher substances implanted in the earth's crust. . . . [By] our efforts, renouncing all bodily comfort, we gained entry into this new world. So it seemed to us. But we learned later that if we were able to reach the foot of Mount Analogue, it was because the invisible country had been opened for us. . . . Those who see us, even though we cannot see ourselves, opened the door for us . . . answering our puerile calculations, our unsteady desires, and our awkward efforts with a generous welcome.[67]

Fig. 17. Alexandre de Salzmann (1874–1934) was a true Renaissance man—artist, world-reknowned authority in lighting and set design, teacher of jiu-jitsu, and later in his life, a follower of the teachings of G. I. Gurdjieff.

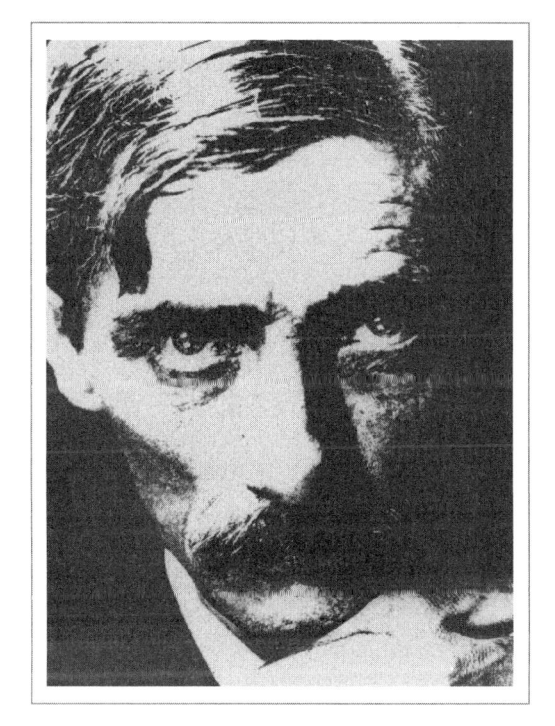

Fig. 18. A later photograph of Alexandre de Salzmann. His encounter with René in 1931 changed the course of the young poet's life forever.

Fig. 19. Madame Jeanne de Salzmann (1889–1990), René's spiritual guide, worked with Gurdjieff in Russia and assisted him in establishing his Institute for the Harmonious Development of Man in Fountainebleau, France. In a 1979 interview, she states: "The search is the same for all religions and spiritual ways. It is searching for something in yourself, something that is missing in your usual state. There are many different ways and different masters who have tried to show the way."

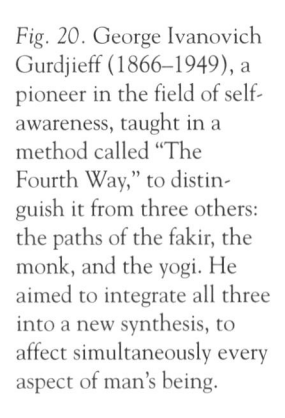

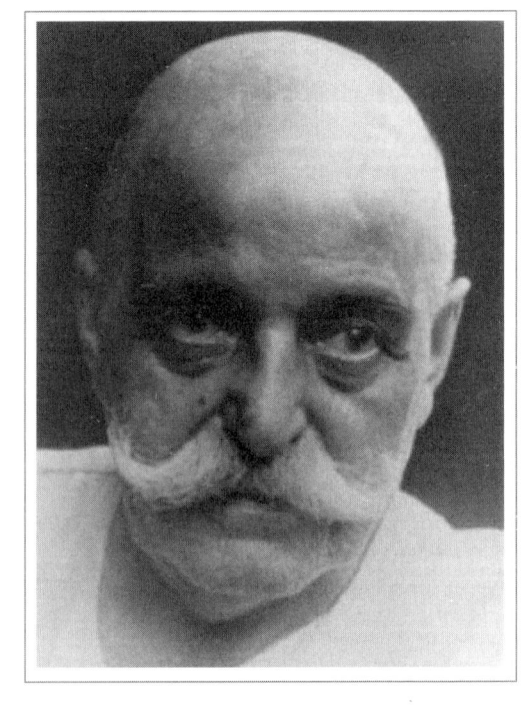

Fig. 20. George Ivanovich Gurdjieff (1866–1949), a pioneer in the field of self-awareness, taught in a method called "The Fourth Way," to distinguish it from three others: the paths of the fakir, the monk, and the yogi. He aimed to integrate all three into a new synthesis, to affect simultaneously every aspect of man's being.

Fig. 21. René Daumal (right), Luc Dietrich (center), and Lanzo del Vasto (left), 1942. These poets and seekers of the metaphysical realm were all students of Jeanne de Salzmann, but del Vasto soon returned to his own spiritual path. In 1939, Dietrich and René established a close friendship that continued up to their premature deaths in 1944.

Fig. 22. Painting of Mount Analogue by Kathleen Rosenblatt, 1992.

Fig. 23. Painting of the flora on Mount Analogue by Kathleen Rosenblatt, acrylic and pastel, 1992.

Fig. 24. The last photograph of René taken by Luc Dietrich, four days before René's death on May 21, 1944.

V
MAIN WORKS

10

The Poetry of *Le Contre Ciel*

Death and Her Consort

> **To God**
> If you have formed a Circle to go into
> Go into it yourself & see how you would do.
> —William Blake

René Daumal's dense, visionary poetry deals obsessively with the apparent rift between spiritual and physical life. It has a monotheme of death and rebirth through self-abnegation and renunciation. The rationale behind the theme of renunciation is the self-transformation or awakening of the poet himself and his reader. This awakening entails a knowledge of one's inner workings.

> Name if you can your shadow, your fear, and measure the circumference of its head and the size of your world.
> It only takes a word.
> If you dare break the silence woven with mute laughter—if you dare break the bubble without complicity.
> ("It Only Takes a Word")[1]

His earliest poems written between 1924 and 1935 were collected into a book entitled *Le Contre-Ciel* (*The Counter-Heaven*) (1936), for which, as previously mentioned, he won the Prix Jacques Doucet in 1935, awarded by three of France's preeminent writers, Valéry, Gide, and Giraudoux. A second edition, published in 1970, included earlier and later poems as well as prose poems of particular interest. All of the following poems and essays mentioned here are contained in *Le Contre-Ciel*.

Among the earlier poems is a long meditation on consciousness entitled "The Keys of a Great Poetic Game" ("*Clavicules d'un grand jeu poétique*") (1929) made up of cosmological and hermetic aphorisms. It is a composite of verse and prose expressing the same recurring theme of transformation expressed throughout his work, later echoed in his prose allegories. The verse itself is Daumal's depiction of man's creation myth—how every soul begets its own material dimensions and its extensions in the world, until it becomes immersed in these extensions, inseparable from them and annihilated by them. In Daumal's text, interspersed throughout the poem, "I," the subject, can maintain itself as an entity in the midst of these extensions only by perpetual negation. This *théologie négative* consists of a perpetual "no" to the material plane, including that which is ordinarily considered part of the "I": physical features, attitude, character, job, social position, penchants, opinions, virtues, talent, and genius: "Irony or refusal is the weapon which shatters all these shells."[2] The individual is shrunken from its indulged, bloated space to a more retracted, denser size. Taking full advantage of the French homophones *nom* (name) and *non* (no), he underlines the absurdity of existence with a play on words:

> Retreat back behind yourself and laugh:
> The Laugh is pronounced on your No.
> Renounce your Name, laugh at your No.
>
> *Recule encore derrière toi-même et ris:*
> *Le rire est prononcé sur ton* NON
> *Renie ton Nom, ris de ton* NON.[3]

Daumal called this phenomenon of retraction "metaphysical suicide": the voluntary destruction of the outer covering that surrounds the inner man. The negated world, the non-I, is the world of all the disarming extensions—the female principle, according to Hindu theory and according to Daumal.

> laugh at your Name
> and from there contemplate
> A boiling sea before you
> the word Yes shines unnamable, reflected by each bubble.
> Male-the-No, he watches the female.[4]

One sees a reflection of the biblical creation myth, as well as the Vedic myth of the first primal being, Purusha, creating all things out of himself. Daumal seems to be saying that every individual does this in a primal way. We each create this female principle, the world of appearances, as Adam conjured up Eve out of the wish fulfillment of his very bones:

> She is his sacrifice and his creature, since she is all the outer skin that he has shed.[5]

Daumal cites three rapports that can exist between the subject "I" and the extensions: causality, knowledge, and love. However, these only exist if the separation, the negation of the outer world, is maintained by the I.

> Absurd to be included in the lowest of innumerable
> bubbles—provoked, evoked, projected—a No
> is pronounced "I" and I observe.
> I am the cause of All this if I am No.
> I am the knower of All this if I am No.
> I am the lover of All this if I am.[6]

Using the Vedic hymnal mode of enumeration, Daumal then follows the evolution of this creation myth, as the bubbles of *maya*, the world of appearances, begin to take living forms:

> Under my glance which negates, a knot of bubbles affirms and organizes itself into systems of cooperating circular movements.[7]

In the interspersed commentary, Daumal explains that these material bubbles, organized into durable forms, are called appetites and desires. Soon the subject, realizing that he also is a form, feels isolation and seeks union with another human being. Daumal allows that:

> Also true love, the kind that is not a mere systematization of individual desires around an object that is physically, psychologically, and sociologically convenient, does not blind but rather illuminates.[8]

In sections 13, 14, and 15, the poet illustrates how the "No" can liberate itself, can know, and can love. Liberation comes in surpassing his individual costume in favor of moving in harmony with the universe.

> How the No, wanting itself to be Other, bursts with love,
> ... he lets suffering lives gush
> from bleeding wounds toward other suffering lives,
> also isolated from the common Sea, painfully separated
> from the single Sea; he allows every leap of the
> multiple animal toward the primal Grandmother,
> being born again in different forms, this single
> irresistible leap of love.[9]

In the prose gloss, Daumal explains that under the light of perpetual watching and negation, the multiple forms and desires can unravel and loosen their grip on the burgeoning consciousness:

> Since I stop thinking of them as *my* nature and *my* property, they tend to reunite with nature, which in turn ceases to be considered exterior. They appear as animals long imprisoned in human skin and which, once liberated, seek to rejoin the herd of their own kind.[10]

We see that the concept of contraction and expansion presented in this poem corresponds to the creative momentum that spans all of Daumal's literary production. In prose section 16, the basic act of consciousness is considered to be the synthesis of three aspects: first, the act of negation, a dissociation of the "I" from the external world in order to reduce or refine the "I." This characterizes most of the poetry of *Le Contre-Ciel*. This negation includes an "evoking of the renounced forms" and a "knowledge of the negated forms" that characterizes *La Grande Beuverie*, wherein Daumal deals with all the "bubbles" of man's illusions. Second, Daumal considers the most loathsome aspects of individuals and society, illustrating an important teaching of many esoteric doctrines: that every man must face his baser instincts before he can alchemically transform lead into gold. He must integrate his lower animal nature with his higher self. This leads into the third and final aspect, "Integration of the forms through love." In his introduction to *Mount Analogue*, Roger Shattuck describes this movement:

> Then, however, beginning a vibratory rhythm that must follow if self-annihilation is not to result, the pure consciousness expands again into all things, experiences the world subjectively once more, loses itself in the mystery of creation. Baudelaire describes

> the rhythm of consciousness in the terse words that open "My Heart Exposed" ("*Mon coeur mis à nu*"): "The Vaporization and Centralization of Me. Everything Is There." (*De la vaporisation et de la centralisation du moi. Tout est là.*). Daumal would accept the terms and reverse the order. Centralization or concentration: elimination of everything exterior in order to arrive at the intensity of self-awareness. Vaporization: reassimilation of all the universe in the amplitude of sympathy and action.[11]

This is the essence of *Mount Analogue*—ascension through one's effort and in integration with other seekers. And where, according to "Clavicules," does this expansion and contraction take place?

> The battlefield is a human being, the poet. His being is the junction of creative mystery where the atrocious sadness of contradiction encounters the correlative joy of resolution.[12]

For the poet, the moments of illumination are brief, for he cannot maintain the state of transcendence. "He who sees the absurd suffers this torture: to have the Final Word on the tip of his tongue but to be unable to pronounce it."[13] The prose sections lengthen as the verse section decreases, while Daumal outlines in detail his dialectical theory of poetics. For him, creating poetry is the perfect example of abnegation of the material expansion of "I."

> All poetry has its root in the immediate act of negation. The poet becomes conscious of himself by making the forms appear that he is renouncing. Through this act they become the symbols, palpable aspects of his asceticism. He expresses himself by what he rejects and projects from himself, and if one finds his proposed images admirable, it is always to the "No" hidden behind them that our admiration goes.[14]

The theme of renunciation or nonattachment that echoes throughout all the poetry of *Le Contre-Ciel* takes on a particular bent: renouncing attachments to life means embracing death. Many of Daumal's early poems reflect this continuing obsession. Two sections of *Le Contre-Ciel* are entitled "Death and Her Man" ("*La mort et son homme*"). He wrote in a letter, "I believe in the horrible (*Je crois à l'horrible*), just as someone else might say, 'I believe in God.'" He seems not to have suffered so much the traditional fear of annihilation—the grim reaper as being the end of everything. Rather, he longed for death as the closest thing to infinity, union with the All. Death was the final shedding of identity leading to the ultimate cosmic vitality.

Using the name "Nathaniel," he wrote to Gilbert-Lecomte in 1928:

> Death, always brutal and vulgar, a pure event. But death remains naked with its odor of garbage. It is not a terrible thing. Consider creating a school where one teaches how to die: that is, to see death in its total nakedness.[15]

He was convinced that the seeming importance of any individual's existence was a mirage and that one can only achieve absolute reality by melding with the universe. In life, this can only be achieved partially, temporarily, and asymptotically, never completely. In keeping with the Hindu concept, according to the philosopher Aruni, death can potentially be an elevation to a higher state. "In death, a man's speech becomes merged with the mind which merges with the breath (*prana*) which merges in light which itself becomes merged in the deity."[16] If this absolute reality is beyond both existence and nonexistence, then the passage betwixt them—the moment of death—is the most favorable for apprehending this absolute reality. This positive attitude toward death is expressed in one of Daumal's personal letters:

> On August 1st, 1929, I realized I was in love with my death.
> On August 1st, 1930, I named it nothingness.[17]

To Maurice Henry he wrote:

> Therefore, from this life on, I want to get used to picturing myself in death, thinking of the dead man that I will be, of the dead man that I am.[18]

The frequently occurring image of death, *la mort*, is more than the angel of death; she is the bounteous Mother, the only pure entity in a world of contingencies, often sinister and avaricious in her search for beings to extinguish, forcing upon them further metamorphoses. Daumal throws himself into the embrace of "The Only One" (or "Single Lady" in Kelton Knight's translation) ("*La seule*") (1929), "the mistress of the end, the Mother who reigns in the inverse of day."[19] In one poem after another, the poet denudes himself, divests himself of all extensions: "I burned my wheat fields, I starved my Babylon" ("Oath of Loyalty").[20]

> What beautiful carnage without anger in your honor . . .
> when I amputated myself from myself,
> here I am, words stopped, me minuscule,
> lost in the vertigo of your breast, all that was for nothing.
>
> "To Nothingness"[21]

The violence and fire of these images express the seriousness of Daumal's commitment. In form and feeling, these poems come closest of any of his works to being prayers to a personal anthropomorphized Goddess. He feminizes the word for "nothingness" (*le néant*) by changing it to *la néante*. As he beseeches "mother Nothingness," he uses a litanical structure, made up of a mantric repetition:

> Where I have no eye she sees
>   Let them be the only Visions!
> Where I have no ear she hears
>   Let them be the only Charm![22]

The poet addresses this queen of the night, always in the "*tu*" form, imploring her mercy. Here we see the Surrealist/Pataphysical influence as Daumal creates a Dantesque or Faustian vision of hell. Through a coruscating use of language, the material world is portrayed in its most cancerous, horrific aspects, a Sartrian world of *de trop*. Extreme violence is directed against the body, the symbol of the individual conscience. In all these poems, there is a continual juxtaposition of terrestrial elemental forms, dismemberment and death—"lilacs of living skin," "her skin of pulp," "carcasses of plaster," "jaw of death," bits of red flesh, and the single mythic image of the Void, receptive yet devastating, the figure of Kali eating her children: "For you sucking my marrow, you without dimension and free of frontiers, I take you to bed on this grotesque nuptial bed" ("To Nothingness").[23] Since it is the act of writing that symbolizes the renunciation of material forms, it is not surprising that the hand becomes a privileged image: "hands of iron," "hands of the black ocean." While the nose and ears bleed and the body is dismembered, the hand remains to carry out the act of testifying: "I can only speak with my hands" ("Panic Sweat").[24]

The nightmarish atmosphere of these poems may be explained in part by his experimentation with mind-altering drugs during this period. Daumal was methodically following Rimbaud's formula for "upsetting all the senses" and was focusing on the darkest side of reality. These poems were written at a period when he seemed to be falling deeper into despair and alluded to suicide on several occasions. In *"Disillusion,"* he writes:

> Pay attention, I am going to teach you how to die.
> Close your eyes and grit your teeth, bang!
> You see, it's not difficult, there are no surprises.
> When I want to drink from the spring
> I find the water changed to stone.
> Where is this emptiness which draws me?[25]

In these poems, he appears to already be among the dead.

> I am trying to look like someone
> Among you who is alive
> It is only good manners
> To laugh a little.
> Just between us, it's finished, isn't it?
> Either alone or together,
> My beard continues to grow,
> It is the only sound you can hear.
>
>   "The Famous Surprise"[26]

Images of animals abound, symbols for visceral reactions and organic functions, the "beast passions" according to Daumal. Everywhere they are famished and devour each other: "the lion which is drawn out of your breast," "the elephant which knocks against the lining of your forehead," and animals that growl and leap, and animals that evoke human faculties and behavior:

> And a thousand other animals growl, stretch out, and lunge forward toward the orifices of this man. ("Keys")[27]

Although Daumal was probably influenced by the various Surrealist poets around him, most of these poems were written before he was twenty years old, while he was still attending the lycée. So his brand of surrealistic flourishes was, for the most part, "homegrown." Many of his images are juxtaposed in definite anti-rational "Surrealist fashion":

> But the safety valve of chaos with its rubber lips waxed the imbecile's moustache and the wise man had to wear suspenders. (Poem to Debone Philosophers entitled, "The Miserable Beyond")[28]

We see the Surrealist dreamscape in a spontaneously dictated poem, "Dictated in 1925":

> the stairs without end, the broken mirror . . . the enfeebled crawling under the rubbish, under the moist beams, in the empty attics.[29]

He spontaneously recorded all his mental states and juxtaposed random phrases according to some inner logic:

> Singing shock of tears falling from the sky, immediately covered by an enormous laugh of metallic structures.[30]

Yet his images were almost always presented within a traditional sentence structure containing a subject and predicate (even if in French the subject can alternately follow the verb). Nowhere do we find anything like Guillaume Apollinaire's sunburst effect of images juxtaposed without a syntactical connection. Nor does Daumal employ strange typographic techniques such as those invented by Apollinaire. Yet Philip Powrie points out Daumal's techniques of "subversive dislocation" that seek to disorient the reader in order to loosen his habitual modes of perception. He employs negative images like "The Great Day of the Dead" or "the palace with no doors," as well as oppositional hyphenated terms, for example, "anti-king," "anti-sun," "contre-ciel," and oxymorons such as, "'I' am the viewer of the night, the hearer of silence." The protagonist of his poems is never clear, for Daumal usually obscures any notion of a fixed identity.

The majority of his poems are written in free verse or in prose. Often a poem will begin with a semblance of regularity in rhyme or meter (rarely both together), and then gradually become irregular; an example is the meter change in "Brief Revelation on Death and Chaos." In "Single Lady" ("*La seule*"), the first four lines have an alternating rhyme while the second quatrain has random rhyming.

Although Daumal and the Pataphysicians, as well as the Surrealists, purported to incorporate humor into their work, there are actually few humorous Surrealist poems extant, nor is there much to laugh about in Daumal's poetry. These poets were all intensely serious about their spontaneous creations and outpourings of the soul. If most Surrealist poems tried to capture short moments of perception and disquiet, Daumal's often captured painful yet timeless moments of eternity.

It was not until later in his career that Daumal truly encompassed the full range of Hindu poetics. Early on, however, he began to incorporate some Vedic imagery and theory that emerged amid the heavy layer of surrealistic imagery. He himself recognized the danger of confusion inherent in the Surrealist technique.

As early as 1926, at the age of eighteen, he wrote to Maurice Henry:

> Surrealistic automatic writing furnishes the material of chaos: in order not to let oneself get smothered in this sludge, you need the Word (or the divine will or the unconscious, inspiration, revelation).[31]

He refers to the *Bhagavad Gita* in "Keys" and speaks of the "the function of magical procedures" such as "maniacal repetitions, primitive chants and rounds, which were first inscribed in the Vedas. I remember the primitive rondos . . . like a very old cosmic ritual, this circular dance is also that of the world."[32]

If early Vedic literature often provides glimpses of eternity full of joy and abundance, moments of blissful *samadhi* or Buddhist *satori*, this was generally not Daumal's vision. At this point in his life he seemed generally to focus on the harrowing aspects—he felt the painful vibration of this experience—the restless longing for death. Instead of moments of heaven, it was rather a hell on Earth. Daumal makes few concessions to the reader's desire for diversion; all his poems deal with this theme of salvation through dying to oneself. His work is characterized by extremes of emotion—fire and water—because he allows no middle road; he makes a consummate effort to see the lies of his life and wake himself out of the accepted human stupor.

> . . . I am . . . I know . . . I want . . . Lies!
> Lies grafted onto my flesh, an abscess which screams at me:
> "Don't slaughter us, we are of the same blood!"
>
> "The Holy War"[33]

The uncompromising fervor of these lines seems to correspond to the Vedic concept of ardor or fire (*gaudi*) as a quality of poetry outlined by Vishvanatha: "an expansive embrace of the spirit . . . an emotion which enflames us, exalts us, and provokes in us an active response."[34] In more than a dozen poems, the imagery of fire predominates: "the fire of your enslaved voice,"[35] "I have set the storehouses on fire,"[36] "this devastated heart of fire and ice,"[37] and "the cruel fire of this lucid love devours me slowly."[38] In "Willed Fire" he writes: "Subjected to the languages of fire, turn your face to the flames, towards the divine kiss which will suck out your teeth with one smack."[39] Not only does this fire image recall the Hindu concept of the initiatory fire that transforms, the fire of austerity, it also conjures up typical Surrealist imagery—the fire that erupts, melts, and liquifies, as seen in the poems of Breton or the paintings of Salvador Dali.

In a 1938 poem in Daumal's essay "Black Poetry and White Poetry" ["Poésie noire, Poésie blanche"] (1954), at the end of *Le Contre-Ciel*, one can see the application of a fundamental Hindu philosophical concept. Contrary to Aristotelian theory, the Hindus believe that it is possible for $A=B$ and $A \neq B$; that is, for A to equal and not equal B at the same time.) Something can both be and not be without any real contradiction. Daumal employs paradoxical equations six times in the poem.

> Twelve times the moon affirms itself
> and twelve times negates itself
> it is, but it is not
> she devours and recreates herself in four periods.[40]

Likewise in the poem "How Everything Begins Again" ("Comment tout recommence"), he refers to the Prime Mover as "Himself-no-not-Him."[41]

In "The Distribution" ("Le Partage"), Daumal uses the myth of the creation of the world of nature out of the many parts of the primal god, Purusha's body.

> I give my brain to the storm.
> O white lightning, my knees on the ice.[42]

In his essay "Powers of the Word in Hindu Poetics" (1938), Daumal mentions the necessary requirements to produce "*sauvité*" (*vaidarbhi*): "easily pronounced sounds, frequent breaths, such that the listener is put into a state of relaxation and prepared to taste the liquefying emotions."[43]

Accordingly, sounds and images of fluidity abound in the original French text and almost as much in the English translation.

> Barges glide
> through liquid skies
> and wolves' gums bleed
> in the green velvet night.
>
> Des barques glissent
> dans des cieux liquides
> et les gencives des loups saignent
> dans la nuit de velours vert.
>
> "The Panic Sweat"[44]

Just as he began to receive some prominence from the publications of his poems and the Prix Jacques Doucet, he abruptly stopped writing poetry altogether. "I no longer know how to write poetry," he wrote to Jean Paulhan.[45] If Daumal's poetry had always had more than a literary aim, why were these other aims suddenly no longer served by poetry? Here we see again how much his life continued to unfold according to the legendary saga of his idol Rimbaud, who ended his career as a poet at the age of nineteen.

Like Daumal, the teenage Rimbaud had run off to Paris from the Ardennes, but after three years, he rejected the literary scene of Paris. This revolutionary genius burned all the copies of his recently published "A Season in Hell," in which he had written, "No more words!" Starting in 1874, he left France eight times, often on foot, seeking the non-Christian, non-bourgeois innocence of the Orient and Africa. His disillusionment with the limitations of poetry drove him to seek an active life in the here-and-now, the gritty natural world of preindustrial age countries. He worked in Abyssinia for twelve years—unaware that his poems had made him a legend in Paris—until an infected tumor in his leg brought on his premature death at age thirty-six, a similar demise and at the same age as Daumal.

Like Rimbaud, Daumal saw the poet's role as a seer and a "stealer of fire." But he too lost faith for a while in the efficacy of his own words. René not only left Paris physically (to study with Jeanne de Salzmann), but spiritually he turned his back on the Parisian avant-garde, as well as on his own ability to create true poetry. He too sought the East and returned to a simpler path, beginning again to learn how to live and to write.

He continued to work on *A Night of Serious Drinking* (*La Grande*

Beuverie), study Sanskrit, and began his *Treatise of Sanskrit Grammar and Poetics* (*Traité de grammaire et de poétique sanskrites*), which he continually worked on the rest of his life. In 1936 he began to write about poetry by writing several essays on Hindu poetics. This led to the writing of several prose poems, "The Last Words of the Poet," "Black Poetry, White Poetry," and "The Holy War."

Around the same period he succeeded in mastering another literary form, the prose allegory, as in *A Night of Serious Drinking*. In all this new material we see the incorporation of the rich imagery of his surrealist phase, Hindu ideas on poetics, and the new material and practices of the Gurdjieff teaching. As a result, Daumal's poetry gained in intensity while it diminished in quantity. More and more his writing took on the quality of an event or a sacrament.

In the prose poem, "The Last Words of the Poet" (1936), Daumal returned to one of his favorite themes: the role of the poet and poetry:

> You have to be two to make a poem. The one who speaks is the mother, the poem is the egg, and the one who listens is he who fertilizes the egg.[46]

Then the poet, condemned to death, speaks his mind, giving vent to Daumal's annoyance with the "sussuralism" [sic] and "psychic parlor games" of his own past and of the literati of his entourage.

> As soon as I will have opened my mouth,
> you will see all those return into the ground,
> those who conduct seances,
> those who use pendulums,
> those who look to the stars for reasons to do nothing,
> the daydreamers, the suicides,
> the maniacs of mystery,
> the maniacs of pleasure,
> the imaginary voyagers,
> the beaux-arts maniacs who don't know why they
> sing, dance, paint or build,
> the maniacs of the beyond
> who do not know how to be here.[47]

These lines illustrate Daumal's intolerance of facile occultism, intensified after ten years of experiencing what he felt was "the real thing." Like

Guénon, Gurdjieff had little tolerance for the current and past European attempts to understand Eastern philosophy. He sweepingly described all the occult and spiritual societies as "workshops for the perfection of psychopathism."[48]

In "The Holy War" (1940), another prose poem, Daumal uses the Muslim theme of the holy war in its original sense: the war against "the complacent traitors of dream and convenient illusion."[49] As in the preceding poem, there is a dire sense of urgency: there are no irrelevant images to distract from the dramatic themes of war, or of the poet waiting to be hanged. Only images of death, murder, arms, and war are strong enough to support Daumal's call to arms, to "Wake up!" and fight the internal war. He addresses the enemy—the little vanities and laziness that insinuate themselves:

> You rebels, one day I shall put you in your place. I shall bend you under my yoke, I will feed you hay, and groom you every morning. But as long as you suck my blood and steal my words, it would be better to never write a poem![50]

He even acknowledges the current implications of the word *war* in that war-scarred year of 1940, feeling that the new meaning will provide the needed weight to put force into his message: "Because in a real poem the words carry their things."[51]

In "Black Poetry, White Poetry" Daumal seems to distill the essence of Hindu theories of poetics into a telling comparison of the typical and the ideal poet.

> Black poetry is fertile with prestige like dreams and opium. The black poet tastes all pleasures, decks himself with every ornamentation, exercises all his powers—all in his imagination. The white poet prefers reality, even bleak reality to rich lies. His work is an incessant battle against pride, imagination and laziness.[52]

This contrast also reflects Gurdjieff's distinction between subjective, accidental art and objective, conscious art. The subjective artist is in the power of ideas, thoughts, and moods over which he has no control whatsoever. In the same essay, Daumal poses the question to himself: Is he a white poet? "Often I doubt it, sometimes I am sure of it. But in the past if I was a poet, for sure I was a black poet, and if tomorrow I am to be a poet, I want to be a white poet."[53]

Here and elsewhere he seems to denigrate the early poetry in *Le Contre-Ciel*. In his brief epilogue entitled, "The Poet's Warning" for the 1935 publication, he expresses his hesitation at publishing these poems, hating to "make a spectacle of his apprenticeship." He claims that the beliefs expressed in "Keys" (1929) have only recently begun to be incorporated into his being. He further adds that he is no longer encumbered by "the philosophical jargon and the facile pathos" of that essay-poem. In characterizing these "lyric pieces,"[54] he writes:

> Closer to a scream than a song. They were bursts from an escape valve while waiting for better. I have since found better ways to dissipate most of the torments, which those outpourings calmed so poorly. Better and simpler... to unlearn daydreaming and learn to think, to unlearn philosophizing and learn to speak—that is not accomplished in a day.[55]

By the time Daumal cautioned us about his early poems, he had been reading Hindu philosophy for twelve years. Apparently he characterized as "black poetry" the Surrealist techniques of automatic and oniristic writing that he used in *Le Contre-Ciel*. He viewed his early poetry as today's reader might: that mixed in with the exciting imagery is an unrelentingly torturous bombardment of claustrophobic anguish. There is too little regard for life, too much focus on putrefaction and death. These themes indicate that he felt he had to lose life to understand death in order to really live... a painful dialectical pilgrimage. Poetry was the hammer that he used to crack the shell around him. It is evident that Daumal was overwhelmed by his thirst for infinity. Had he toxified his emotional center by his sampling of chemical and emotional elixirs? The physical effects of the various drugs and his innate mental fever had left him walking on a tightrope between two chasms or choices: becoming conscious or going insane. His natural ascetic bent had driven him to focus on the most extreme aspects of Advaita Vedanta concerning the reality and value of the material world. Eventually he would chose the middle road.

Although most critics of Daumal agree that his later works display a greater maturity, Maurice Desselle prefers Daumal's early poetry to his later novels and essays. Desselle felt that the medium of poetry was more conducive to expressing the inexpressible. Only poetry could break through the confines of rational thought to the cutting edge of self-discovery.[56]

In 1941 Daumal revived his comic sense of irony to put across his ideas about poetics. In his essay "Quelques poètes français du XXVème siècle" ("A Few French Poets of the Twenty-Fifth Century"), he discusses five imaginary future poets and gives excerpts of their poems. He reflects back to the twentieth century "when poets did not need an apprenticeship for this interior vocation," and claims that often people were called poets who were "confused intellectuals, drunks, talkers, or ambitious climbers."[57] His humorous examples only partially conceal his sharp critical satire of modern literature.

Daumal borrows Gurdjieff's metaphor "between two stools" (being neither awake nor asleep) for the title of one of his essays "Entre deux chaises,"[58] another discussion about poetry as a means of "relearning how to speak." He proposes silence as the best means of preparing to utter the poetic word. No longer is silence synonymous with death; now there appears a dawning awareness that Silence is active, not passive, the "luminous seed" of eternity. Through his silence, Daumal would remain the inveterate listener. Just as the contemporary poet George Quasha describes poetry as "speaking with listening,"[59] so Daumal was able in silence to hear himself. Later, the modern French philosopher Gaston Bachelard quoted Daumal's lines from "Black Poetry, White Poetry": "Listen to the tumult in your heart when you listen to yourself."[60] Only in silence can we hear our inner voice.

Two poems remain: "Mémorables" (1942) and "The Four Cardinal Seasons" (1943). Although Daumal was still actively writing prose poems in 1943, this latter poem seems to be the first poem in verse in eight years, and his last poem, completed a year before his death. This short poem in verse is unlike any other, in that it is peaceful, even joyous—a veritable ode to dawn, noon, sunset, and midnight. Jack Daumal called it a song of rediscovered innocence. Warm colorful images of the natural world abound.

La poule noire de la nuit
vient encore de pondre une aurore.
Salut le blanc, salut le jaune,
salut, germe qu'on ne voit pas.

The black hen of night
just laid the egg of dawn again.
Hail white, hail yellow,
Greetings, seed that we cannot see.[61]

Daumal creates the peaceful ambiance of this poem by relying on sonorities and subtle rhymes from his own French literary heritage as well as those suggested by the Hindu treatise, Mirror of Composition. In the above stanza he links the sounds of *poule, encore, pondre une aurore*, and continues the nasalized vowels of the graceful "on" sound with *blanc, jaune*, and *qu'on ne voit pas*. The following stanza continues this sound, the final words of each four lines being: *instant, gong, dents*, and *dévorant*, and the next stanza continues similarly. He even creates a regular meter and strong rhyme: of *minuit* and *s'agit(ent)*. Unfortunately, the translation loses both the rhythm and the rhyme:

> *Mais en silence je salue le grand minuit,*
> *celle qui veille quand les trois s'agitent.*
>
> But in silence I greet the grand midnight,
> the one who keeps watch while the other three are moving.[62]

The poem appears to be a final greeting and farewell to our great star and an affirmation of its time-positioning, so elemental to our life. It is the only poem in which he sings the sun's praises for its own sake rather than as a symbol for some aspect of human torment or evolution. Sounding like St. Francis greeting his brother sun, Daumal shows himself a lover of earth as well as heaven, in contrast to the existentially tragic images of the following lines from an earlier work

> The great black anti-suns, pits of truth in the essential plot, in the gray veil of the curved sky. ("Willed Fire")[63]

For the first time, an emotion of warmth and familiarity is present in these last poems of the early forties: The sun is greeted as symbol ("hail, he who burns up our contaminations"), and as friend, ("the red fruit of memory"). Here we see Daumal truly creating images that radiate *rasa*, that have a strong sensory and emotional taste. In the terminology of Hindu poetics, he has passed through the process of idealization (*sadharanikarana*) from his troubled personal emotion to the serenity of contemplation. He achieves *maitri* or "mutual friendship" of verbal and ideal elements, using images that distinguish poetic speech from the matter-of-fact speech of everyday life: "the black hen of night laying the bright golden egg of the sun."[64] This is called *vakrokti*—an expressionistic deviation proper to poetry that creates its complex significance and aesthetic charm. Another example would be the red fruit of memory (the sun) sitting "on the cushions of the horizon," a warm visually textural image, with an immediate *rasa*.

Still the poem is not without some reference to his inner life: Daumal speaks of great midnight as he often spoke of darkness and nothingness, only here it is serene and dreamlike, without the usual terror and despair.

> Closing my eyes I see it without seeing anything
> > through the shadows.
> Closing my ears I hear its step which never goes away.[65]

Daumal is describing the inner eye and ear that he had developed toward the end of his life, both tuned to new frequencies and picking up finer emissions. Through his own hard work and austerity, without the aid of the drugs of his early years, he could "see without seeing." Thus this poem follows the Hindu ideal of intuitively externalizing the internal spiritual activity. At the same time there is a hint here of the waning of his earthly life—closing his eyes and seeing without seeing through the shadows. It is as if he were slowly tuning in to the reality that was to come.

Although every one of Daumal's poems had some kind of *rasa* or taste, this taste varied and intensified as the years went by. If the early poems expressed an anguished despair, his later poems expressed a visionary contemplation and perspicacity. In "Mémorables" he can now review his life with detachment, examining the crucial moments of his development and the extremes of emotion that colored them. Finally, the earthly spirituality of "The Four Cardinal Seasons" expresses the poet's renewed humanism, achieved in a hard and true way.

11

La Grande Beuverie

A Night of Drunken Delusions

> Philosophy teaches how man thinks he thinks;
> but drinking shows how he really thinks."
>
> —Aham Egomet quoting Oinophilus
> in *A Night of Serious Drinking*[1]

Daumal began writing *A Night of Serious Drinking* (*La Grand Beuverie*, literally "The Great Drinking Bout"), during his 1932 sojourn in the United States. Claudio Rugafiori, the editor of Daumal's posthumous publications, reported that the misery and squalor of New York City during the Depression opened Daumal's eyes to the grim reality of the world. He realized how narrow was his little circle of intellectuals and poets in Paris. Upon his return he began to meet regularly with Alexandre de Salzmann.

Among Daumal's notes written on the steamer returning to France in 1933, is his self-questioning as to the reasons for his voyage. He asks, "Why New York?" "I know that Paris was too full of my old trappings, my old clothes, the failures of my deliriums. I needed a cleaning. I needed a cruel city." His earnings as press sectretary for the Indian dance troupe were not sufficient to provide for adequate food and lodging. Consequently, his U.S. stay was problematic and uncomfortable. He continued in his notes to describe the sleepless nights and nightmarish days spent in New York writing *A Night of Serious Drinking*. His account is more than just an imaginative series of metaphors for mild depression: "this same, untenable, bitter and just suffering struck its steel rays through my flesh, cut through my stomach, quartered my ribs, burst in my head, and caused spasms in my Adam's apple and my lower lip."[2]

179

This is the suffering of a man "between two stools," Gurdjieff's term for the state of one who has had a taste of a higher consciousness but who cannot maintain it. He cannot go back to "sleeping" comfortably, taking life on the level of appearances and ordinary pleasures (one stool), nor can he summon the strength needed to remain continually "awake" (the other stool). Furthermore he is surrounded by resistance, that is, temptations to dreamy, pleasant sleep, as well as the depressing example of all the sleeping people around him. This will be the stuff of which *A Night of Serious Drinking* is made: the bric-a-brac and eternal fidgeting of the world of sleep and the frustration of the struggle to awaken. While still on the ship, he wrote:

> Nevertheless, there still remains the big drinking bout. It is a myth. This morning, forging through on this advancing steamer, which implacably cuts through the water, is also myth. There is never anything but the big question to resolve; all the rest, life and thoughts, is the necessary myth, the revolving expression of my battle with that.[3]

In Daumal's day-to-day life, even while far away in New York, the first stool to give up was, more specifically, the belief in Le Grand Jeu and their ability to affect society and politics. As the group now began to lose energy and disintegrate, he went through a period of disillusionment, forever arbitrating the jealousies and internecine quarrels. Practically all the responsibilities of the review rested on his shoulders. Furthermore, Lecomte's intoxication and ill health caused him great distress.

As he struggled through this period of transition, from the womb of Le Grand Jeu into adulthood, he decided to write a humoristic chronicle of the avatars of Le Grand Jeu. Just as Jarry's Dr. Faustroll traveled to strange islands whose inhabitants were based on real life characters— Aubrey Beardsley, Gaugin, Malarmé, and others, so Daumal had most of his friends appear—Lecomte is Ergehel, "pale as a dead man," Maurice Henry is "Marcellin, the anarchist," Monny de Boully—"Salomon," Antonin Artaud—Othello, etc.[4] Eventually this chronicle developed into *La Grande Beuverie*.

In the final 1938 version, published in English in 1979, under the title *A Night of Serious Drinking*, Daumal reveals his sense of the comic, the marvelous, and the repugnant—or, shall we say, the bizarre, the incongruous, and the perverse—all of which serve to touch on a higher truth by looking at its underside. Daumal chose the *recit* or initiatic tale as his mode of expression in both *A Night of Serious Drinking* and *Mount Analogue*. This form had been used by many great writers, including Francois Rabelais, the sixteenth-century erudite, free-thinking monk, whose humanistic spirit and proto-Surrealism was greatly appreciated by Alfred Jarry and Daumal. In his 1934 review of Rabelais's *Complete Works*, Daumal wrote: "A pocket-size book of Rabelais—the best reason to go off on vacation. There is no one other than Plato that I reread so willingly."[5]

Serious Drinking is a cross between Rabelais's *Pantagruel*, Swift's *Gulliver's Travels*, and Jarry's *Exploits and Opinions of Dr. Fautroll, Pataphysician*, as it leads us on an itinerary of strange persons and places. The book is made up of three sections, entitled:

   I. A labored dialogue on the power of words and the frailty of thought [an Ionesco-like comedy of words that presents the language of confusion].
  II. The Artificial Paradise [the longest and most developed section—a corrosive critique of modern society, presenting the experts in the world of language substitutes].
 III. The Ordinary Light of Day [man carries out the ritual fire sacrifice—the metamorphosis of the body/machine expressed finally through a language of clarity].

Although there are virtually endless possibilities of interpretation, the most obvious is this: Daumal is conducting his readers on a tour through the labyrinth of the mind's convolutions. Using thirst as a metaphor, he reveals normal life to be a state of endless intoxication. He conveys us through a topsy-turvy, comic inspection of Dante's realm of Hell, a voyage into the center of the self. It is a book about the psychology of consciousness that dumps the reader right into the maelstrom. In an article on Daumal, Marcel Lobet writes:

> This misunderstood writer revives "novelistic esotericism," which, according to Pierre de Boisdeffre, prefers over the seductions of realism, "a symbolic representation of life, pushed sometimes to the point of myth." With Daumal, literature becomes a metaphysical experience, an exploration of the invisible, a descent into what Boisdeffre calls the infra-world. Like Rimbaud,

Daumal applies himself to the disarrangement of all his senses [often incorrectly translated as "derangement"] and he spends a "season in hell." He is a seeker of the Absolute.[6]

In this book, we now enter the contractive stage of Daumal's evolution. After delineating the "I" from external forms in his early poetry, here he has us descend like Orpheus into the underworld, in order to inspect man in his lowest state.

In the first section, the state of dreaming and drunkenness is used as a parody for our usual waking state. The characters are so besotted with liquor that their functioning is impaired. They move in a thick haze. The continual drunken banter of section I is reminiscent of the fifth chapter of Rabelais's *Gargantua*, entitled "The Remarks of the Drunkards." In *Serious Drinking*, we hear "bacchic litanies" such as:

Oh! the thirst . . .
(Chorus: which may which may which might)
. . . of the stomach
(Chorus: which reeks which reeks which rots)
. . . of the chest
. . . of the brain.[7]

In *Gargantua*, we find six pages of similar inane drunken repartees, also without narration:

"Drink up!"
   "I drink, I wet my whistle, I sprinkle my throat, and all out of fear of dying."
   "Keep on drinking and you'll never die."
   "If I don't drink, I'm dry, and that means I'm dead already. My soul flies away to some frog-pond. For the soul never inhabits a dry spot."[8]

In *Serious Drinking*, one of the drunken responses is:

We all know that thtuff! We've read Pantagruel ath well, you old thoak!
   "If only you knew how much I'd like to stop talking, you wouldn't be so thirsty."[9]

In the lengthy second section, Daumal's critique concerns individuals more than institutions, since Daumal was more concerned with the rehabilitation of man. With a sort of wild hilarity, he passes in review the "Fidgetors," "Fabricators of Useless Objects," the "Pwatts," the "Nibblists," the "Kirittiks," the "Sophes," and the "Scienters." Daumal shows us the human machine in its most degenerate, unredeemed state, wherein none of the characters are conscious of anything other than their current mood or their most recent ambition. They are blind puppets, *prakriti*, pushed around by nature and society. The concept of renunciation in order to evolve is beyond their scope. What we see in *Serious Drinking* is a parody of our present day era, Kali Yuga, the Age of Confusion, mentioned in the *Sahittya Darpana*, during which "men engage in activities only for their external fruits."[10]

In this book we see all the many sides of Daumal in action: the poet, the philosopher, the Surrealist, the Pataphysician, the political activist, the Hinduist, and the Gurdjieffian, each in turn parodying his favorite bête noire. In the first section he picks on them all and epitomizes the entire decadent age of *Kali Yuga* in one sentence. It rings more current than the year 1935:

> Then he jotted down the rudiments of an extraordinary poem which would be plagiarized the following day and betrayed in every language by two hundred and twelve minor poets; from it sprang the same number of avant-garde artistic movements, twenty-seven historic brawls, three political revolutions on a Mexican farm, a famine in Gibraltar.[11]

He is particularly ferocious about the abstract theorizing of modern-day intellectual art critics and their cant. One of the Fabricators of Useless Objects states: "Art is a synthetic transference of the dynamism of volume into its relativist reabsorption,"[12] a statement reminiscent of the Pataphysical geometric theorems of Alfred Jarry.

In a procedure reminiscent of the eighteenth-century writer, Jonathan Swift, Daumal divides artists into several groups, including the Fabricators of Useless Objects. Some live in "glass houses" that they call "ivory towers," some live in "dark rooms" that they call "nature," and in "vampire caves," or in "flea circuses" that they call "the world." They succeed in rendering unusable even the most usable things, and this they call the "triumph of art." One architect described the perfectly uninhabitable house:

> The bird is the parasite of the tree as man is the parasite of the house. The edifice I built has its own meaning. See the simplicity and the audacity of the lines; a cement pole sixty meters high which supports rubber spheres. No walls, no ceiling, no windows; we rejected those superstitions long ago.[13]

He further explains that the Fabricators all dote and pamper one of their own internal bodily organs, usually one with something wrong with it, embellishing it with flowers and jewels and calling it "my soul" or "my life":

> Into each unusable object that he creates he hides a small fragment of that organ. When it is all used up the man dies. But this darling sickly organ lives on, sometimes for centuries.[14]

Here and there the tongue-in-check attitude gives way to a serious description of how things should be, but these are rare:

> In reality, a true painter, as you know, possesses within himself—in his muscles, his sensibility, even in his thinking—the golden number or numbers and the law of color. He makes them live through everything he experiences and sees, not just on canvas; his work is, therefore, useful and universal.[15]

These straightforward statements of Daumal's serious beliefs are brief; in *Serious Drinking*, Daumal generally uses the underhanded method of humor to deliver the same message indirectly. In a 1942 response to a disgruntled female reader, four years after the book's publication, he explains why this is so:

> You didn't notice that each time I exposed one of the fakes, I immediately gave a definition of the real thing. The alphabetical index will help you in tracking my thoughts about scientists, artists, religion, love and philosophy. I wanted to do a satire, not a panegyric. That is why my positive affirmations take little space typographically compared to the rest but they're there.
>
> What remains unfinished, unsaid in the book is something else: the practical method to get out of this hell (laughter is the faint trace of the first step out). I wanted to make it known that this practical method could not be put in a book.[16]

Nothing in their society goes unparodied; there is hardly a single sentence that is not mock serious or deliberately silly. Professor Mumu administers holy water intravenously to reconcile Faith and science in "contaminated Scienters." At the first inoculation he admits the reality of the miracle of Lourdes. At the second, the Blessed Mother appears to him. At the third, he recognizes the infallibility of the pope. At the seventh, Faith speaks in him: "Seek no more to understand."[17]

Another group in society that receives the Daumalian treatment are the actors, here known as "Actées" or Preactors in the current English version (*les Agis*, i.e., those who are passively acted upon). First the narrator's guide gives a straightforward description of how actors used to be:

> In ages past, an actor knew how to call up the gods and allowed them to enter him. Through him the gods conversed with men. . . . They danced and played together, men and gods. They lent their bodies to the gods, whereas today we fabricate gods according to size to fit the actees.[18]

Daumal had just experienced the performer's sensibility first-hand, having spent long months with the entourage of Shankar. Yet this satire is most likely a send-up of the Parisian theater scene. In the early forties, when he would have begun to hear readings from Gurdjieff's book, *All and Everything*, he would have heard reiterated the same attitude toward the presumption of contemporary actors. In his twenty-four-page tirade, Gurdjieff is equally ruthless against their "swaggering" and "dramatizing." He claims their complete vacuity and self-conceit are clothed in "such a fairy-like exterior" that they are treated like gods. "Their arrogance is such that the only thing they carry with modesty is their hemorroids."[19]

In a similar fashion, Daumal has a field day picking on the writers or Pwatts. He gives a comic treatment to one of his favorite themes: the role of the poet and poetry. He presents the Pwatts's definition of lyricism:

> a chronic disorder of an individual's internal hierarchy, which is manifested by an irresistible urge, called "inspiration," to make useless, rhythmic utterances. Unconnected with what the ancients called "lyricism," which was the art of drawing harmonies from the human lyre suitably attuned by long and patient effort.[20]

In his final essay "Black Poetry, White Poetry," Daumal describes the black poet as one who exploits poetry for his personal satisfaction, who believes himself to be either the true originator of his poems or better yet, "the chosen" spokesman of a higher being. His poetry is the result of pride, fallacious imagination, or laziness. He gives a comic depiction of the black poet, here called a passive Pwatt: in the process of practicing automatic writing he first waits for the initial phase of inspiration—a state of uneasiness induced by eating too much or too little, letting oneself be deceived by one's wife, or losing one's wallet. And then?

> Next you shut yourself up in your room, take your head in your hands and start bellowing until the bellowing brings a word to your throat. You spit it out and write it down. If it is a noun, you start bellowing until an adjective or a verb turns up. But above all, never think about what you mean or better still, never mean anything at all, but let whatever wishes to be said, be said through you. We call it the fine poetic frenzy.[21]

In contrast to the passive Pwatts, the active Pwatts have a poeticizing machine implanted into their pineal gland. One Pwatt lifted off the top of his skull to reveal a metal sphere hung on gimbals; it was hollow, filled with thousands of tiny aluminum strips on each of which was engraved a different word. The sphere turned on its two axes and it grew still, allowing a word to drop through an aperture underneath. In this manner the Pwatt can achieve the certainty

> that a sentence arrived at will be a phenomenon without precedent and that it will have no useful meaning whatsoever. It will be the pure materia prima of poetry.[22]

Sometimes his cold humor turns to indignation and anger, as it does toward politicians, when he considers the devastating effects of colonialism, which was reaching its peak in the thirties. [In 1939, the Exposition Coloniale de Paris was a venue where the imperialists could show off the booty from their conquests.] Daumal was troubled by the current hegemony of certain countries over much of the world. He gets in a political jab, by describing a parlor game about mother countries and their colonies, and men with national flags stuck in their skulls. René mocks the Communist philosophizing by depicting a group who lock themselves in a cupboard with a lighted wax taper and bottles of beer, to compose a treatise in ten volumes entitled "Errors Yet to Be Made in Deciding What Materialistic Dialectics Is Not."[23]

Daumal, the philosopher of consciousness, picks on the Fidgeters, who keep exceedingly busy doing one thing or another, and if one of them "flounders and acknowledges his inner being,"[24] he usually ends up by blowing his brains out.

He parodies the fashionable Orientalism and followers of cult diets of the thirties, particularly the Theosophist followers of Krishnamurti, as well as pseudo-Hinduists, Vedantists, and others (although Daumal's opinion of Krishnamurti altered favorably when he met with him in 1930). He lists their behaviors as one of the methods of population control along with drug taking and other forms of suicide:

> Other literati compose treatises, supposedly translated from Oriental languages in which they explain the art of becoming rapidly neurasthenic, neuropathic, demineralized, and finally cadaverish, by the practice of dietary regimes and respiratory practices. But it only works on the so-called artistic and intellectual youth.[25]

He also describes the organized destruction of young people as another means "to organize death without which life would be nothing but a perpetual, vicious circle."[26] It is clearly a description of Hitler's Youth or any other fascist mobilization of children:

> The method is straightforward; the children are taken at a time when their intelligence is not fully developed, and their passions respond to the slightest stimulation; they are made to live in companies, dressed and armed uniformly, and by means of magical speeches and collective physical exercises, whose secret is ours alone, we give them what we call "the cult of the common ideal"; this is an absolute devotion to a loud-mouthed, authoritarian person. Then they let two opposing groups go at each other, for after all "The young man who is not killed in the flower of his youth . . . is the old man of tomorrow."[27]

Almost exactly halfway through the book, the inmate guide Aham Egomet suddenly explains the philosophical basis of the three sections within the limits of the "drinking" metaphor. He tells the narrator that he is going to write a book and call it *A Night of Serious Drinking*. The first section will depict the nightmare of lost souls who seek ways of feeling a little more alive, but instead, remain drunken, stupefied, and thirsty. In the second, he will describe the phantasmal lives of the Escapees and the illusory drinks of their illusory paradise. In the third, he will hint at the existence of subtler, more real drinks "which must be earned with the glow of your brow, the anguish of your heart, and the sweat of your limbs."[28] Why does Daumal save this bit of structuring until halfway through this meandering dream? This appears to be an example of his focus-blur technique: let the reader flounder a bit without familiar conventions; let him really be in a dream.

In the third and final section, the main character falls through a trap door and lands on a straw mattress in a room without doors—out of that whirlwind dream tour into part 3 and "the cold light of day." Yet the dream continues, even as the author questions, "Which is the dream?"[29] As he mimics Shakespeare's "Perchance to dream," when the narrator cries, "Perchance to wake!" the author Daumal suddenly intrudes over the narrator and discusses the advisability of waking his hero from the dream, casting doubt on the traditional literary convention that assumes that dream states are false and waking states true. Then the phantasmagoria intensifies. There is a huge conflagration, wherein the narrator burns all the trappings of his former life—his books, his clothes and his furniture in a sacrifice by fire, a ritual of renunciation. He chants four prayers to the sun reminiscent of the *Rig Veda*. Then the element of water comes in to complete this ritual cleansing.

> The walls and floors began to deliquesce like wax in an oven, puckered, ran in deepening grooves which closed over and became flaccid pipes which oozed viscous, lukewarm liquids.[30]

Thus Daumal returns again to the collective myth of death through sacrificial fire (*agni* or the Greek *ekpyrosis*), then rebirth and purification by water. So much of Daumal's youth had been focused on the idea of liberation through death. He had seen it evoked in Rimbaud's "A Season in Hell" and Nerval's "Aurelia" where the personal image of hell is more frightening than the traditional Christian version. This emotionally charged concept of dying and being reborn, symbolized in ancient times by the image of the serpent biting its own tail, is everywhere present in Daumal's tale. Just as fire and death are mentioned in virtually every one of his poems, so in *Serious Drinking* the fireplace is ever present in the background as the drinkers sit around it. Then at the climax, everything goes up in smoke.

Overall, *A Night of Serious Drinking* is so swift and compact, so poetic and multimeaningful, it can hardly be absorbed in one reading. And Daumal achieves this effect, not by convoluted French existential complexities, but rather by imaginative leaps often rendered in simple words and images.

His style is crisp. He likes beginning his brief numbered sections with short, clipped sentences. The book itself begins with "It was late when we drank," dropping us right into the midst of the perpetual conversation that man carries on with himself. The second section starts with "We were in thick smoke," and section eight, "We were drinking like fish."[31]

In some places, on the other hand, the text is a cornucopia of elaborate surrealistic imagery. In his desire to amplify the effects, he gives us frequent barrages of inventories that, as we saw in his poetry, have an incantatory effect on the reader. Whereas *Le Contre-Ciel* was filled with imagery of geophysical elements, anatomical parts, and macabre violence, here we have colorful lists of household items, foods, flowers, and scientific details. Among the Sophers (Scientists) of every kind, and very much in fashion, were the Astromancers, Idyllomancers, Palmologists, Iridomancers, Flatulencers, Astragalomancers, Molybdomancers, Fritillarists, and Rhabdologists, all of whom were skilled in telling the past and the future and in conjuring away the present. This verbiage is the literary evidence of the endless multiplicity of the phenomenal world; it contrasts with his sparse selective wording when describing the simple overall scene. Daumal the set designer creates a full stage for each farce he presents: "Couches deep as coal trucks, covered in cascades of artificial silk, bright fountains gushing verbena, chamomile, mint, and lemonade."[32]

Daumal also costumes his characters with exacting Pataphysical detail. His three favorite writers make a gratuitous appearance: Francois Rabelais, Alfred Jarry, and Leon-Paul Fargue. Rabelais is disguised in a nun's habit with a large, floating coif like a sea manta, while Jarry had "a thin oval belly like a long fish, and the tips of his mustache painted green."[33]

We owe the theatrical quality of *A Night of Serious Drinking* undoubtedly to the influence of Bharata, "who felt that the dramatic form was the most perfect fruition of aesthetic creativity . . . the embodiment of feeling in sensuous tissue."[34] Almost any page in the book could be staged. Each particular vignette has its own internal logic and parody-message, always presented in a sensually palpable context, a requirement of Hindu poetics. There is a definite variation of tone throughout the novel. In her essay,

"Regarding *La Grande Beuverie*," Helen Maxwell quotes Daumal's own comments about his book: "The leaps in tone are deliberate—it was for me an experiment; I didn't want to be dominated by *a tone, a style*, so I ventured a work in three distinct tones, dominant in each of the three sections respectively.[35] The *rasa* of the overall composition seems to be comedy-parody with a subtle mixture of seriousness, mock heroic, tragedy, and faint optimism.

He achieves a kind of realistic surrealism by juxtaposing the nebulous atmosphere of the dream world with the journalistic, matter-of-fact reportage of the narrator. Daumal continually injects dislocations of identity, time, and place—the smokey darkness and dirtiness of the tavern, the view of the people through the trap door, the confusion of "I" with the collective "we" and "one."

Daumal the Gurdjieffian is everywhere present in the book, and always has the final word. On virtually every page there are allusions to man's sleep state and weak thinking. Gurdjieff contended that we hardly ever think; "it" thinks. What we call thoughts are merely mental associations endlessly linked together. Here Daumal calls them "little creepy crawlies," and elsewhere "inner ticklings."

Daumal skillfully depicts man's habit of negative thinking. When the main character runs into his black thoughts, he anthropomorphizes them as animated cartoonlike characters, little creatures called pride, vanity, fantasy, greed, and illusion. They are the same ones depicted in "The Holy War," who whisper, "We dress you up; without us, what kind of presentation would you make in society?"[36] Here in *Serious Drinking*, the narrator recounts:

> They threw their arms around my neck with cries of joy, calling me "dear uncle" and shrieking all manner of endearments, words like: " At last you're back!" . . . They clung to my hair, ears, and fingers, removed my spectacles, etc.[37]

Both Daumal and Gurdjieff are very concerned with the whole undertaking of writing a book, as well as communication in general. Gurdjieff's preface is entitled, "The Arousing of Thought," while Daumal's foreword begins with the sentence, "I refuse to accept that a clear thought can ever be inexpressible." Then he proceeds to discuss the three conditions necessary for clear discourse: "a speaker who knows what he wishes to say, a listener in a state of wakefulness, and a language common to both."[38] Then follows part 1 entitled: "A labored dialogue on the power of words and the frailty of thought." Neither author employed whimsy and fantasy just to appear clever; these elements were a deliberate part of their arsenal for effective communication.

Daumal was influenced not only by the philosophy of Gurdjieff but also by his literary style. The similarities are unmistakable between *A Night of Serious Drinking* and Gurdjieff's opus, *All and Everything*. Daumal took part in numerous readings of this book until the time of his death. (*All and Everything* was published in 1948, a year after Gurdjieff's death.) Certain corollaries also link Daumal's *Mount Analogue* with *All and Everything* and with Gurdjieff's *Meetings with Remarkable Men*. All four works share in common the inclusion of fantasy elements: in *All and Everything* we find extraterrestrial myths and fictions, in *Serious Drinking* we find surrealistic dreamscapes; in the two authors' later works we find inexplicable marvels and improbable events, such as the crossing of the Gobi desert on stilts (*Meetings*), and talking plants (*Mount Analogue*).

Gurdjieff's work has rarely been considered from a literary point of view, apparently because its style is so foreign and indecipherable to the Western critical mind. In his book, *Notes Inédits*, Charles Duit places *All and Everything* in a long line of traditional humorous fables, along with Montesquieu's *Persian Letters* and Voltaire's *The Ingenue*, to which I would add *The Exploits and Opinions of Dr. Faustroll, Pataphysician*. Just as Jarry created the planet Haldernablow, so in *All and Everything*, Beelzebub, an old man from the planet Karatas, exiled to Mars, makes several connoitering visits to Earth to observe the strange ways of the "three-brained beings" there. His visits occur over millennia; he visits the ancient civilization of Atlantis, Babylon at its height, and then visits present-day countries, documenting their current state of degeneration.

Duit points out that the baroque and preposterous form of *All and Everything* belongs to the very old tradition of *The Thousand and One Nights*. Since Beelzebub is addressing a child, his grandson Hassein, he narrates the cosmic tale in the Oriental style designed to give a "childish" pleasure. This kind of storytelling was familiar to Gurdjieff, growing up in the Caucasus; his own father had been a bard, capable of relating hundreds of tales from memory. Duit tries to isolate the element that most deters the modern reader:

> What for a "childish" mind constitutes the charm and strength of Beelzebub—as of the Iliad, the *Chanson de Roland* and the *Thousand and One Nights*—namely the constant harping on the same

images, the same expressions, and the tide-like ebb and flow—is just what the intellectualized reader finds hard to take.[39]

Daumal uses this same primitive technique as he constantly harps on the theme of drinking, deliberately choosing the most earthly, even plebeian behavior of wanting to get drunk, in order to camouflage, by contrast, his more important theme of waking up.

The comparisons that Duit makes in reference to *All and Everything* could also be applied to *Serious Drinking*. He compares Gurdjieff's book to James Joyce's *Finnegans Wake*, as "a work which speaks of all and everything; refuses to make any haste at all, and imposes its own pace on the reader."[40] Both Gurdjieff's and Daumal's books are extended satires of the modern mind of science and literature. While Gurdjieff uses Greco-Armenian jargon, for instance, "saliakorriap" for "water," "Havatvernouis" for "religions," or "perambarrsasidean" for "tuning fork," Daumal mocks the scientific mind of the "Politologists," the "Anthropographers," the "Philophasists," and the "Clarificators of clarifications." By such means, they both attempt to achieve an effect of absolute disorientation. Since Beelzebub speaks in the language of the planet Karatas, the reader is forced to consider Earth vocabulary and the behavior of mankind from the viewpoint of the inhabitants of Karatas. Duit shows how this comic ethnology thoroughly "exoticizes" us until the very structure of our everyday lives is questioned, "for in 'explaining' all phenomena by laws unknown to Earth science, Gurdjieff insinuates a fundamental doubt."[41]

With much Jarryesque dark humor, Gurdjieff hardly conceals his sarcasm when he seeks to "defend" the denizens of our planet. The following examples of the forty-eight chapter headings express both his humor and seriousness:

Chapter X: Why "Men" Are Not Men;

Chapter XIII: The Impudent Brat Hassein, Beelzebub's Grandson, Dares to Call Men "Slugs";

Chapter XI: A Piquant Trait of the Peculiar Psyche of Contemporary Man;

Chapter XLIII: Beelzebub's Survey of the Process of Periodic Reciprocal Destruction of Men, or Beelzebub's Opinion of War.[42]

In the case of *Serious Drinking* Daumal's chapter headings, though not as provocative, do help to interject bits of structuring into the randomly flowing dream. The categorizing of nonsensical persons and places makes the categorizing itself seem nonsensical. Yet it does provide the minimal structure necessary to allow Daumal's imagination to run free. Jean Richer writes: "The influence of India is noticeable in Daumal's penchant for arranging notions and persons in neat categories; it is both Cartesian and Hindu to classify, to order and to analyze."[43]

As in *Dr. Faustroll*, *All and Everything*, and in Joyce's *Finnegan's Wake*, so in this pataphysical enterprise, Daumal creates numerous new word entities. In *Bharata* he writes:

> In the dialogues of the Upanishads, the speakers decompose and recompose words, marry them in new ways and present them at different angles . . . in order to charge them up with power. This will create many different relationships for the man which will engage him in a real act and incite him to rise above his merely verbal understanding.[44]

He also applies the Hindu science of etymology (*Nirukta*) in order to make a point in a humorous way: he claims the term *Scients* comes from *scier* (to saw), a sly comment on how the sick bay's scientists (whom he refers to as "failed Cannibals") like to slice up a subject in order to study it.

Daumal shows no timidity in his book. He seems to be able to let loose every last vestige of Surrealist flamboyance remaining in him, yet controlling it with consummate adroitness to serve his aim. With his fingers again on a literary focusing lens, he focuses and blurs, focuses and blurs, pulling us in and out of a dream state. He describes Leon-Paul Fargues's get-up:

> One minute on his chin and the next in his hand was a false Armenian beard, and depending on the various phases, curves and knots of the conversation, his face went from smooth to hairy and from hirsute to shaved just like the amazing evolution of a human shooting star.[45]

In the final pages Daumal presents an allegory of the human machine. As parts of the body are immolated, in a ritual conflagration shaken loose and melted away, the narrator climbs into the upper story or cockpit representing the human head. He peers through two lenses embedded in the walls (eyes). Then he describes all the levers, dials, pumps, and bellows and the anthropomorphic apes that run the machinery.

Then suddenly Daumal ends the dream and finally ends the book with a straightforward message. The narrator abruptly walks out into the street, musing on the interconnectedness of all things, "the infinity of unities which joined once more into oneness,"⁴⁶ as each element changes into the next:

> the river was lost in the sea, the sea in the clouds, clouds in rain, rain in sap, sap in wheat, wheat in bread, bread in man—but at this point there was resistance, as man looked on with that air of bewilderment and discontent, which sets him apart from all other animals on our planet.⁴⁷

He describes the turning gyre of evolution from protoplasm to elephant:

> And the turning of this circle would have been without impediment for all time but for mankind that, resisting transformation, attempted with great travail to live for itself in the tiny, cancerous tumor it made on the universe.⁴⁸

Suddenly Daumal pulls us out of the book's long metaphor of bedlam, to examine man's situation as if through a telescope. Gurdjieff had a very complex, un-Darwinian, unconventional concept of evolution that Daumal draws upon here. Gurdjieff felt that European thought was incorrect in perceiving man's evolution as apart from nature or as a conquest of nature. Ouspensky quotes him as saying, "Humanity neither progresses nor evolves. What appears as progress or evolution is in fact, a partial modification which can be immediately counterbalanced by a corresponding modification in an opposite direction."⁴⁹ This should seem evident to any observer of our technical and industrial progress, which is counterbalanced by ever-increasing violence and barbarism in the world. Gurdjieff taught that, in order to evolve to a state higher than that of a thinking, feeling animal in the chain of organic life, we humans have to deliberately choose to oppose the forces of nature in a new way; not in the usual sense of abusing the ecology, but in the sense of overcoming the internal and external forces that would have us remain asleep. Man must voluntarily go against his penchants; he must swim upstream.

The final summation of the book comes out of the mouth of Totochabo, who returns again. He presents a simple, poetic myth of "larval man." Man is a caterpillar who will not take the necessary steps to evolve into a butterfly. Rather he clings to his caterpillar appetites, caterpillar passions, and caterpillar metaphysics. Totochabo says:

> But what could be more comforting than to discover that we are nothing? It's only by turning ourselves inside out that we become something. Is it not a great comfort to the caterpillar to learn that she is a mere larva, that her time spent being a semi-crawling digestive tube will not last, and that after a period of confinement in the mortuary of her chrysalis she will be born again as a butterfly—not in a nonexistent paradise dreamed up by some caterpillary, consoling philosophy, but here in this very garden.[50]

The transition from the surface world of a caterpillar to the three-dimensional world of a butterfly is clearly an allegory for the concept of man's possible evolution. It is similar to Gurdjieff's image of man as a technically advanced airplane that always tries to maneuver on the ground and is unaware that it can fly. Totochabo gives two more beautiful analogies; he refers to an example of an actual tadpolelike creature in Mexico, the *axolotl*, that like man inexplicably remains in its embryonic state. As an experiment, some *axolotles* were injected with thyroid extract and they were seen to change into a species of salamander. Unfortunately, such outside intervention is not generally available to effect a metamorphosis in man. He has to want to give up his caterpillariness of his own volition.

On the final pages, Totochabo discusses how we always see everything upside down (another Gurdjieffian concept). He considers for example how we reverse the concepts of love and hate, and submits as evidence, headlines such as:

> Tragedy of a Jealous Husband—"I loved her too much, so I killed her"
>
> Accused Woman Kills Lover with Hammer before Death-Leap into Well with Two Babies[51]

We call these "crimes of passion," or as Totchabo says, "the cause of such instances of stupid, pointless mutual destruction is what we call 'love.'" And at the other extreme, when we wish to express the idea of hatred, we use the symbol of "water and fire"; for us this is the idea of two irreconcilable enemies. But the one exists only through the other:

> Without fire, all the water in the world would be an inert lump of ice. Without water, fire would die for all eternity, since for all eternity it has consumed and scorched everything around it.[52]

He points out how we are always observing the wonders of steam, the perfect balance between fire and water, yet we continue to say "as incompatible as fire and water, and we continue to call double suicides and murders of passion "love."[53] Thus, in the final moments of the book, Daumal has returned to the archetypal symbols of fire and water to elucidate his final message: like steam, we too can achieve the integration of our own duality.

In closing he reechoes the classic endings of *Plato's Symposium* and Voltaire's *Candide*. Instead of "Let us go and cultivate our garden," his closing lines are "We all got up, for there were several pressing things to do. There were many things to be done toward the business of living."[54]

12

Mount Analogue

Non-Euclidian Mountain Climbing

> **Eternity**
> He who binds himself to a joy
> Does the winged life destroy
> But he who kisses the joy as it flies
> Lives in eternity's sun rise
>
> —William Blake

Mount Analogue is generally considered René Daumal's masterpiece, for it combines his poetic gifts and philosophical accomplishments in a way that is both entertaining to read and profound to contemplate. It is a many-leveled symbolic allegory of man's escape from the prison of his robotic, egoistic self. At the same time, it is well-grounded in scientific data and the facts of our physical existence.

After conducting his readers on an adventure into the depths of human materialism and spiritual ignorance in his previous book, Daumal turns our attention to the heights of self-knowledge. The catharsis of the contraction phase of Daumal's life, as depicted in *A Night of Serious Drinking*, is followed by the phase of expansion and hope in *Mount Analogue*, a book dedicated to Alexandre de Salzmann. Looking away from the lower depths of the Counter-Heaven of *Le Contre-Ciel*, the peak of the holy mountain emerges out of the fog.

In a letter he described his passage from the drinking bout to the mountain, a place where the caterpillar could transform itself into a butterfly:

> After having described a chaotic, larval, illusory world, I undertook to speak of another world more real and coherent. It is a

long *récit* about a group of people who realized that they were in prison and who realized that they had to renounce this prison (the drama being that they [we] are attached to it).[1]

The book is subtitled *A Novel of Symbolically Authentic Non-Euclidean Adventures in Mountain Climbing.* Jack Daumal relates that René first began serious mountain climbing in 1937. Jack was better trained professionally and was able to pass his knowledge on to his brother. He says that René was a natural in the mountains and a quick learner. They made many climbs together in the two years preceding the outbreak of World War II. In a 1987 interview that I conducted for *Parabola* magazine, Jack said that in 1939 to 1940, the doctors recommended mountain air for René but no more climbing due to his tuberculosis. That is when the idea of Mount Analogue crystallized. Now that he was stuck in the lower climes, he remembered his métier was that of a writer:

> If I couldn't scale the mountains, I would sing of them from below. Then I began to think seriously with the heaviness and awkwardness with which one jostles one's thought processes, when one has conquered one's body by conquering rock and ice. I will not speak about the mountain but through the mountain. With this mountain as language, I would speak of another mountain which is the path uniting the earth and heaven. I will speak of it, not in order to resign myself but to exhort myself.[2]

Daumal's real-life passion for the mountains allowed him to transpose to the page the *rasa* of his own experience. This serves as an analogy expressing Daumal's own experience of a seeker's initiation into the "Path" (*Dharma*). A more specific interpretation is that it is an allegory for Daumal's experience in the Gurdjieff Work. The leader of the group, Sogol, like Totochabo of *A Night of Serious Drinking,* is generally considered to be a character based on Alexandre de Salzmann or Gurdjieff himself.

The narrator recalls an article he had written on "The Symbolic Significance of the Mountain," and this gives Daumal the opportunity to discuss various interpretations of this symbol from the Old Testament, Egypt, Islam, Greece, and especially from India, drawing on Guénon's study of symbolism of the mountain. The narrator recounts:

> I had written in substance that in the mythic tradition, the Mountain is the bond between Earth and Sky. Its solitary summit

reaches the spheres of eternity and its base spreads out in manifold foothills into the world of mortals. It is the way by which man can raise himself to the divine and by which the divine reveals itself to man.[3]

Throughout the entire novel there will be an interpenetration of symbols and concrete reality. The Hindus were the first to describe this way of seeing the world. According to Jan Gonda, the author of *Vedic Literature*, Vedic authors were always convinced of the existence of a correlation between the visible and invisible world—ritual acts, natural phenomena, and phenomena of divine agency: "The hold that nature has over man comes from the unseen powers within it."[4] This explains the Vedic tendency to avoid unequivocalness for reasons of taboo. Ambiguities help to blend the two spheres together. Daumal's text is imbued with this same parallelism between the visible and the invisible—the trek, the characters, and obstacles are all symbolic of the blending of the lower and the higher. Guénon had devoted an entire book, *La Grande Triade* (*The Great Triad*), to exploring this symbology. According to him, the base of the mountain, earth (passive perfection—*prakriti*), is a symbol for personality, designated by the personage Arjuna, the anxious warrior hero of the *Mahabharata*. The peak of the mountain connects with heaven (active perfection—*purusha*) and is a symbol for the evolved spirit, designated by the god Krishna, Arjuna's counselor. This symbology is perfectly enacted in the course of Daumal's story.

Among the many references to myths, Daumal's narrator recalls "those obscure legends of the Vedas in which *Soma*—the nectar which is the seed of immortality—is said to reside in its luminous and subtle form within the mountain. Now, based on this symbolism, he proposes the physical existence of the ultimate mountain, which must be inaccessible to ordinary human approaches. While existing earthly mountains, even the mighty Himalayas, have been demystified by the profane, he finds the mythic mountains also inadequate because they have no geographical existence. He feels that Mount Meru of the Hindus, lacking real physical coordinates, "loses its persuasive significance as a way of uniting earth and heaven." Accordingly, he believes in the material existence of Mount Analogue: "whose summit must be inaccessible but its base accessible to human beings as nature has made them. The doors to the invisible must be visible."[5]

With deliberate brushstrokes, Daumal sketches in the essential details of plot and character. One of France's most eminent literary critics, André

Rousseau, in a lengthy chapter, "L'Avenement de René Daumal" ("The Accession of René Daumal") of his book *Littérature du XX ième siecle* (*Literature of the Twentieth Century*), recalls René's description of the effort involved in producing what he called *la Chose-a-dire* ("the Thing-to-say"). "The Thing-to-say appears then in the most intimate part of oneself, like an eternal certainty."[6] Rousseau felt that there was not a single line in *Mount Analogue* where *la Chose-a-dire* does not hit us. Immediately, the proposed mountain-climbing expedition becomes intertwined with a quest for knowledge. The narrator and his soon-to-be-teacher, Sogol, are kindred souls, discovering each other in a manner reminiscent of Breton's "objective chance," that is, finding a kindred soul in an anonymous way— in response to an article. Here we see the synchronicity that will occur many times throughout *Mount Analogue*, the randomness and hidden order that surrounds us. Their chance encounter is also reminiscent of Daumal's lines in his essay "Nerval Le Nyctalope": "I was thus being observed! I was not alone in the world! This world which I had thought was only my fantasy!"[7] Contrast this with Sogol's note to the narrator: "Monsieur, I have read your article on *Mount Analogue*. Until now I had believed myself the only person convinced of its existence," and the narrator's surprise: "And here was someone taking me at my word! And talking about attempting an expedition! A lunatic? A practical joker? But what about myself?"[8]

The teacher/seeker figure, Pierre Sogol, "with the tranquillity of a caged panther," is a character drawn larger than life, who combines "a vigorous maturity with the freshness of a child"[9] His thinking is described as being

> like a force as palpable as heat or light or wind. This force seemed to consist of an exceptional faculty for seeing ideas as external objects and establishing new links between ideas that appeared totally unrelated. [He would] treat human history as a problem in geometry, the properties of numbers in terms of zoological species, and illustrate how language obeyed the same laws as celestial mechanics.[10]

Sogol's varied background recalls both de Salzmann and Gurdjieff, each of whom had many areas of expertise. The seeds of this character were sown back in 1934 when René was sent to collect de Salzmann's material effects at the Hotel Jacob in Paris after his death in Switzerland on May 3, 1934. He described the experience in a letter to Vera:

It was certainly sad to undo all these balls of string that he planned to unwind himself one day. And to find so many projects started. There were mostly books: algebra manuals, adventure novels, old history books, dictionaries, some perhaps of value, but I felt it useless to take them except for three or four. There remains: pieces of wood, paint supplies, an ax, plus his papers—sketches, studies, projects, plans, etc., and a magi marionnette.[11]

When we meet the composite character Sogol, he is currently an inventor and teacher of mountaineering, accepting students only if they first scale his Parisian apartment building and enter through the window.

The narrator accompanies Sogol through his laboratory, which he calls his "park." They meander down a pebble path through plants and shrubs, among which are dangling hundreds of little signs, "the whole of which constituted a veritable encyclopedia of what we call human knowledge, a diagram of a plant cell, the keys to Chinese writing, musical phrases, maps, etc." The narrator finally realizes the brilliant logic of this information path:

> All of us keep a fairly extensive collection of such diagrams and inscriptions in our heads; and we have the illusion we are "thinking" the loftiest scientific and philosophical thoughts when, by chance, a few of them fall into a pattern which seems neither too conventional nor too novel. Here, all this material was displayed before us; we could not confuse it with ourselves. As a garland is strung from hooks, we hung our conversation on these little images, and each of us could see the mechanism of the other's mind and of his own with equal clarity.[12]

Here, and many times throughout the book we see Daumal's rejection of busy behavior, overintellectualizing, and his general preference for quality over quantity. This reflects Daumal's study of Guénon (especially his book *Quantity and Quality*), and the Hindu preference for being rather than information gathering. In Buddhist literature, the material world is often referred to as the "10,000 beings." Daumal loves to evoke this image by making long lists of things, both in his novels and in his poetry.

Sogol and the narrator bare their souls for thirteen pages of the first chapter, entitled "The Meeting." They each share their disinterest and apathy for "this monkey cage agitation which people so dramatically call life."[13] Sogol recounts that after having experienced almost every pleasure and disappointment, happiness and suffering, he felt he had completed one cycle of existence. He joined a monastery where he applied himself to inventing instruments, which rather than making life easier, would rouse men out of their torpor. Two such examples were a pen for facile writers that spattered every five or ten minutes, and a tiny portable phonograph equipped with a hearing-aid-like earpiece that would cry out at the most unexpected moments: "Who do you think you are?"[14] With hilarious inventiveness, Daumal applies Gurdjieff's theory of "alarm clocks"—employing reminding factors and resistances, little tricks to wake ourselves up. It also harks back to the Lilliputians of *Gulliver's Travels* who wore elaborate flappers to keep themselves roused. Finally, Sogol then relates that he left the monastery, continuing always to question this "grown-up" existence:

> Fearing that death I suffer every moment, the death of that voice which, out of the depths of my childhood, keeps questioning me as it does you: "Who am I?" Whenever that voice is silent—and it doesn't speak often—I'm an empty body, a perambulating carcass.[15]

The narrator relates similar existential anxieties from his own childhood, echoes of Daumal's early experience:

> That evening in bed with the light out, I tried to picture death, the "no more anything." In my imagination I did away with the outward circumstances of my life and felt myself confined in ever tightening circles of anguish; there was no longer any "I." What does it mean "I"? Then one night, a marvelous idea came to me: Instead of just enduring this agony, try to observe it, to see where it comes from and what it is. I perceived that it all seemed to come from a tightening of something in my stomach, as well as under my ribs and in my throat. I forced myself to relax, especially my abdomen. The anguish disappeared. When I tried again to think about death, instead of being clawed by anxiety I was filled with an entirely new feeling. I knew no name for it—a feeling between mystery and hope.[16]

By the fifteenth page, Daumal has posed the question three times: Who are you? or Who am I? Together the two characters agree that there must be an answer to this question, there must exist, according to Sogol, a superior type of man, possessing the keys to everything which is a mystery to us. This idea of a higher and unknown strain within the human race was not something I could take simply as an allegory. Experience had proven, I told myself, that a man cannot reach truth directly, nor all by himself. An intermediary has to be present, a force still human in certain respects yet transcending humanity in others.[17]

This excerpt echoes Gurdjieff's belief in an "Inner Circle of Humanity," a group that maintains an inner sanctuary of esoteric knowledge and secretly mediates in human events. It also reflects Daumal's personal experience in his early years of having failed on his own to find what he was seeking. He thus shares with us his own fortune to have found three of these intermediaries in the persons of the de Salzmanns and Gurdjieff. For him this allegorical tale is less farfetched than it might appear. Just as Sogol suggests, Daumal would not take *Mount Analogue* "simply as an allegory."

In chapter 2, entitled "Suppositions," Sogol spends ten pages providing the scientific data, complete with diagrams, to explain the anomalous properties of Mount Analogue. Because of the invisible closed shell of curvature that surrounds the island, it remains protected from human detection, but not always, not everywhere, and not for everyone. At a certain moment and in a certain place, certain persons (those who know and have a real wish to do so) can enter. This phenomenon is a scientifically embellished metaphor for Gurdjieff's explanation of how esoteric knowledge is not truly hidden but simply imperceptible to those who are not seeking it. "The sun has the property of uncurving the space which surrounds the island. At sunrise and at sunset it must in some way penetrate the shell, and through that same breach we shall enter!"[18] Sogol presents the potential of synchronicity; his logic convinces the group of interested candidates and they all declare themselves willing to make the unprecedented journey.

Daumal provides a biographical profile as well as an actual ink sketch of each crew member, possibly attempting to create each of the twelve archetypes of human beings, as delineated by Gurdjieff. The eight remaining crew members together seem to represent different aspects of a single being. Among them we find the American artist (Judith Pancake), the Russian linguist (Ivan Lipse, probably based on Lavastine), the Austrian brothers—scientist Hans and metaphysician Karl. Four others drop out, epitomizing the stumbling blocks on the path to enlightenment. One is caught up in the joyous dance of *maya* (illusion), another is trapped in the veil of self-pity, and the others are too full of worldly concerns to leave the dream they inhabit.

By chapter 3, Daumal puts this cast of characters to sea, realistically and metaphorically. "We were by no means cut out to be sailors. Several of us were seasick. The path to our highest desire often lies through the undesirable."[19] Finally, in chapter 4, by a kind of syncretism of logic and magic, the sailors manage to penetrate the impenetrable envelope of curved space by doing nothing except being ready. In the true spirit of nonaction, the spirit of the *Bhagavad Gita*, the sailors are pulled in by a higher force:

> A wind arose without any warning, or rather a powerful suction suddenly pulled us forward, space opened ahead of us, a bottomless emptiness, a horizontal abyss of water and air impossibly intertwined. The boat creaked in all its timbers, was hurled forward unerringly along a rising slope as far as the center of the abyss, and was suddenly set adrift in a wide, calm bay, in sight of land.[20]

They land, and are welcomed as though they had been expected. When they try to answer Daumal's favorite question, "Who are you?" they realize that, with the guides (who are in an advanced state of evolution), "We could no longer get away with just words."[21] They gradually orient themselves, wondering why the port of arrival is called "Port O' Monkeys." The narrator muses, "that name summoned up in my mind, rather disagreeably, all my heritage as a twentieth-century occidental—something curious, imitative, shameless, agitated."[22] Looking out into the port, they view "Phoenician barks, triremes, galleys, caravels; along with two paddle-steamers and an old wood and steel sloop from the last century."[23] The search for consciousness knows no barrier of time, culture, or age; all come as "monkeys."

As they prepare to ascend the mountain, they get carried away with their research and analyses of the Asiatic origins of local myths, the peculiar optical conditions of the island's atmosphere, and endless linguistic, sociological, and religious aspects. Suddenly they are roused by their guide from these preoccupations ("dreams" in Daumal's words) and realize how their idle curiosity was holding them back from their primary goal.

> We all knew too well that vile creature of intellectual cupidity, and each of us had his own owl to nail to the door along with a few chattering magpies, parading turkeycocks, and lots of fat

geese! But all those creatures are so securely anchored, grafted so deeply into our flesh, that we cannot cast them away without tearing out our very insides. We had to go on living with them for a long time, enduring them, coming to know them well, until they fell from us, just as the scabs of an eruptive disease come off, of themselves, when the system becomes healthy again. It is damaging to rip them off prematurely.[24]

Here again we see the same little creatures that we met in "The Holy War" and *A Night of Serious Drinking*—the same physical imagery of foibles and fretting "grafted to the flesh." Only now, in Daumal's maturity, he understands that they too play a role in the process of evolution. Each individual had to renounce his current activities to go off on the journey. Later they had to give up their alpinist gadgetry and exploratory instruments for simpler provisions, as they prepared themselves for the mountain ascent.

> We began to call one another by our first names ... the change was not the effect of mere intimacy. For we were beginning to shed our old personalities. At the same time as we decided to leave our heavy equipment on the coast, we were also preparing to leave behind the artist, the inventor, the doctor, the scholar, the writer. Beneath the old disguises, new men and women began to show the tips of their ears. Men and women, and all kinds of creatures as well.[25]

This concept of removing the trappings of one's personality and penchants that Daumal alludes to from his earliest writings onward is a common theme to all great works about the spiritual quest. A Sufi tale relates how the little stream succeeds in crossing over the desert by evaporating and allowing itself to be carried by the wind (dying in order to be reborn). In *The Divine Comedy*, Dante uses a metaphor similar to Daumal's: "One climbs to the summit of Bismantua with only one's feet: but here one has to fly; I say, fly with light wings and the feathers of a great desire,"[26] and, of course, in the Gospel, it is written: "Except a kernel of wheat die, it bringeth forth no fruit."[27]

Finally, Father Sogol declares that he gives up "my cap of authority ... a crown of thorns for the person I used to be. Far within me, where the memory of what I am is still unclouded, a little child is waking up and making an old man's mask weep."[28] Father Sogol was trying to become *sanskrita*, "one who remakes himself," one who has an interior being and measure for judging. Only then could the mysterious synchronicity occur: at that moment he discovers a "peradam," the precious curved crystal hidden in the slopes of Mount Analogue "with an index of refraction so close to that of air in spite of its great density, that the inexperienced eye barely perceives it."[29] The paradam was considered to be a miraculous material entity, a little bit of evidence that slips through from another dimension of reality. Only when Father Sogol humbled himself, could he detect the tiny peradam, the highest material reward of a seeker's sincerity on Mount Analogue. Truly, this was the quintessential philosopher's stone, representing the activation of true insight, the reconciling energy that can reconnect man's two disparate natures. Pierre Sogol, whose very name meant *Stone Word*, could now touch the material evidence of his inner work.

If there is any doubt about the meaning behind Daumal's allegory, he provides short variations to drive home his message. Woven into the narrative are two beautiful mythic tales, "The History of the Hollow Men and the Bitter Rose," based on an old folktale of the Ardennes, and the "Myth of the Sphere and the Tetrahedron." The first story is a poetic allegory about man's place in the universe. "The Hollow Men live in solid rock and move about in it in the form of mobile caves or recesses. In ice they appear as bubbles in the shape of men."[30] The four pages that follow give free rein to his vast store of imagery, and express his inklings of another reality concurrent with our usual one. "Others say that, as a sword has its scabbard or a foot its imprint, every living man has in the mountain his Hollow Man, which he will seek out in death."[31]

He draws upon Gurdjieff's theory that the energy we expend, especially that of our thoughts and emotions, is always used, eaten up by something else in nature's chain (the biggest consumer being our moon). "They eat only the void, such as the form of corpses; they get drunk on empty words and all the meaningless expressions we utter."[32]

Then follows the drama of the twin brothers Mo and Ho and their battle with the Hollow Men in their search for the elusive Bitter Rose: "Whoever eats of it finds that, whenever he is about to tell a lie, aloud or to himself, his tongue begins to burn."[33] Finally Mo and Ho are forced to inhabit the same body and become a composite being, "Moho." If they continue to evolve, they might even become a *homo* (a man). This transformation recalls the metamorphosis of the caterpillar in *A Night of Serious*

Drinking. The tale of the Hollow Men is yet another vision quest—a story of a search for knowledge encapsulated in Daumal's larger one, both in the tradition of the grail and the holy mountain.

Here, as throughout *Mount Analogue*, Daumal combines a lightness of poetic imagery with a weightiness of thought reminiscent of the poetry of the most Eastern of our Western literary ancestors, the Greeks. One line will be light as air, likening the Bitter Rose to a swarm of butterflies. Another has a weight as if it were carved in stone: "The Hollow Men cannot enter our world, but they can come up to the surface of things. Beware of the surface of things."[34]

In his imagery, Daumal achieves the Hindu ideal of *suavité* (liquidity) which Visvanatha likened to flowing liquid. The Vedic literary scholar, Jan Gonda, believes that the Hindus achieved this suavity through the use of concise, elliptical phraseology, and vocabulary that was nuanced, melodious, and dignified. Daumal's imagery is not only liquid, but limpid—the quality of light passing through liquid. Visvanatha called limpidity the "evidence" produced by fire and water, the interaction of ardor and flow. Gonda also points out that Vedic writers often made graphic references to natural phenomenon, and showed a keen power of observation and pictorial expression. Likewise, Daumal presents a poetic, nuanced vision of the natural world. Now that he had achieved a certain security of having found a "path," it seems that he was finally able to see the holy in earthly images as well, rather than often denouncing them as in his early poetry. It bespeaks of his sense of joy as he was preparing to leave the earth. He graphically details Mo's movements:

> Like a lizard, sometimes like a spider, he inches upwards across the high precipice, between white snow below and the blue-black sky. Little swift-moving clouds envelop him from time to time, and then expose him suddenly to the light again. And now at last, a little distance above him, he sees the Bitter Rose, shimmering with unearthly tints.[35]

The second myth is a prose poem that was also included in a 1954 collection of Daumal's poetry entitled, "Black Poetry White Poetry." It is another creation myth, similar to his earlier poem, "The Keys of a Big Game," reflecting the Vedic myth of primordial man multiplying himself into all forms and species. As in the earlier poem, this growth is conceived in terms of contraction and expansion. "In the beginning, the Sphere and the Tetrahedron were united in a single inconceivable form: Concentration and Expansion mysteriously fused in a single will."[36] Daumal describes the familiar theme of the One multiplying into the many that he had experienced in his drug-induced death experience:

> The Sphere becomes Primordial Man, who, wishing to realize separately all his desires and possibilities, scattered himself into all the animal species and men of today. Man received the light of understanding. He wished to see his light and delight in its changing shapes. He was driven out by the force of the One.[37]

The form of *Mount Analogue* is a first-person narrative written in an understated, documentary style. It is the same style that we find in a dozen of his letters written to Vera, Jack, Jean Paulhan, Renéville, and others, while in the mountains during the years 1937 to 1943. Comprising thirty-two pages, these letters give lyrical, firsthand accounts of life in the mountains and include his experiences with the hardy mountain people. He describes his mountaineering training and how he would climb every other day, until walking on horizontal land seemed a little strange:

> There is nothing quite like the mountains for teaching slowness and calmness; there are climbs which take an hour of absolute slowness: left foot, right hand, walking stick here, right foot, walking stick there, body weight left, left hand . . . and here nervousness would kill. Once on top, the body discovers its paradise, which is taking off one's shoes and drinking a mouthful of wine mixed with snow gathered along the way.[38]

His description of the *névé* or glacier snow in *Mount Analogue* is lifted right out of his epistolary description to Rolland de Renéville where he lists ten different kinds, such as "wheat snow," "diamond snow," and "carpet snow."[39] One ten-page letter to his brother Jack is so replete with technical, montagnard jargon, that Daumal included thirty-six explanatory footnotes. Likewise, the detail of *Mount Analogue* reflects his expert knowledge of the subject, yet he never overburdens the novel with excess technical jargon that would intrude on the main poetic thrust.

The lightness and lyrical quality, reminiscent of Vedic poetry, is especially present in these mountain letters. It is clear that, in spite of his tubercular condition, Daumal was in his element several thousand feet up:

his natural humor bubbles up everywhere to celebrate the mountainscape. These qualities emerge in *Mount Analogue* in a particular pattern: the beginning chapters are pervaded by a subtle humor, the middle chapters become more technical and scientific, and the final chapters achieve a joyful lyricism and exaltation. This progression gives a certain dramatic momentum to the voyage and climb.

The overall taste (*rasa*) of the book would fall into the Hindu category of "marvel," as in *A Night of Serious Drinking*, for a sense of marvel and strangeness is intended, in a very matter-of-fact way, from the first page. Whenever a camera was used on Mount Analogue, nothing would appear on the developed film. Some of the flora of Port O'Monkeys include the incendiary *lycoperdon*, which would spontaneously ignite through intense fermentation, and the talking bush, whose fruit in the shape of resonant gourds could reproduce all the sounds of the human voice when rubbed by its own leaves. Yet the down-to-earth reporting makes the strange phenomena—such as herds of unicorns, seem absolutely plausible. The casual tone belies the weightiness of the ideas behind the bare facts of the allegory.

> I nibbled a biscuit. A donkey kept fanning a cloud of flies in my face with its tail. My companions were as pensive as I was. After all, there was something mysterious about the ease with which we had landed on the continent of Mount Analogue; it still seemed that we had been expected.[40]

In this book Daumal presents, in a veiled manner, many aspects of the teacher-disciple relationship of the esoteric tradition and of the Gurdjieff Work in particular. One important concept is the linkage that exists between seekers. One can never advance farther up unless one prepares for those behind. In the narrative, the guides explain to Sogol's band that each passing group must leave their encampment stocked with provisions for the next caravan. When the party sees the distant white smoke from the group ahead, they feel a mutual support: "From now on the trail linked our fate to theirs, even if we were never to meet."[41] In the notes that he made for future additions to the novel, he talks further about the traces left by one seeker for another, warning the climber not to leave traces of false starts and mistakes. "Be ready to answer to your fellow men for the trail you leave behind you."[42]

All seekers are linked through a hierarchy of evolved souls such as "the high mountain guides." Everything happens through the unfolding of a divine plan. When they wonder how they came to land, "we were to learn later that it was not by chance, and that the wind which had carried us there was no natural and fortuitous wind, but had blown in accordance with a will."[43]

In the last paragraph of the notes, the narrator lists the many factors that contributed to their successful entry: their calculations, their efforts, and their renunciation of bodily comforts. "So it seemed to us. But we learned later that if we were able to approach Mount Analogue, it was because the invisible doors of the invisible country had been opened to us by those who guard them. Those who see us even though we cannot see them.[44]

The interpenetration of the symbolic and the concrete—of fiction, fantasy, and the actuality of Daumal's own experience of the Gurdjieff Work and even of mountain climbing—makes the novel a real manual for the aspiring seeker. It is an itinerary of Daumal's many paths, showing how they all come together in one.

Thus Daumal uses fiction to present another crucial aspect of the teacher-disciple relationship. According to Ouspensky, "The first and most important feature of groups is the fact that groups are not constituted according to the wish and choice of their members. Groups are constituted by the teacher, who selects types which, from the point of view of his aims, can be useful to one another."[45] Yet the teacher does not clear the same single path for all disciples. Each person must find his own with the help of the teacher. In a letter to Ribemont Dessaignes, he wrote:

> The first sentence of the *Tao Tei King* is: "a path that is a path already traced is not the Path." I told you that I have encountered in my life a true teaching. One of the signs of its truth for me is that he never proposes a path already traced. No, at each step, the whole problem is posed. Nothing is resolved for me, once and for all.[46]

The novel remained unfinished with only meager notes to indicate the direction in which it might have gone. In the postface added by his wife, Vera, she discusses the preparation for the successive encampments: "Probably René Daumal would have made clear what he meant by this work of preparation. For in his daily life he devoted himself to preparing many minds for the difficult voyage toward Mount Analogue."[47]

The novel is truly a new embodiment of the Hindu concept of the mountain being the point where Heaven and Earth meet. In *A Night of*

Serious Drinking, Daumal suggests "madness and death" as two escape exits, while the entire *Mount Analogue* constitutes the diary of an escape through the unnameable third exit alluded to in the previous novel. It is the log of someone on his way, a record left behind for others to read and follow. His proposed final chapter was to be entitled "And You, What Are You Seeking?"

Daumal indicates the preliminary stages of a true path as depicted in many traditions, a practical method for perfecting one's life here on this planet. Thus *Mount Analogue* represents the culmination of Daumal's expansion as a poet and perfectly reflects the esoteric teachings of Hinduism and Gurdjieff, both literary and philosophical. This final work is the consummation of all his years of honing his craft and his soul, surrendering his ego in order to ascend the holy mountain.

Conclusion

Looking back on the life and work of René Daumal, his story is all the more vivid for its unfolding against the backdrop of *les années folles*—the crazy years following World War I. He experienced the communal postwar disillusionment and taste for the bizarre shared by all those disaffected moderns who converged on Paris at that time. Yet, if Daumal and the Simplistes spawned the first and youngest youth movement, he himself was never just another *enfant terrible*, or wild child. He went to extremes in a youthful way, in his intransigence and his risk taking, yet somehow the delicacy of his "pataphysics" and the rare sobriety of his intoxication lifted him above the rest. Quickly, he went beyond the purely literary, philosophical, and political levels, to seek out a way of living that was above both the distractions of the abstract and the contingencies of personal life.

Like tangential circles, Daumal's life in the twenties and thirties has a consonance with life in the sixties and its aftermath. The interwar years are considered to be the most creative moment in history since the Renaissance. Many historians consider the 1960s the next resurgence to occur. To truly understand Daumal's place in history, one must view him not only in his own context but from the standpoint of our experience and time sequence in the twentieth century. Many influences, creative movements, and freedoms that we now take for granted or believe to be of recent origin were hard-won breakthroughs in his era. Thus, exploring the parallel processes and proclivities of our eras will allow us to better understand Daumal and better explain why we feel such a natural empathy for him.

While studying at the University of the Sorbonne (which Daumal had attended), it seemed to me that the atmosphere in the ancient student quarter had remained virtually unchanged since the twenties. It was still the hotbed of intense political thinkers and revolutionaries, only now the leftist-leaning youths were reading Mao's Little Red Book and had Che Gueverra posters on their walls. The tenor of the literary scene was as Surrealistic as it was Existential, traditions carried on by the Theatre of the Absurd. The Surrealists and other early writers were still in vogue and the plays of Giraudoux, Anouilhl, and the later Absurdists were made affordable to students in the innumerable theaters of Paris, such as the Theatre Alfred Jarry. André Gide's earlier *Les Nourritures Terrestres* was still considered a manifesto for youth. Abstract Expressionists and Pop artists carried on the tradition of the Cubists and Surrealists, only now they were revered by a larger segment of the mainstream audience.

More and more, the same issues that concerned Daumal were firing up an entire generation of students. Like Daumal and his coterie, young people in the sixties gradually began to distrust conventional doctrines, be they social, economic, or religious. Colleges began offering courses in Eastern religions, and many spiritual teachers such as Krishnamurti, Sachidananda, and Pir Vilayat Khan attracted Western followers, while the popular Maharishi Mahesh Yogi used television to spread his message of "God Consciousness."

As in the twenties, so in the sixties, there was an expansive quality that made everything seem possible, as well as a sense of angst in the face of war, assassinations, inequalities, and "isms." When one reads about the synergistic energy of the Grand Jeu, it conjures up those same qualities of the sixties—fraternity, commitment to causes, psychic exploration, creativity, innocence, and naiveté—among the small enclaves of extremely dedicated young people who felt committed to aid the disenfranchised and change the world. As with the Surrealists, such an aura of innocence invaded all activities that any outlandish folly could be pursued with purity and impunity. Joy and celebration seemed to pervade the atmosphere, as new forms of art and music exploded everywhere.

In May 1968, tear gas enveloped the Sorbonne during the student uprisings, as French students fought the stringent university format and other rigid laws of bourgeois capitalist society. Among the angry messages I saw scribbled on the walls were iconoclastic quotes by a seminal writer, René Daumal, that exclaimed: "Destroy! Tear off the masks! Pull down all the ridiculous scaffoldings!" It was at this moment in history that Daumal's star truly began to rise. His work suddenly became known to a whole new generation of listeners who were ripe to hear his message. His own earnest dedication to societal transformation was now matched by theirs. Daumal's words from 1928 vehemently expressed the tenor of 1968. Yet, if these messages brought him fame, they did not represent the best of René, for, in the end, René Daumal's true aim was not political but metaphysical.

From our own vantage point in the last hours of the century, Daumal's explorations of the spirit and psyche might seem all too old and familiar. But beware the Law of Familiarity, which prevents us from hearing afresh certain messages that we think we have already learned. This information is as fresh and timely today as it was sixty-five or a thousand years ago. Daumal's writing remains a legacy for us, even in the midst of the self-development programs available in today's psychotherapeutic marketplace.

In reviewing the life of this poet-priest, one may wait in vain for a consensus as to which of the influences proved the most significant—Surrealism, Hinduism, or Gurdjieff—or whether his original mind would have continued to articulate his own philosophy based on his personal experience of the cosmos. Indeed, Daumal's unquenchable intellect produced a seminal synthesis of many ancient sources of knowledge. He revered the old traditions in the books but was open to the Gurdjieff teaching when it suddenly appeared before him—a new voice and another new synthesis.

As an adolescent, Daumal had an innate sense of the importance of renunciation and self-negation to delineate the self from its ego desires and extensions. As he passed through a dark period in his early probing years, he slowly began to see that true philosophy is self-inquiry—that it was through his own efforts, moment to moment, that he created the fuel for his being. After reading the Vedas he was able to summarize its message in his own words: "Man cannot live without fire; and you cannot build a fire without burning something"—that is, only through personal efforts, knowledge, and discipline can man attain a higher level of being.

Carrying a copy of the *Bhagavad Gita* with him always during the last ten years of his life, he never forgot that "A man of true renunciation is he who neither craves nor hates; for he who is above the two contraries soon finds his freedom" (5.3). Daumal struggled with the same issue of contrary forces and freedom, and learned from Gurdjieff that the valuable element is not the indifferent detachment but the struggle itself. Inner unity or fusion is obtained by means of "friction"—the struggle between yes and no in man. This fusion creates the energy to crystallize the freedom of true consciousness and union with God.

Although Daumal rarely considered the possibility that grace might intervene in this struggle, he did believe that Alexandre de Salzmann's intervention in his own life was a miraculous turning point. He hints at this in *A Night of Serious Drinking*. A character talks of "the golden touch and the hand of gold that opens all doors," and then he questions the number of keys and doors needed, and what it costs to acquire "the golden touch." Certainly René had passed through several crucial doors—the Surrealist doors of perception and the Hindu Sun-Gate of wisdom. He had used various keys—experiments in perception, the writings of René Guénon, and his own writing—but it appears safe to accept his own verdict that the Gurdjieff teaching opened the major door for him, thus shedding light on all the other rooms and passage ways.

The first and final key was always the practice of direct awareness of his interior forces, exposing the dark ignorance of the self-centered personality. When he came to accept the necessity for slow, humbling self-study and patient self-observation, he gave up any pretensions to enlightenment and faced his nothingness. He was able to shed light on his inner processes and reveal the many layers of self and psyche. He found a means of awakening. In a beautiful final poem he seems to sum up the dilemma of each moment of life, as well as the progressive stages of his own life, a final summation of all his efforts on Earth:

> I am dead because I lack desire;
> I lack desire because I think I possess;
> I think I possess because I do not try to give.
> In trying to give, you see that you have nothing;
> Seeing you have nothing, you try to give of yourself;
> Trying to give of yourself, you see that you are nothing;
> Seeing you are nothing, you desire to become;
> In desiring to become, you begin to live.

Notes

Introduction

1. R. Daumal, *Le Contre-Ciel* (1970), p. 95.

Chapter 1. An Anarchist of Perception

1. R. Daumal, *Essais et Notes*, p. 224.
2. Jack Daumal, letter to the author, 1992.
3. R. Daumal, *Essais et Notes*, p. 225.
4. R. Daumal, *The Powers of the Word*, p. 113.
5. Luc Perin, *Lettre à La Grive*, p. 19.
6. R. Daumal, *Correspondance* I, p. 125.
7. Robert Meyrat, in Sigoda, *René Daumal et ses Abords Immédiats*, p. 37.
8. R. Daumal, *Correspondance* Vol. 1, p. 125.
9. Meyrat, in Sigoda, *René Daumal et ses Abords Immédiats*, p. 40.
10. R. Daumal, *Le Grand Jeu* 1, p. 16.
11. R. Daumal, *Correspondance*, Vol. 1, p. 193.
12. Ibid.
13. R. Daumal, *A Night of Serious Drinking*, p. 89.
14. Ribemont-Dessaignes, in *L'Originel*, p. 38.
15. Jean Jacques Leveque, "Une quête romantique," p. 6.
16. Alfred Jarry, *Selected Works of Alfred Jarry*, p. 192.
17. R. Daumal, *Le Grand Jeu* 1, p. 2.
18. Jack Daumal, letter to the author, 1992.
19. R. Daumal, "Concerning Uday Shankar," *Rasa*, p. 35.
20. Jacob Needleman, *The Heart of Philosophy*, p. 129.
21. R. Daumal, "Mémorables," *Le Contre-Ciel* (1970), p. 213.
22. R. Daumal, letter to Vera, *Correspondance*, Vol. 2, p. 292.
23. Philippe Lavastine, interview with author, 1977.

24. Alain Rolland de Renéville, "Souvenir de René Daumal," p. 505.
25. Monny de Boully in l'Originel, p. 39.
26. André Gide, Les Nourritures Terrestres, p. 30.
27. Ibid.
28. R. Daumal, Correspondance Vol. 2, p. 167.
29. Gide, Les Nourritures Terrestres, p. 40.
30. R. Daumal, Lettres à ses amis, p. 107.
31. R. Daumal, "Nénie," Le Contre-Ciel (1970), p. 65.
32. R. Daumal, "Lettres de la Montagne," p. 189.
33. Ibid., p. 194.
34. Emile Dermenghen, in A. Rolland de Renéville, "Souvenir de René Daumal," p. 268.
35. Philippe Lavastine, interview, 1977.
36. Monny de Boully, unpublished letter, 1968.
37. Alexandre de Salzmann, Der Rhythmus, 1912. Excerpt reprinted in "Light, Lighting and Illumination," Material for Thought (Summer 1972): 22–24.
38. R. Daumal, letter in Jack Daumal, Cahiers Daumal, No. 1, p. 28.
39. Ibid., p. 29.
40. Ibid. p. 30.
41. Jean Schlumberger, letter in Jack Daumal, Cahiers Daumal, No. 1, pp. 30–32.
42. Simone Weil, letter to Daumal in Cahiers Simone Weil, p. 4.
43. R. Daumal, unpublished notebook, in Random, Les puissances du dedans, p. 237.
44. R. Daumal, "Mémorables," Le Contre-Ciel (1970), p. 215.
45. Luc Dietrich cited in Random, La puissances du dedans, p. 238.
46. Rolland de Renéville, "Souvenir de René Daumal," p. 509.
47. Vera Daumal, letter to Pierre Granville, in R. Daumal, Correspondance, Vol. 3, p. 405–406.
48. Vera Daumal, quoted in Camille, "René Daumal et Le Grand Jeu," in Sigoda, René Daumal, L'Age d'Homme, p. 235.

Chapter 2. Daumal and Renunciation

1. R. Daumal, Lettres à ses amis, p. 34.
2. Jacques Masui, "La voie de René Daumal," p. 57.
3. R. Daumal, in Le Grand Jeu 1.
4. Gilbert-Lecomte, Le Grand Jeu 1, p. 16.
5. R. Daumal, "Freedom without Hope," in The Powers of the Word, p. 1.
6. R. Daumal, Powers of the Word, p. 5.

7. Arthur Rimbaud, "A Season in Hell," in Angel Flores, *An Anthology of French Poetry*, p. 124.
8. R. Daumal, *Powers of the Word*.
9. Ibid., p. 4.
10. R. Daumal, "Freedom without Hope," in *The Powers of the Word*, p. 23.
11. R. Daumal, "La Revolte et l'Ironie," in *Essais et Notes*, *L'Evidence Absurde*, vol. 1.

Chapter 3. Drug Experimentation

1. R. Daumal, "The Determining Memory," in *The Powers of the Word*, p. 163.
2. R. Daumal, *The Powers of the Word*, p. 166.
3. Ibid., p. 167.
4. Ibid., p. 169.
5. R. Daumal, "Asphyxia and Absurd Evidence," *The Powers of the Word*, p. 70.
6. R. Daumal, "Mémorables," *Le Contre-Ciel* (1970), p. 213.
7. Phil Powrie, *René Daumal: L'Etude d'une obsession*, p. 14.
8. R. Daumal, "The Determining Memory," *The Powers of the Word*, p. 169.
9. O. V. de Milosz, *Ars Magna*, p. 12.
10. *Bhagavad Gita*, XI, 23–13, p. 15.
11. R. Daumal, "The Determining Memory," *The Powers of the Word*, pp. 170–71.
12. R. Daumal, "Mémorables," *Le Contre-Ciel* (1970) p. 215.

Chapter 4. Surrealism and *Le Grand Jeu*

1. R. Daumal, *Le Grand Jeu*, p. 2.
2. R. Daumal, *Correspondance* Vol. 1, p. 127.
3. Anthony Hartley, *The Penguin Book of French Verse*, p. xlviii.
4. R. Daumal, *Lettres à ses amis*, p. 304.
5. R. Daumal, *Correspondance* Vol. 1, p. 116.
6. Roger Shattuck, *The Banquet Years*, p 195.
7. Maurice Nadeau, *The History of Surrealism*, p. 72.
8. Shattuck, *The Banquet Years*, p. 239.
9. Ubu Cocu, in Alfred Jarry, *Selected Works of Alfred Jarry*, pp. 28–30.
10. Roger Shattuck in Nadeau, *History of Surrealism*, p. 21.
11. Salvadore Dali, "La Femme Visible," in Nadeau, *History of Surrealism*, p. 184.

12. Michel Random, *La Puissances du Dedans*, p. 269.
13. Robert Meyrat in Sigoda, *René Daumal et ses abords immédiats*, p. 39.
14. Pierre Minet, in Sigoda Exposition de Charleville-Mezières.
15. Robert Meyrat, in Sigoda, *René Daumal et ses abords immédiats*, p. 44.
16. R. Daumal, "Mémorables," *Le Contre-Ciel* (1970), p. 214.
17. André Breton, *Manifestes du Surrealisme*, p. 50.
18. Robert Vitrac and Max Morise, in Nadeau, *History of Surrealism*, p. 81.
19. Louis Aragon, "Traité du Style," in Nadeau, *History of Surrealism*, p. 90.
20. Tristan Tzara, quoted in Nadeau, *History of Surrealism*, p. 69.
21. Anna Balakian, *André Breton*, p. 16.
22. René Daumal, *Lettres à ses amis*, p. 45.
23. Ibid., p. 304.
24. Jack Daumal in R. Daumal, *Le Grand Jeu* 1, p. 56.
25. R. Daumal, "Pataphysics and the Revelation of Laughter," in *The Powers of the Word*, p. 20.
26. Alfred Jarry, "Exploits and Opinions of Dr. Faustroll, Pataphysician," *Selected Works of Alfred Jarry*, p. 193.
27. R. Daumal, "Pataphysics," *Powers of the Word*, p. 17.
28. R. Daumal, "Traité des Patagrammes," *Essais et Notes, L'Evidence Absurde*, pp. 209–40.
29. R. Daumal, "en gggarrrde!," in Rosset, *Evergreen Review*, pp. 211–13.
30. Julien Torma, "Letter to René Daumal," quoted in Rosset, *Evergreen Review*, p. 120.
31. Charles Baudelaire, *Les Paradis Artificiels*, p. 143.
32. Anna Balakian, *Surrealism: The Road to the Absolute*, p. 100.
33. Freud, quoted in André Breton, *Les Vases Communicantes*, p. 163.
34. Pierre Reverdy, "La Révolution Surréaliste," in Nadeau, *History of Surrealism*, p. 93.
35. Helen Maxwell, "Bergson et le Grand Jeu," in *L'Originel* 7, p. 8.
36. R. Daumal, *Lettres à ses amis*, p. 91.
37. Ibid., p. 112.
38. Nadeau, *History of Surrealism*, p. 25.
39. R. Daumal, *Le Grand Jeu* 3, pp. 76–83.
40. Monny de Boully, in *l'Originel* 7, p. 39.
41. R. Daumal, *Lettres à ses amis*, p. 48.
42. R. Daumal, "Nerval the Nyctalope" in *The Powers of the Word*, p. 38.
43. Meyrat, in Sigoda, *René Daumal et ses abords immédiats*, p. 46.

44. Monny de Boully, unpublished letters, Paris, 1947.
45. Nadeau, *History of Surréalism*, p. 144.
46. Breton, "Les Chants du Maldoror," *Les Pas Perdus*.
47. Ribemont Dessaignes, in *l'Originel* 7, pp. 43–44.
48. R. Daumal, *Lettres à ses amis*, p. 187.
49. R. Daumal, *Le Grand Jeu* 3, pp. 81–83.
50. Ibid. pp. 187–89.
51. R. Daumal, "Surréalism and the Grand Jeu," *The Powers of the Word*, p. 58.
52. Balakian, *André Breton*, p. 95.
53. de Boully, in *L'Originel* 7, pp. 39, 45.
54. Marianne Lams in *L'Originel* 7, p. 11.
55. Ibid.
56. de Boully, in *L'Originel* 7, p. 39.
57. Ibid.

Chapter 5. The Avant Garde and Party Politics

1. H. Stuart Hughes, *Consciousness and Society*, pp. 402–405.
2. "Le Surréalisme et Le Grand Jeu," in R. Daumal, *Le Grand Jeu* 4, p. 11.
3. Louis Aragon, "La Révolution d'abord et toujours," p. 23.
4. Declaration of January 25, 1925, cited in Nadeau, *History of Surrealiam*, p. 103.
5. Philip Rahv, "Proletarian Literature: A Political Autopsy," *Literature and the Sixth Sense*, p. 10.
6. Jean Jacques Brochier, *L'Aventure des Surréalistes*, p. 11.
7. Pierre Naville, "La Révolution et les Intellectuels," in Brochier, *L'Aventure des Surrealistes*, p. 255.
8. Ribemont Dessaignes, "Entretien," *L'Originel*, no 7. December 1978 special edition of *Le Grand Jeu*, p. 44.
9. André Breton, in Brochier, *L'Aventure des Surréalistes*, p. 254.
10. Roger Vailland, *Le Surréalisme Contre la Révolution*, p. 12.
11. Leon-Gabriel Gros, "René Daumal, et le Grand Jeu," p. 356.
12. R. Daumal, *Lettres à ses amis*, p. 203.
13. R. Daumal, *Tu t'es toujours trompé*, p. 186.
14. R. Daumal, *Lettres à ses amis* p. 298.
15. Ibid., p. 255.
16. Rolland de Renéville, in R. Daumal, *Tu t'es toujours trompé*, p. 254.
17. R. Daumal, "Lettre de Paris," in *Essais et Notes, L'Evidence Absurde*, p. 265.
18. R. Daumal, *Tu t'es toujours trompé*, p. 205.

19. R. Daumal, letter quoted in Pascal Sigoda, *René Daumal*, p. 194
20. R. Daumal, *Tu t'es toujours trompé*, p. 270.
21. R. Daumal, "Mémorables," *Le Contre-Ciel* (1970), p. 214.
22. Jeanne de Salzmann, quoted in letter from Jack Daumal, 1992.
23. Gurdjieff, quoted in Ouspensky, *In Search of the Miraculous*, p. 342.
24. R. Daumal, *Correspondance 3*, p. 238.

Chapter 6. The Influence of Hindu Thought

1. André Rolland de Renéville, "L' Elaboration d'une méthode," in R. Daumal, *Le Grand Jeu*, Vol. 2, p. 11.
2. *Rig Veda*, 5.95.
3. William Blake, *The Poetry and Prose of William Blake*, p. 481.
4. *Rig Veda*, 8.9.
5. Ibid., I.1,9.
6. Ibid., X.129, 1–7.
7. Kapil Tiwari, *Dimensions of Renunciation in the Advaita Vedanta*, p. 19.
8. Alexandra David-Neel, *Buddhism*, p. 48.
9. *Arthava Veda*, 11.5.5, cited in Theodore de Barry, *Sources of Indian Tradition*, p. 17.
10. Ibid.
11. Gurdjieff, *All and Everything*, p. 1176–1177
12. de Barry, *Sources of Indian Tradition*, p. 20.
13. Ibid., p. 18.
14. Ibid.
15. Kapil Tirwari, *Dimensions of Renunciation*, p. 24.
16. *Manusmriti* (The Laws of Manu).
17. *Mandukya Upanishad*, 1.2.1, p. 396.
18. *Brihadaranyaka Upanishads*, I.3. 12–22, p. 145.
19. *Bhagavad Gita*, VI.1, p. 32.
20. Ibid., III.6.
21. Samkara, "Le Marteau de stupidité," translated by R. Daumal in Jacques Masui, ed, *Port des singes*.
22. Philippe Lavastine, "Vedanta," *Material for Thought*, p. 4.
23. R. Daumal, "Metaphysical Intuitions in History," *You Were Always Wrong*, p. 58.
24. Ibid., p. 60.
25. Ibid., p. 66.
26. Ibid., p. 58.
27. R. Daumal, "Poem to God and Man," in *You Were Always Wrong*, pp. 76–80.
28. Jacob Needleman, *Lost Christianity*, pp. 136–139.

29. R. Daumal, letter to Raymond Christoflour, in Masui, "René Daumal et l'Inde."

Chapter 7. Daumal in the Labyrinth of Pathways

*The epigraph was used as the heading of Daumal's œuvre, *La Langue Sanskrite: Grammaire, Poésie, Théâtre* [The Sanskrit Language Grammar, Poetry, Theater].

1. Anna Balakian, *The Literary Origins of Surrealism*, p. 56.
2. Charles Baudelaire, "Correspondances," *Anthology of French Poetry*, p. 297.
3. R. Daumal, *Correspondance*, Vol. 1, p. 216.
4. R. Daumal, *Le Grand Jeu 2*, p. 73.
5. Guénon, *Introduction to the Study of Hindu Doctrines*, p. 12.
6. Ibid., p. 23.
7. Ibid., pp. 59–60.
8. Ibid., p. 60.
9. Guénon, *East and West*, p. 42.
10. R. Daumal, *Grand Jeu 2*, p. 2.
11. Ibid.
12. Guénon, *Introduction to the Study of Hindu Doctrines*, p. 118.
13. Ibid., p. 120.
14. R. Daumal, "L'Origine du théâtre," *Bharata*, p. 13.
15. Guénon, *Introduction to the Study of Hindu Doctrines*, pp. 102–103.
16. Guénon, *Apercus sur l'initiation*, p. 27.
17. André Gide, quoted in Bosco, "Trois Rencontres," p. 68.
18. Gide, *Les Nourritures Terrestres*, p. 122.
19. Ibid., p. 1.
20. Guénon, *Introduction to the Study of Hindu Doctrines*, p. 147.
21. Philippe Lavastine, "Vedanta," *Material for Thought*, p. 4.
22. André Breton, "René Guénon, jugé par le Surréalisme," p. 68.
23. Wendy Doniger O'Flaherty, "Hard and Soft Reality," p. 23.
24. Ouspensky, *A New Model of the Universe*, p. 264.
25. Guénon, *Symboles fondamentaux*, pp. 64–65.
26. Sri Aurobindo, quoted in Guénon, *Symboles fondamentaux*, p. 66.
27. R. Daumal, "Essais sur l'introspection," *Essais et Notes, L'Evidence Absurde*, p. 172.
28. Gurdjieff, quoted in Ouspensky, *In Search of the Miraculous*, p. 19.
29. Guénon, *Le Règne de la quantité*, pp. 318–19.
30. Breton, *Manifestes du Surréalisme*, p. 92.
31. R. Daumal, *Mount Analogue*, p. 112.
32. Guénon, *Etudes sur le franc maconnière*, p. 16.

33. Guénon, *Introduction to the Study of Hindu Doctrines*, p. 249.
34. Lecomte, *Le Grand Jeu* I, p. 52.
35. R. Daumal, letter in Masui, "René Daumal et l'Inde," p. 61.
36. R. Daumal, letter in Sigoda, *René Daumal*, p. 198.
37. Masui, "René Daumal et l'Inde," p. 61.
38. Ibid., p. 62.
39. Jack Daumal, letter to the author, 1992.
40. R. Daumal, *Mount Analogue*, p. 194.

Chapter 8. Daumal and Hindu Poetics

1. *Brihadaranyaka Upanishad* (IV. 4. 12), p. 142.
2. Edwin Gerow, *History of Indian Literature*, p. 38.
3. R. Daumal, "To Approach the Hindu Poetic Art," *Rasa*, p. 14.
4. Ibid., p. 8.
5. Ibid.
6. Ibid. p. 9.
7. Krishna Chaitanya, *Sanskrit Poetics*, p. 190.
8. R. Daumal, *Rasa*, p. 44.
9. Ibid., p. 45.
10. Ibid., p. 46.
11. Ibid.
12. R. Daumal, "La Nature essentielle de la poésie," *Bharata*, p. 57.
13. Ananda Coomaraswamy, "Theory of Art in Asia," p. 59.
14. R. Daumal, *Bharata*, p. 59.
15. Ananda Coomaraswamy, "Theory of Art in Asia," p. 59.
16. S. K. De, *Sanskrit Poetics as a Study of Aesthetics*, p. 13.
17. R. Daumal, *Bharata*, p. 88.
18. Ibid.
19. Ibid., p. 41.
20. Ibid., p. 44.
21. Jan Gonda, *Vedic Literature*, p. 265.
22. R. Daumal, review of *The Tibetan Book of the Dead* in *Les Pouvoirs de la Parole*, p. 175.
23. Ibid., p. 175.
24. R. Daumal, "On Oriental Music," *Rasa*, p. 21.
25. Ibid., p. 22.
26. Ibid., p. 24.
27. *Taittirya Upanishad*, 2.7.
28. R. Daumal, "Dialogue du Style par René Daumal et Lanzo del Vasto," *Les Pouvoirs de la Parole*, p. 265.
29. R. Daumal, *Message Actuel de l'Inde*.
30. Ibid.

Chapter 9. Daumal with Gurdjieff and the de Salzmanns

1. Georgette Camille, "René Daumal et le Grand Jeu." in Sigoda, *René Daumal*, pp. 234–35.
2. Jacques Masui, "René Daumal et l'expérience Gurdjieff," p. 34.
3. P. L. Travers, *New York Times Magazine* (July 29, 1979): 30.
4. P. D. Ouspensky, *In Search of the Miraculous*, p. 188.
5. Michel de Salzmann, "Seeing: The Endless Source of Freedom," pp. 17, 18, and 23.
6. Pierre Schaeffer, "Maitre de Danse," *Dossier*, p. 24.
7. Gurdjieff, *Meetings with Remarkable Men*, p. 70.
8. Catholicos Vazken I, *An Introduction to the Armenian Liturgy*, pp. 61, 62.
9. Gurdjieff, quoted in P. D. Ouspensky, *In Search of the Miraculous*, p. 274.
10. Ibid.
11. R. Daumal, "Le Nondualisme de Spinoza," *Essais et Notes, L'Evidence Absurde*, p. 91.
12. R. Daumal, in Jack Daumal, *Cahiers Daumal*, No. 1, p. 24.
13. Ibid., p. 25.
14. R. Daumal, "Nerval the Nyctalope," *The Powers of the Word*, p. 47.
15. Jack Daumal, *You Were Always Wrong*, p. 5.
16. Ibid., p. 12.
17. Ibid., p. 19.
18. Ibid., p. 22.
19. Ouspensky, *In Search of the Miraculous*, p. 351.
20. Gurdjieff, *Life is Real, Only Then When I Am*, pp. 140–42.
21. R. Daumal, "The Role of Movement in the Complete Education of Man" in *The Powers of the Word*, pp. 72–75.
22. Ibid., p. 280.
23. Gurdjieff, quoted in Ouspensky, *In Search of the Miraculous*, p. 26.
24. Ibid., pp. 296–97.
25. Ibid.
26. Frank Lloyd Wright, quoted in James Moore, *Gurdjieff and Mansfield*, p. 208.
27. James Moore, *Gurdjieff: The Anatomy of a Myth*, pp. 228–29.
28. Ravi Ravindra, "Gurdjieff et l'enseignement de Krishna," in Bruno de Panafieu ed., *George Ivanovitch Gurdjieff*, p. 12.
29. R. Daumal, autobiographical notes, quoted in Michel Random, *La Puissance du Dedans*, p. 270.
30. R. Daumal, unpublished letter to Jean Paulhan, 1936.
31. R. Daumal, *Correspondance*, Vol. 2, p. 175.
32. R. Daumal, "Mémorables," *Le Contre-Ciel* (1970), p. 215.

33. Alexandre de Salzmann in R. Daumal, *Correspondance*, Vol. 2, p. 230.
34. Ibid., p. 232.
35. R. Daumal, unpublished letter to Jean Paulhan, 1936.
36. R. Daumal, letter, in J. Daumal, *Cahiers Daumal*, No. 1, p. 34.
37. Ibid.
38. R. Daumal, *Correspondance*, Vol. 3, p. 57.
39. Jean Biès, "René Daumal et l'expérience Gurdjieff," in Masui, ed., "La Voie de René Daumal," p. 37.
40. R. Daumal, letter to Christoflour, in Masui, "La Voie de René Daumal."
41. R. Daumal, unpublished letter to Jeanne de Salzmann, 1940.
42. R. Daumal, letter to Renéville, *Correspondance*, Vol. 2, p. 87.
43. R. Daumal, letter to J. Paulhan, *Correspondance*, Vol. 3, p. 97.
44. Ibid. p. 98.
45. R. Daumal, letter to E. Dermenghen, *Tu t'es toujours trompe*, p. 207.
46. Rolland de Renéville, "Souvenir de René Daumal," p. 506.
47. Ibid.
48. R. Daumal, Letter to Renéville, in Masui, "La Voie de René Daumal," p. 48.
49. Michel de Salzmann, "Footnote to the Gurdjieff Literature," in J. Walter Driscoll, *Gurdjieff: An Annotated Bibliography*, pp. xvi–xx.
50. R. Daumal, letter to J. Paulhan, in Sigoda, *René Daumal*, pp. 290–92.
51. R. Daumal, *Correspondance*, Vol. 3, p. 312.
52. Philippe Lavastine, personal interview, 1977.
53. R. Daumal, *Correspondance*, Vol. 3, pp. 351–53.
54. Ibid., p. 340.
55. Ibid., p. 364.
56. Ibid., p. 362.
57. Ibid.
58. Ibid., pp. 369–70.
59. Ibid., pp. 377–79.
60. Ibid., pp. 355–56.
61. Ibid., p. 360.
62. R. Daumal, unpublished letter to Louis Lief, 1942.
63. R. Daumal, unpublished letter to Genevieve Lief, 1943.
64. R. Daumal, in Mark Polizzatti, Introduction to *Le Contre-Ciel* (1990).
65. R. Daumal, unpublished letter to Jack Daumal, 1943.
66. R. Daumal, unpublished letter to Louis Lief, 1943.
67. Personal conversations with Jack Daumal 1995.

Chapter 10. The Poetry of *Le Contre Ciel*

1. R. Daumal, "It Only Takes a Word," *Le Contre-Ciel* (1990), p. 61.
2. R. Daumal, "The Keys to a Great Poetic Game," *Le Contre Ciel* (1990), p. 8. R. Daumal, "Les clavicules d'un grande jeu poetique," *Le Contre Ciel* (1970), p. 25. In subsequent references, page numbers in parentheses will refer to the French version.
3. R. Daumal, "The Keys to a Great Poetic Game," *Le Contre Ciel*, p. 9; (= p. 26).
4. Ibid., p. 9; (= p. 27).
5. Ibid., p. 10; (= p. 28).
6. Ibid., p. 10-11; (= p. 29).
7. Ibid., p. 11; (= p. 30).
8. Ibid., p. 14; (= p. 34).
9. Ibid., p. 15; (= p. 36).
10. Ibid.
11. Roger Shattuck, Mount Analogue, p. 23.
12. R. Daumal, "The Keys to a Great Poetic Game," *Le Contre Ciel*, p. 21; (= p. 43).
13. Ibid., p. 21; (= p. 44).
14. Ibid., p. 17; (= p. 37).
15. R. Daumal, *lettres à ses amis*, p. 119.
16. R. Daumal, quoted in Ramada, *Survey of Upanishadic Literature*, p. 122.
17. R. Daumal, *Lettres à ses amis*, p. 204.
18. Ibid., p. 154.
19. R. Daumal, "The Single One," *Le Contre-Ciel*, p. 40; (= p. 62)
20. R. Daumal, "Oath of Loyalty," *Le Contre-Ciel*, p. 51; (= p. 76).
21. R. Daumal, "To Nothingness," *Le Contre-Ciel*, p. 54; (= p. 79).
22. R. Daumal, "Oath of Loyalty," *Le Contre-Ciel*, p. 52; (= p. 77).
23. R. Daumal, "To Nothingness," *Le Contre-Ciel*, p. 54; (= p. 79).
24. R. Daumal, "Panic Sweat," *Le Contre-Ciel*, p. 94.
25. R. Daumal, "Disillusion," *Le Contre-Ciel*, p. 52; (= p. 73).
26. R. Daumal "The Famous Surprise," *Le Contre-Ciel*, p. 47. (= p. 72).
27. R. Daumal, "Keys to the Great Poetic Game," *Le Contre-Ciel*, p. 18. (= p. 39).
28. R. Daumal, "Poem to Debone Philosophers," *Le Contre-Ciel*, p. 69; (= p. 103).
29. R. Daumal, "Dictated in 1925," *Le Contre-Ciel*, p. 79; (= p. 114).
30. Ibid.
31. R. Daumal, letter to Maurice Henry, 1926, *Correspondance*, Vol. 1, p. 24.

32. R. Daumal, "Keys to the Great Poetic Game," *Le Contre-Ciel*, p. 22. (= p. 34).
33. R. Daumal, "The Holy War," *Parabola* 6 (12), p. 13.
34. R. Daumal, *Rasa*, p. 135. R. Daumal, *Bharata*, p. 75.
35. R. Daumal, *Le Contre-Ciel* (1990), p. 36.
36. Ibid., p. 51.
37. Ibid., p. 54.
38. Ibid., p. 58.
39. R. Daumal, *Le Contre-Ciel*, "Willed Fire," p. 61; (= p. 89).
40. R. Daumal, *Poésie noir, poésie blanche*, p. 201.
41. R. Daumal, "How Everything Begins Again," *Le Contre-Ciel*, p. 142, (= p. 96).
42. R. Daumal, "The Distribution," *Le Contre-Ciel*, p. 127; (= p. 177).
43. R. Daumal, "The Powers of the Word in Hindu Poetics," *The Powers of the Word*, p. 121.
44. R. Daumal, "The Panic Sweat," *Le Contre-Ciel*, p. 94; (= p. 136).
45. R. Daumal, letter to J. Paulhan, in Random, "Le Grand Jeu."
46. R. Daumal, "The Last Words of the Poet," *Le Contre-Ciel*, p. 193.
47. Ibid., p. 195.
48. Gurdjieff, *All and Everything*, p. 249.
49. R. Daumal, "The Holy War," p. 13.
50. Ibid.
51. Ibid.
52. R. Daumal, "Black Poetry, White Poetry," *The Powers of the Word*, p. 156.
53. Ibid., p. 157.
54. R. Daumal, "The Poet's Warning," *Le Contre-Ciel*, p. 3.
55. Ibid.
56. Maurice Desselle, letter to the author, January, 1996.
57. R. Daumal, "Some French Poets of the 25th Century," *The Powers of the Word*, p. 148; (= *Essais et Notes, L'Evidence Absurde II*, p. 99).
58. R. Daumal, "Between Two Stools," *The Powers of the Word*, p. 115; (= *Essais et Notes, L'Evidence Absurde II*, p. 147).
59. George Quasha, personal interview, 1997.
60. R. Daumal, "Black Poetry, White Poetry," *The Powers of the Word*, p. 156.
61. R. Daumal, "The Four Cardinal Seasons" *Le Contre-Ciel*, p. 217.
62. Ibid.
63. R. Daumal, "Willed Fire," *Le Contre-Ciel*, p. 61; (= p. 89).
64. R. Daumal, "The Four Cardinal Seasons," *Le Contre Ciel*, p. 217.
65. Ibid.
66. Ibid.

Chapter 11. La Grand Beuverie

1. R. Daumal, "Letter from New York," *Argile*, p. 33.
2. Ibid., p. 32.
3. Ibid., p. 33.
4. Phil Powrie, in R. Daumal, *Une Etude d'une Obsession*, p. 46.
5. R. Daumal, review of Rabelais's *Complete Works*, in *La Nouvelle Revue Française*, p. 1031.
6. Marcel Lobet, "L'Expérience spirituelle de René Daumal."
7. R. Daumal, *A Night of Serious Drinking*, pp. 22–23. R. Daumal, *La Grande Beuverie*, p. 45. In subsequent references, page numbers in parentheses will refer to the French version.
8. Rabelais, *Gargantua*, p. 42.
9. R. Daumal, *A Night of Serious Drinking*, p. 19; (= p. 39).
10. *Sahitya Darpana*, in "To Approach the Hindu Poetic Art," in R. Daumal, *Rasa*, p. 82.
11. R. Daumal, *A Night of Serious Drinking*, p. 9; (= pp. 19–20).
12. Ibid., p. 48; (= p. 89).
13. Ibid., p. 45; (= p. 82).
14. Ibid., p. 46; (= p. 85).
15. Ibid., p. 49; (= p. 90).
16. R. Daumal, letter quoted in Accarias, *Retour à Soi*, p. 183.
17. R. Daumal, *A Night of Serious Drinking*, pp. 71–72; (= p. 129).
18. Ibid., p. 62; (= p. 113).
19. Gurdjieff, *All and Everything*, p. 504.
20. R. Daumal, *A Night of Serious Drinking*, p. 53.
21. Ibid., p. 54; (= p. 98).
22. Ibid., p. 56; (= p. 101).
23. Ibid., p. 26; (= p. 51).
24. Ibid., p. 43; (= p. 78).
25. Ibid., p. 90; (= p. 159).
26. Ibid.
27. Ibid.
28. Ibid., p. 59; (= p. 107).
29. Ibid., p. 103; (= p. 182).
30. Ibid., p. 104; (= p. 183).
31. Ibid., pp. 5, 13 (= pp. 15, 28).
32. Ibid., p. 36; (= p. 64).
33. Ibid., p. 20; (= p. 40).
34. R. Daumal, "Bharata," in *Bharata*, p. 51.
35. R. Daumal letter, quoted in Helen Maxwell, "Regarding La Grande Beuverie," in Accarias, *Retour à Soi*, p. 174.

36. "The Holy War," *Parabola* p. 12.
37. R. Daumal, *A Night of Serious Drinking*, p. 17.
38. Ibid., p. 1.
39. Charles Duit, "Notes Inédites," quoted in Michael Waldberg, *Gurdjieff: An Approach to His Ideas*, p. 21.
40. Ibid., p. 22.
41. Ibid., p. 24.
42. Gurdjieff, *All and Everything*, Introduction.
43. Jean Richer, "Sur le sentier de la Montagne: René Daumal, conteur," *Hermès* (Spring 1967) :91.
44. R. Daumal, "Bharata," in *Bharata*, p. 51.
45. R. Daumal, *A Night of Serious Drinking*, p. 20; (= p. 41).
46. Ibid., p. 107; (= p. 191).
47. Ibid.
48. R. Daumal, *A Night of Serious Drinking* p. 108; (= p. 192).
49. Gurdjieff, quoted in Ouspensky, *In Search*, p. 58.
50. R. Daumal, *A Night of Serious Drinking*, p. 109; (= p. 194).
51. Ibid., p. 111, 112; (= p. 200).
52. Ibid.
53. Ibid.
54. Ibid.

Chapter 12. Mount Analogue

1. R. Daumal, letter to Renéville, *Hermès* 5 (1967): 93.
2. R. Daumal, quoted in Rosenblatt, "Interior Resonances: A Conversation with Jack Daumal," *Parabola*, p. 90.
3. R. Daumal, *Mount Analogue*, p. 40. R. Daumal, *Le Mont Analogue*, p. 15. (In subsequent references, page numbers in parentheses will refer to the French version.)
4. Jan Gonda, *Vedic Literature*, p. 43.
5. R. Daumal, *Mount Analogue*, p. 42; (= p. 18).
6. Andre Rousseau, "L'Avènenment de René Daumal," *Littérature du vingtième siècle*, p. 67.
7. R. Daumal, "Nerval the Nyctalope," *The Powers of the Word*, p. 38.
8. R. Daumal, *Mount Analogue*, p. 40; (= pp. 14, 19).
9. Ibid., p. 46; (= p. 27).
10. Ibid.
11. R. Daumal, *Correspondance*, Vol. 3, p. 57.
12. R. Daumal, *Mount Analogue*, p. 49; (p. 34).
13. Ibid.
14. Ibid., p. 52; (= p. 39).
15. Ibid., p. 59; (= p. 37).

16. Ibid., p. 51; (= p. 40).
17. Ibid., p. 52; (= p. 40).
18. Ibid., p. 67; (= p. 67).
19. Ibid., p. 76; (= p. 84).
20. Ibid., p. 88; (= p. 110).
21. Ibid., p. 89; (= p. 112).
22. Ibid., p. 89; (= p. 113).
23. Ibid., p. 90; (= p. 114).
24. Ibid., p. 97; (= p. 128–29).
25. Ibid., p. 99; (= p. 134).
26. Dante, *The Divine Comedy* 4, v. 27–29.
27. Gospel of John 12:24.
28. R. Daumal, *Mount Analogue*, p. 100; (= p. 135).
29. Ibid., p. 91; (= p. 117).
30. Ibid., p. 83; (= p. 128).
31. Ibid.
32. Ibid.
33. Ibid., p. 84; (= p. 101).
34. Ibid., pp. 84–85; (= p. 103).
35. Ibid.
36. Ibid.
37. Ibid.
38. R. Daumal, "Lettres de la Montagne," *Argile*, p. 184.
39. Ibid., p. 192.
40. R. Daumal, *Mount Analogue*, p. 104; (= p. 141).
41. Ibid., p. 106; (= p. 144).
42. Ibid., p. 116; (− p. 163).
43. Ibid., p. 89; (= p. 113).
44. Ibid., p. 120; (= p. 175).
45. Ouspensky, *In Search of the Miraculous*, p. 222.
46. R. Daumal, letter to Dessaignes, in Sigoda, *René Daumal*, p. 233.
47. Vera Daumal, in *Mount Analogue*, additional notes, p. 112.

Bibliography

Accarias, Jean Louis. *René Daumal, ou le Retour à Soi.* Paris: Editions l'Originel, 1981.
Aragon Louis. "La Révolution d'abord et toujours," *La Révolution Surréaliste* 5 (August 1925).
Attal, Jean Pierre. "René Daumal et le veritable emploi de la parole." *Critique*, 1968.
Balakian, Anna. *André Breton.* New York: Oxford University Press, 1971.
———. *The Literary Origins of Surrealism.* New York: New York University Press, 1947.
———. *Surrealism: The Road to the Absolute.* New York: Noonday Press, 1959.
de Barry, Theodore, ed. *Sources of Indian Tradition.* Vols. 1 and 2. New York: Columbia University Press, 1958.
Baudelaire, Charles. "Correspondances," *Anthology of French Poetry*, ed. Angel Flores. New York: Doubleday, 1958, p. 297.
———. *Les Paradis Artificiels.* Paris: Gallimard, 1964.
Berman, Morris. *Coming to Our Senses.* New York: Simon and Schuster, 1989.
Bhagavad Gita, by Vyasa. Trans. Franklin Edgerton. Cambridge: Harvard University Press, 1972.
Biès, Jean. *René Daumal.* Paris: Editions Seghers, 1967.
Blair, Chauncey J. *Heat in the "Rig Veda" and "Arthava Veda."* New Haven, Conn.: American Oriental Society, 1961.
Blake, William. *The Poetry and Prose of William Blake.* Ed. David V. Erdman. New York: Doubleday, 1970.
Bosco, Henri. "Trois Rencontres." *La Nouvelle Revue Française*, November 1951.
Boue, Pascal, "Le narrateur et ses doubles dans *La grande beuverie* de René Daumal." *Le Mirail*, Spring 1988.

Bowie, Malcolm. "Raising the Glass." *The Listener*, 22 November 1979.
Breton, André. *Anthologie d'humour noir*. Paris: Sagittaire, 1940.
———. *Manifestes du Surréalisme*. Paris: Gallimard, 1967.
———. *Les Pas Perdus*. Paris: Gallimard, 1970.
———. "René Guénon, jugé par le Surréalisme." *La Nouvelle Revue Française*, July 1953.
———. *Les Vases Communicantes*. 4th ed. Paris: Gallimard, 1970.
Brihadaranyaka Upanishad. Trans. Robert Ernest Hume. London: Oxford University Press, 1979.
Brochier, Jean-Jacques. *L'Aventure des Surréalistes, 1914–1940*. Paris: Editions Stock, 1977.
Camille, Georgette, "René Daumal et le Grand Jeu." In *René Daumal, L'Age d'Hommes*, edited by Pascal Sigoda. Paris: Dossiers H, 1993.
Chaitanya, Krishna. *Sanskrit Poetics*. New York: Asia Publishing House, 1965.
Ciordeau, Jean Claude. *Théorie de la connaissance et philosophie de la parole dans le Brahmanisme classique*. Paris: Mouton, 1964.
Clancier, Georges Emmanuel. *De Rimbaud au surréalisme*. Paris: Editions Seghers, 1959.
Coomaraswamy, Ananda. "The Theory of Art in Asia." In *Introduction to the Art of Eastern Asia*. Palo Alto, Calif.: Stanford Academic Reprints, 1953.
Dante Alighieri. *The Divine Comedy*. Baltimore: Penguin, 1963.
Daumal, Jack, ed. *Cahiers Daumal*. Nos. 1–7. Cairo: L'Organization Egyptienne Générale du Livre, Corniche du Nil, 1987–1994.
———. Letter to author, 1992.
Daumal, René. *Bharata, L'Origine du Théâtre, la Poésie et la Musique en Inde*. Paris: Gallimard, 1970.
———. *Chaque fois que l'aube paraît: Essais et notes*. Paris: Gallimard, 1953.
———. *Le Contre-Ciel*. Paris: Gallimard: 1970.
———. *Le Contre-Ciel*. Trans. Kelton Knight. New York: P. Lang, 1990.
———. *Correspondance*. Vol. 1, 1915–1928. Paris: Gallimard, 1992.
———. *Correspondance*. Vol. 2, 1929–1932. Paris: Gallimard, 1993.
———. *Correspondance*. Vol. 3, 1934–1944. Paris: Gallimard, 1996.
———. *Critique de la raison impure; et les paralipomènes de la comédie psychologique, composés sous forme de dialogues avec Joe Boussquet et René Daumal*. Brussels: Stock, 1955.
———. *Essais et Notes, L'Evidence Absurde*, Tome I (1926–1934), Paris: Gallimard, 1972.
———. *Essais et Notes, Les Pouvoirs de la Parole*, Tome II (1935–1943), Paris: Gallimard, 1972.
———. *Fragments Inédits de La Grande Beuverie*. Paris: Editions Eolienne, 1996.

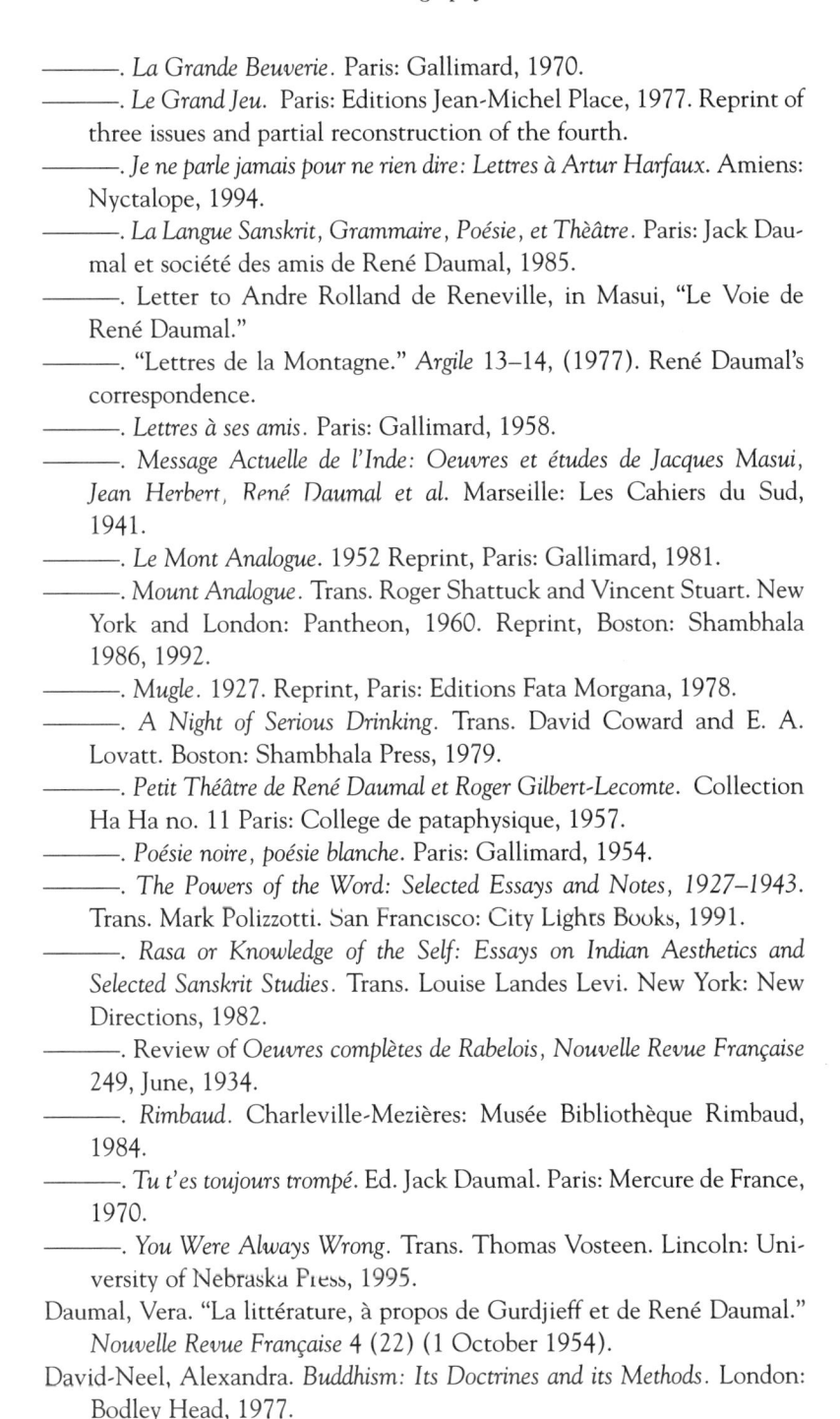

———. *La Grande Beuverie*. Paris: Gallimard, 1970.

———. *Le Grand Jeu*. Paris: Editions Jean-Michel Place, 1977. Reprint of three issues and partial reconstruction of the fourth.

———. *Je ne parle jamais pour ne rien dire: Lettres à Artur Harfaux*. Amiens: Nyctalope, 1994.

———. *La Langue Sanskrit, Grammaire, Poésie, et Thèâtre*. Paris: Jack Daumal et société des amis de René Daumal, 1985.

———. Letter to Andre Rolland de Reneville, in Masui, "Le Voie de René Daumal."

———. "Lettres de la Montagne." *Argile* 13–14, (1977). René Daumal's correspondence.

———. *Lettres à ses amis*. Paris: Gallimard, 1958.

———. *Message Actuelle de l'Inde: Oeuvres et études de Jacques Masui, Jean Herbert, René Daumal et al*. Marseille: Les Cahiers du Sud, 1941.

———. *Le Mont Analogue*. 1952 Reprint, Paris: Gallimard, 1981.

———. *Mount Analogue*. Trans. Roger Shattuck and Vincent Stuart. New York and London: Pantheon, 1960. Reprint, Boston: Shambhala 1986, 1992.

———. *Mugle*. 1927. Reprint, Paris: Editions Fata Morgana, 1978.

———. *A Night of Serious Drinking*. Trans. David Coward and E. A. Lovatt. Boston: Shambhala Press, 1979.

———. *Petit Théâtre de René Daumal et Roger Gilbert-Lecomte*. Collection Ha Ha no. 11 Paris: College de pataphysique, 1957.

———. *Poésie noire, poésie blanche*. Paris: Gallimard, 1954.

———. *The Powers of the Word: Selected Essays and Notes, 1927–1943*. Trans. Mark Polizzotti. San Francisco: City Lights Books, 1991.

———. *Rasa or Knowledge of the Self: Essays on Indian Aesthetics and Selected Sanskrit Studies*. Trans. Louise Landes Levi. New York: New Directions, 1982.

———. Review of *Oeuvres complètes de Rabelois*, *Nouvelle Revue Française* 249, June, 1934.

———. *Rimbaud*. Charleville-Mezières: Musée Bibliothèque Rimbaud, 1984.

———. *Tu t'es toujours trompé*. Ed. Jack Daumal. Paris: Mercure de France, 1970.

———. *You Were Always Wrong*. Trans. Thomas Vosteen. Lincoln: University of Nebraska Press, 1995.

Daumal, Vera. "La littérature, à propos de Gurdjieff et de René Daumal." *Nouvelle Revue Française* 4 (22) (1 October 1954).

David-Neel, Alexandra. *Buddhism: Its Doctrines and its Methods*. London: Bodley Head, 1977.

De, S. K. *History of Sanskrit Poetics*. Calcutta: Oriental Press, 1960.

———. *Sanskrit Poetics as a Study of Aesthetics*. Berkeley and Los Angeles: University of California Press, 1963.

Defourny, Michel. "Des phrères simplistes au *Grand Jeu*, une page d'histoire littéraire." *Marche Romane* 21 (1971).

Dessaignes, Ribemont. "Entretien." *L'Originel*, December 1978.

Deussen, Paul. *The Philosophy of the Upanishads*. New York: Dover Press, 1965.

Didier, Alexandre. "Frontières de René Daumal." *Courrier du centre internationale de la poésie, Maison internationale de la poésie*, September–October 1987.

Dort, Bernard. "Un penseur révolutionnaire." *Cahiers du Sud* 322 (1953).

Driscoll, Walter. *Gurdjieff: An Annotated Bibliography*. New York: Garland, 1985.

Edgerton, Franklin. *Beginnings of Indian Philosophy: Selections from the "Rig Veda," "Arthava Veda," "Upanishads," and "Mahabharata"*. London: Allen and Unwin, 1965.

Esslin, Martin. *The Theater of the Absurd*. New York: Anchor Books, 1961.

Etiemble, H. "René Daumal: *Le Mont Analogue*." *La Nouvelle Revue Française*, January 1953.

Gerow, Edwin. *A History of Indian Literature*. Wiesbaden: Otto Harrassowitz, 1977.

Gide, André. *Les Nourritures Terrestres*. Paris: Gallimard, 1897.

———. *La Porte Etroite*. Paris: Mercure de France, 1909.

Gilbert-Lecomte, Roger. *Correspondance*. Paris: Gallimard, 1971.

Gonda, Jan. *Vedic Literature*. Wiesbaden, Germany: Otto Harrassowitz, 1975.

Gros, Leon-Gabriel. "René Daumal et Le Grand Jeu." Special edition, *Cahiers du Sud* 28, March, 1954.

Guénon, René. *Aperçus sur l'initiation*. Paris: Vega, 1928.

———. *La Crise du monde moderne*. Paris: Editions Bossard, 1927.

———. *East and West*. Trans. William Massey. London: Luzac, 1941.

———. *Etudes sur le franc maçonnière*. Vol. 2. Paris: Vega, 1941.

———. *La Grande Triade*. Paris: Gallimard, 1957.

———. *L'Homme et son devenir selon la Vedanta*. Paris: Editions Traditionelles, 1974.

———. *Initiation et réalisation spirituelle*. Paris: Editions Traditionnelles, Quai Saint Michel, 1980.

———. *Introduction to the Study of Hindu Doctrines*. Paris: Vega, 1925.

———. *Le Règne de la quantité et les signes des temps*. Paris: Gallimard, 1945.

———. *Symboles fondamentaux de la science sacrée*. Paris: Vega, 1929.

———. *Le Théosophisme, Histoire d'une Pseudoreligion*. Paris: Villain et Belhomme, 1969.

Guiomar, Michel. "Aux jeux des vents et des saisons." Review of *René Daumal au dela de l'horizon*, by K. Rosenblatt. *Arts Sciences Techniques, Connaissance des Hommes* 5 (1992).

Gurdjieff, George. *All and Everything: Beelzebub's Tales to His Grandson*. New York: Dutton, 1950.

——— *Life Is Real Only Then When I Am*. New York: Dutton, 1978.

———. *Meetings with Remarkable Men*. New York: Dutton, 1970.

———. *Views from the Real World: Early Talks of Gurdjieff*. New York: Dutton, 1973.

Hartley, Anthony, *The Penguin Book of French Verse*. New York: Penguin Books, 1969.

Hughes, H. Stewart. *Consciousness and Society*. New York: Alfred Knopf, 1961.

Jarry, Alfred. *Selected Works of Alfred Jarry*. Ed. Roger Shattuck and Simon Watson Taylor. New York: Grove Press, 1965.

Kane, P. V., *History of Sanskrit Poetics*. Delhi: Motilal Banarsidass, 1965.

La Grive. 135/136 (July/December, 1967). Special edition on René Daumal.

Lavastine, Philippe. Interview with author, 1977.

———. "René Daumal, du Grand Jeu à Gurdjieff." *Nouvelle Revue Française* 22 (1 October 1954).

———. "Vedanta." *Material for Thought* (Spring, 1974).

Lecomte, Marcel. "Chronique littéraire d'une littérature initiatique." *Synthèse* 12 (August–September, 1957).

———. "L'Expérience spirituelle de René Daumal." *Le Journal de Poètes* (February, 1959).

Lepage, Jacques. "'L'Asphyxie et l'évidence absurde' de René Daumal." *Courrier du centre internationale d'études poétiques, Maison internationale de la poésie* (16 September 1971).

———. "Un poète de la connaissance." *Le Bayou* (1962).

———. "A propos de René Daumal." *Courrier du centre international d'études poétiques, Maison Internationale de la poésie* (19 March 1973).

Leveque, Jean-Jacques. "Une quête romantique dans les années vingt." *Le Quotidien des Livres* (January 1993).

Lobet, Marcel. "L'Expérience spirituelle de René Daumal." *Revue Générale Belge* (April 1968).

Mahabharata. Trans. Chakravarthi V. Narasimhan. New York: Columbia University Press, 1965.

Mandukya Upanishad. Trans. Robert Ernest Hume. London: Oxford University Press, 1979.

Manusmriti (The Laws of Manu). Trans. Ganganatha Jha. Calcutta: University of Calcutta, 1920–1926.

Masui, Jacques. "René Daumal et l'Inde." *Cahiers du Sud* 322 (1954). Special issue, including poems, letters, and translations by Daumal.

Masui, Jacques, ed. "La Voie de René Daumel, du Grand Jeu au Mont Analogue." *Hermés: Recherches sur l'expérience spirituelle* 5 (Spring 1967). Special Edition.

Mead, Gerald, *The Surrealist Image: A Stylistic Study*. Las Vagas: Peter Lang Publishers, 1978.

Miguel, André. "Revolte, négation, et abnégation chez René Daumal." *Courrier du Centre International d'Etudes Poétique, Maison Internationale de la poésie* 175 (September– October, 1987).

Milosz, O. V. *Ars Magna*. Paris: Editions Alice Sauerivein, 1924.

Miller, Max. *Sacred Books of the East*. Vol. 42. Delhi: Motilal Banarsidass, 1897–1979.

Moore, James. *Gurdjieff: The Anatomy of a Myth*. Shaftsbury, U.K.: Element Books, 1991.

———. *Gurdjieff and Mansfield*. London, Boston, and Henley: Routledge and Kegan Paul, 1980.

Nadeau, Maurice. *The History of Surrealism*. New York: Collier Books, 1965.

Needleman, Jacob. *The Heart of Philosophy*. New York: Alfred A. Knopf, 1982.

———. *Lost Christianity*. New York: Doubleday, 1980.

O'Flaherty, Wendy Doniger. "Hard and Soft Reality." *Parabola* 7(2), (Spring 1982).

L'Originel 7 (December 1978). Special edition on Le Grand Jeu.

Ouspensky, P. D. *A New Model of the Universe*. New York: Alfred A. Knopf, 1961.

———. *In Search of the Miraculous: Fragments of an Unknown Teaching*. New York: Harcourt, Brace and World, 1949.

de Panafieu, Bruno. "Georges Ivanovitch Gurdjieff." In *René Daumal, L'Age d'Homme*, edited by Pascal Sigoda. Paris: Editions Dossiers H, 1993.

Paulhan, Jean. *Les Fleurs de Tarbes*. Paris: Gallimard, 1941.

Perin, Luc, Lettre à *Le Grive*, 136, 1967 p.19.

Powrie, Phil. *René Daumal, L'Etude d'une obsession*. Geneva: Drox, 1992.

———. *René Daumal and Roger Gilbert-Lecomte: A Bibliography*. London: Grant and Cutler, 1988.

Quasha, George. *Giving the Lily Back Her Hands*. Barrytown, N.Y.: Station Hill Press, 1979.

Rabelais, François. *Oeuvres Complètes*. Paris: Gallimard, 1955.

Random, Michel. "Le Grand Jeu." *Essai*, 1970.

———. *Les puissances du dedans*. Paris: Editions Denoel, 1966.

Reymond, Liselle. *To Live Within*. New York: Penguin, 1973.

Reyner, J. H. *Gurdjieff in Action*. London: George Allen and Unwin, 1981.

Rahv, Philip. *Literature and the Sixth Sense*. Boston: Houghton Mifflin, 1969.

Ravindra, Ravi, "Gurdjieff et l'enseignement de Krishna." In *George Ivanovich Gurdjieff L'Age d'Hommes*, edited by Bruno de Panafien. Paris: Editions Dossiers H, 1992.

Rig Veda. Ed. Ralph Griffith. Delhi: Motilal Banarsidass, 1973.

Rolland de Réneville, Alain. *Rimbaud le voyant*. Paris: René Hilsum and Cie, 1929.

———. "Souvenir de René Daumal." *Cahiers du Sud* 272 (1945).

Rosenblatt, Kathleen. "Interior Resonances: A Conversation with Jack Daumal." *Parabola* 12(4) (1988).

———. Review of *Rasa*, by René Daumal. *Parabola* 7 (1983).

Rosset, Barney, ed. *Evergreen Review Reader: A Ten-Year Anthology* New York: Grove Press, 1968.

Roudaut, Jean. "Sur le chemin de René Daumal." *Critique*, May 1959.

Rousseaux, André. "L'Ascension du Mont Analogue." *Le Figaro Litteraire* 316 (10 May 1952).

———. *Littérature du vingtième siècle*. Paris: Editions Albin Michel, 1955.

———. "L'Oeuvre en marche de René Daumal." *Le Figaro Litteraire* December 1954.

de Salzmann, Michel. "Footnotes to the Gurdjieff Literature." In *Gurdjieff: An Annotated Bibliography* by J. Walter Driscoll. New York: Garland Publishers, 1985.

———. "The Search for Lucidity." *Parabola* 7 (1983).

———. "Seeing: The Endless Source of Inner Freedom." *Material for Thought* 14 (1995).

Satprakashananda. *Methods of Knowledge—Perceptual, Nonperceptual and Transcendental—According to Advaita Vedanta*. London: Allen and Unwin, 1965.

Schaeffer, Pierre, "Maître de'danse." *Dossier* (1977). Special issue on Gurdjieff.

Seghers, Pierre, ed. *La résistance et les poètes (1940–1945)*. Paris: Editions Seghers, 1974.

Shah, Idries. *Tales of the Dervishes*. New York: Dutton, 1970.

Shattuck, Roger. *The Banquet Years*. New York: Vintage Books, 1968.

Shattuck, Roger, and Simon Taylor. *Selected Works of Alfred Jarry*. New York: Grove Press, 1965.

Sigoda, Pascal, ed. Catalogue devoted to René Daumal. Exposition de Charleville-Mezières. Bibliothèque de Charleville, May, 1984.
———. *René Daumal et ses abords immediats.* Paris: 1994.
———. *René Daumal, L'Age d'Homme.* Paris: Editions Dossiers H, 1993.
Swift, Jonathan. *Gulliver's Travels.* New York: Harper and Row, 1970.
Taittirya Upanishad. Trans. Robert Ernst Hume. London: Oxford University Press, 1979.
Tison-Braun, Micheline. *Dada et le surréalisme.* Paris: Bibliothèque Bordas, 1973.
Tiwari, Kapil. *Dimensions of Renunciation in Advaita Vedanta.* Delhi: Motilal Banarsidass, 1977.
Tremolières, François. "Le Mont Analogue." *La Nouvelle Review Française* July–August, 1981.
Upanishads. Trans. Swami Nikhilananda. New York: Harper and Brothers, 1952.
Vailland, Roger. *Le Surréalisme Contre la Révolution.* Paris: Editions sociales, 1948.
Vazken I, Catholicos. *An Introduction to the Armenian Liturgy.* Trans. Tilo Ulbricht and Vartoug Gulbenkian. London: privately published, 1992.
Virmaux, Alain, and Odette Virmaux. *Roger Gilbert-Lecomte et le Grand Jeu.* Paris: Les Dossiers Belfond, 1981.
Visvanatha Kaviraja. *Sahitya-Darpana.* Ed. G. D. Ballantyne. Calcutta: Biblioteca Indica, 1851, 1875.
Vosteen, Thomas. "L'Inconnu Daumal et le Grand Jeu." *Oeuvres et Critiques* 18 (1–2)(1993).
Waldberg, Michel. *Gurdjieff: An Approach to His Ideas.* Trans. Steve Cox. London: Routledge and Kegan Paul, 1981.
Weil, Simone. "Deux lettres de Simone Weil." *Cahiers de Simone Weil.* Paris: Plon, 1978.
Wilson, Colin. *The War Against Sleep: The Philosophy of Gurdjieff.* Wellingborough, U.K.: Aquarian Press, 1980.
Wilson, Edmund. *Axel's Castle.* New York: Charles Scribner's Sons, 1959.
Wilson, Erica. "Metaphysical Laws in the Cosmology of G. I. Gurdjieff." Unpublished paper, 1992.
Wood, Michael. "The Great Game." *The New York Review of Books,* 17 April 1980.

Index

Absurd dream, the, 57
Absurd Evidence (or absurd obviousness), 9, 36–37, 77.
    See also Jarry, Alfred
Absurdity
    of the Communist Party, 73–74
    duality and, 53–56
    of existence, 46, 51, 134, 162, 163
Accarias, Jean Louis, xviii
Action(s), 89–90
Advaita Vedanta, 89–90, 175
Aeneid, The, 57
Aesthetic experience (*rasavadana*), 119–120.
    See also Rasa (savor)
Age of Perfection, 117
Agnosticism, 9
Albigensian crusade, 94
All and Everything, 87, 137, 185, 193
Ambiguity, 46
Amnesia, 9–10
Anarchism, 71–72, 102
Anarchists, of perception, 10
Angel(s), visionary, 8, 17
Anthologie des Philosophes Contemporains, 14
Anticulture, 51
Antiliterature, 51
Antireligiosity, 5
Anti-Sorbonne, 68
A propos d'Uday Shankar (Concerning Uday Shankar), 122
Aragon, Louis, 45, 51, 73, 77
Argile (periodical), 20
Aristotle, 22
Ars Magna, 38
Art
    and artistic elite, 51
    and Bharata's *Treatise on the Theater*, 116–117
    and caste, 117–118
    and communism, 71–79, 76
    and consciousness, 136–137, 174
    individualism in, 98
    and music, 122–123
    of openness/readiness (*la disponibilité*), 18, 23, 53
    poetry and, xiv, 44–45, 117–118, 122–123
    and religion, 45
    and spiritual reality, xv
    and style, 123
    and truth/sacred laws, 116
Artaud, Antonin, 74, 109
Arthava Veda, 86, 87, 115
The Artificial Paradises, 57
Aruni, 166
Aryan life, 86
Ascension, 87, 97
Asceticism, xiii, 134.
    See also Renunciation
"Asphyxia and Absurd Evidence," 35, 37
Association of Revolutionary Writers and Artists (AEAR), 77
Astral body, 84, 155
Astral projection, 7
Astral state, 8
Astral travel, 61
Atonement, 34
Attention, mindful, xv, 129–130, 134–135
    breathing and, 135
Aura, 85
Austerity, 84, 85, 86, 87
Automatic writing, xiii, 7, 46, 51–53, 68, 107, 170

241

Awakening, spiritual, xiv, 13, 133
  Gurdjieff Work and, 129–130, 136
  and poetry, 161–162
Awareness
  art and, xiv
  death and, 36
  Gurdjieff Work and, 129–130
  seven states of, 34
  surrealism and, 45

Balakian, Anna, 57–58, 97
Balzac, 97
Banquet Years, The, 48
Barry, Theodore de, 87
Baudelaire, Charles, 43, 57, 98, 164–165
Beauty, 78, 119–120
Beelzebub's Tales to His Grandson, 138
Being(s), 86
  aesthetic experience and, 120
  divine, 39
  highly evolved, 37
  manifestations of, 121
  multiple states of, 70
Benda, Julien, 77
Bergson, Henri, 58, 109
Beyond, The (*l'Au-delà*), xii, 35, 109
Bhagavad Gita, 12, 34, 39, 78, 170, 215
  Gurdjieff and, 139
  and nonduality, 83–84
  and renunciation, 89–90
Bharata, xiv, xv, 102–103, 116, 189
Bharata: L'Origine du Théâtre, la Poésie et la Musique Hindoues, 12, 193
Bifur (journal), 14
Black humor, 6, 48, 138
  See also Humor, cult of
Black Poetry, White Poetry, 171, 173, 174, 176, 185–186, 207
Blake, William, 35, 85, 161, 197
Body, transformational, 84–85
Boully, Monny de, 17, 22–23, Fig. 4, 60
  and Le Grand Jeu, 67, 69
  and paraoptics, 63
Bourgeois neurosis, 73
Brahmachari (celibate seeker), 86, 87, 88
Brahman, 90.
  See also God
Breath (*prana*), 166
Breathing techniques (*pranayama*), 131, 134–135
Breton, André, 22, Fig. 7, 45, 47, 51
  and Communism, 73
  and Freud, 57, 58

  and Gurdjieff, 138
  and Le Grande Jeu, 60, 64, 65
  and René Guénon, 105–106, 108–109
  style of, 56
Brhadaranyaka Upanishad, 88, 106
"Brief Revelation on Death and Chaos," 169
Brihadaranyaka Upanishad, 89, 114
Brochier, Jean Jacques, 73, 74
Buber, Martin, 147
Buddha, laughing, 56
Buddhism, xiii, 13, 84, 86, 90, 92, 122
  Gurdjieff Work and, 129–130
"Bureau of Surrrealist Research," 52

Candide, 196
Capitalism, 65, 71
Carbon tetrachloride, ingestion of, xiii, 9, 17, 35
  and tuberculosis, 38
Carriacou Island, xvii
Caste system, 92, 100, 117
Cathars, 94
Catholic Church, 5
Certainty, 35, 38
Chaitanya, Krishna, 117
Chance, 46, 49
Chandogya Upanishad, 106
Charcot, Dr. J. M., 52
Chaveau, Dr. Jacques, 149
Childhood, cult of, 46, 48, 53
  and prenatal states, 60
Christianity, 13, 34, 84, 94
  aims of religion and, 93, 94
  Eastern mysticism and, 97–98
  and Luke XIII, 24, 39
  monkhood and, 86
Christoflour, René, 94, 143
Civilization, xv
Clairvoyance, 60, 62
Clarity (*buddhi*), 120–121
Closed-eye vision, 62–63.
  See also Paraoptics
Cocaine, 9
Colonialism, 71
Commerce (journal), 14
Commitment, total, 43–44
Common man, xii
Communion, spiritual, xiii, 35–36
  and *rasa* (savor/taste), 119–120
  sacrifice and, 84
  Self and, 122.
  See also Oneness

Communism, 71–79
Communist Party, 64, 72, 73
Concentration (*dhyana*), 19, 131, 151
Conscience, 48–49, 74
Consciousness, xi
  art and, xiv, 136–137
  and death, 35–36
  dreams and, 58, 106
  evolution of, 34
  experimentations with, 7–8, 9, 32, 35–39, 60–63
  and Gurdjieff Work, 129–132, 136
  and the moment, 31, 33
  rasa (as emotional consciousness), 117
  state(s) of, 8, 32, 35, 58, 60, 103–104, 106, 107
  and time, 122–123
  and toxic substances, 9, 11, 35–39
  and the Void, 9
  woman's, 59
Consciousness and Society, 72
Contemplation, 88, 177
Contradiction, 53
Coomaraswamy, Ananda, 119–120
Corporal body, 85
"Correspondences," Baudelaire, 98
Creation Hymn (*Nasadiya*), 85
The Crisis of the Modern World, 109

Dadaists, xii, 17, 44, 45
  dualism and, 53–54
Dandoy, Xavier, xviii
Dante, 205
Daumal, Antoine, 4
Daumal, Jack, Fig. 10, xvii, xviii, 3, 15, 78, 92–93, 133
  on Gurdjieff, 149
  on René's introversion, 4
Daumal, Jacqueline, xvii
Daumal, Leon, 3, 6
Daumal, Marianne, 3, 5
Daumal, Miriam, xviii
Daumal, René
  biographical background, xi–xv, Fig. 1, Fig. 9, Fig. 12, Fig. 15, Fig. 16, Fig. 21, Fig. 24, 3–29, 45, 58–59, 147–152, 154–158, 172–178, 179–180, 198–199, 213–216
  books by, xiv
  colleagues of, xv–xvi, 7–8, 10, 12, 16–17, 20–21, 24, 26–27, Fig. 2, Fig. 4, 37, 145
  and communism, 71–79

consciousness-altering experiments and, 7–8, 11, Fig. 3, 35–39
and de Salzmanns, 140–141, 142–143, 144, 146–148
and disillusionment, xiv, 11–12, 72
and Gurdjieff Work, 13, 34, 70, 79, 105, 127–158, 190–196
and Hindu teachings/Hindu poetic influences, 12–13, 19, 20, 34, 36, 83–84, 83–95, 91, 101, 113–124, 142, 173, 175, 193
poetry by, xiv, 19, 59, 78, 92, 93, 145, 161–178, 207
psychic abilities of, xii, 18, 60–61, 63
pupils of, 148, 152–153, 158
and René Guenon, 101–111
and renunciation, xiii, 12, 21, 31–34
sketchings/paintings by, Fig. 22, Fig. 23, Fig. 8, 50
spiritual struggle and, xv, 34, 36, 150–152
and study of Sanskrit, 12–13, 27, 110, 113–116, 173
and surrealism, 45–47, 49–51, 56–59, 109–110, 168–169, 193
translations by, Fig. 15, Fig. 16, 14, 114. *See also* individual works and publications by name; *La Grande Beuverie*; *Le Contre-Ciel*; *Mont Analogue*
Daumal, Vera Milanova, Fig. 4, 13, 15, 23, 26–27, Fig. 9, 59, 153
Daumal, Zélie, 3
Daumal, Jijhad, xviii
David-Neel, Alexandra, 86
De, S. K., 120
Death, 166, 167
  consciousness and, 35–36, 134
  daring/pranks and, 50
  and God, 5
  and René Daumal, 29, 166, 167, 173, 202
  and sleep, 36
  and the Void, 9
"Death and Her Man," 165
"Décalogue de l'Ecrivain," 78
Democracy, 72
Depersonalization, 60
Dermenghen, Emile, 20, 77, 145
Der Rhythmus, 24
Descartes, 34, 102
Desire(s), 32, 90, 163
Desnos, 73
Desselle, Maurice, xviii, 23, 175
Detachment, 11

"The Determining Memory," 35
d'Etiévan, Natalie de Salzmann, xviii, 15, 24
Deussen, Paul, 88
"Dictated in 1925," 169
Dietrich, Luc, Fig. 21, 3, 27–28, 149
Dimension of Renunciation in Advaita Vedanta, 88
Discipline, 22, 89–90
  and Gurdjieff Work, 130–132
  Kwajagans and, 128
Disillusionment, xiv, 11–12, 72, 89
"The Distribution," 171
The Divine Comedy, 205
Doniger O'Flaherty, Wendy, 106
Dream(s), 57–59, 182
  absurdity and, 57
  and automatic writing, 52
  categories of, 57
  experimentation with, 7
  and reality, 106–107
  surrealism and, 45, 51, 57, 106
Dream interpretation, xiii, 46
Dualism, 46, 85, 145
  and the absurd, 53–56, 103
Duit, Charles, 191
Duplessis, Yvonne, 62
Dvija (twice born), 84
Dying, 35

Eckhart, Meister, 93–94
Ecole Normale Supérieure, 9
Ecstasy, 105, 120
Editions Eolien, xviii
Editions José Corti, xvii, 44
Ego, xiii, 134
  and atonement, 34
  freedom from, 11, 16
  self-confrontation and, 13
Eluard, Paul, 45, 73
Emotion (*bhava*), 108, 120
  rasa and, 120–121
Energy concentration, xvi
Engels, 59
"*en gggarrde*," 55
Enlightenment, 87, 97–98
Epic poems (*kavya*), 117
"Epistle to Storge," 38
Equivocal interpretation, 46
Essentuki, 134
Ether, 9
Etheric body, 84

Europe, 69
Existence, xi
  absurdity and, 46, 51, 53–56, 162
  and death, 166–167
  futility of, 11–12
  infinite, 97–98
  and meaninglessness, xii, 56
  qualities (*gunas*) of, xiv
  soul and, 32
Exploits and Opinions of Dr. Faustroll, 48, 181, 193
Extra-retinal vision, 7
Extra-sensory perception, 32, 38, 60–63

"The Famous Surprise," 168
Farce, 49
Fargue, Leon Paul, 48, 189
Fascism, 65, 72
"A Few French Poets of the Twenty-Fifth Century," 175
Finnegans Wake, 192
Fiolle, Jean, 78
Fire, xiv, 84, 86, 120–121, 171, 188
The Fire Within, (Castaneda), xvi
Formalism, 45
Fouchet, Max-Pol, 78
"The Four Cardinal Seasons, 176, 178
Free act (*un acte gratuit*), 32
Freedom, 134
  and action, 33
  personal, 32
"Freedom without Hope," 88
Freemasonry, 4
Freud, 57, 59, 79
  and surrealism, 57–58, 106
Freudian psychology, 46
Friendship, 27–28

Gargantua, 182
Gerow, 119
Gide, André, 14, 17, 18, 39, 104, 161
  on voluptuous action, 19
Gilbert-Lecomte, Roger, xvii, 6, 8, 18, 27, 32, Fig. 2, Fig. 4
  daring/pranks and, 50
  and Le Grand Jeu, 69
  and mysticism, 60
  poetic visions and, 38
  and René Guénon, 110
  and renunciation, 83
  surrealism and, 49, 68

Giraudoux, Jean, 14, 161
Gnosis, 100, 115
Gnosticism, 94
God(s), 5
   Christianity and, 94
   and death, 5
   Hindu poetics and, 114, 121
   individual soul and, 90
   laughter and, 53
   Le Grand Jeu and, 64
   omnipresence of, 18
   religion and, 92–93
   revelation and, 39
   Vedas and, 85
Golden Age, 79
Gonda, Jan, 122, 199
Goodness, 78
Gospel of Saint John, 85
Government, xii
   and separation of church/state, 5
Granville, Pierre, 28
Great Depression, 72, 179
Grenada, xvii
Grhastha (householder), 86
Gros, Léon Gabriel, 74
Guénon, René, Fig. 14, xiii, 12, 32, 37, 46, 99
   and Gurdjieff, 138, 139
   and Oriental philosophy, 100–105
   and poetry, 114
   and surrealism, 105–111
Gulliver's Travels, 181
Gunas (qualities/virtues, of existence), xiv
   rajas (neutral), xiv
   and *rasa*, 120–121
   sattva (positive), xiv
   tamas (negative), xiv
Gurdjieff, George I., Fig. 20, xii, xiv, 13, 71, 124, 127–136, 157, 190
   Alexandre de Salzmann and, 24, 141
   and breathing technique, 135–136
   community/followers, xvi–xviii, 21, 23, 24, 27, 138, 142
   and conscious art, 137, 174
   and the Fourth Way, Fig. 20 (legend), 139
   politics and, 78
   psychic powers and, 131
   and René Guénon, 138
   and wartime feasts, 149
Gurdjieff: The Anatomy of a Myth, 138
Gurdjieff Work, 13, 24, 127–158, 128–129
   and Hindu references, 84–85
   Le Grand Jeu work and, 69–70, 139–140
   and mindfulness/self-observation, 129–130, 136
   and relaxation, 134
   and renunciation, 34
   sacrifice and, 131–132
   and yogic postures/breathing techniques, 131–132
   See also Institute for Harmonious Development
Guru(s), 37, 86, 124

Hallucinatory experience, 9, 36–38, 46
   and suicide, 48
Halo, 85, 87
Happiness, 34, 90
Hartley, Anthony, 45
Hartmann, Thomas de, 137
Hashish, 9
Hasidism, 147
The Heart of Philosophy, 13
Heaven, 5
Hedonism, 69
Hegel, 46, 54, 92, 99
Hell, xiv, 5, 167, 170, 181
Henry, Maurice, 8, 45, 47, 170
Heraclitus, 92
Herbert, Jean, 21
Hermès, 110
Hinduism, xiii, xiv, 84, 91, 103, 123
Hindu philosophy, 12–13, 78, 83, 89–90, 102
   and Oneness, 36
   and poetics, 113–115, 116–124
   and *rasa*, 119–122
   and renunciation, 34, 83–95
   Sankya and, 19, 20
   study of, xi, xiii, 12–13, 97–98, 99, 113–124, 142
   yoga and, Fig. 12, 60.
   See also Philosophy; Sanskrit
History of Surrealism, 48
Hitlerism, 72
"The Holy War," 170, 173, 205
"How Everything Begins Again," 171
Hughes, H. Stuart, 72
Humility, 22
Humor, 46, 48, 50, 154, 170, 176
   Hindu poetics and, 121
   pataphysical laughter and, 53, 54.
   See also Black humor
Humor and Its Relation to the Unconscious, 57

Huxley, Aldous, 10
Hypnosis, 62
Hypocrite, 89
Hysteria, 52

Idealism, 71
Idealization (*sadharanikarana*), 177
Identification, 133
Illuminism, 97–98
Illusion (*maya*), 19, 33, 85, 90–91, 164
  religion and, 94
Imagination, 108, 155
  and sacrifice, 131–132
  and suffering, 132–133
Immortality, 99
Impermanence, 53
India, 99, 123
Individual
  and consciousness, 32
  Hindu tradition of renunciation and, 86–87, 90–91
  and soul, xiii, 35–36, 90
  and style, 123
  and Universal Principle, 36–37
Individualism
  and duality, 54
  imbecility of, 8, 31
  Symbolists and, 98
  yogi and, 104–105
Industrialism, 71
Infinity, 5, 6, 38, 134
Initiation, 87, 106
Inner Circle of Humanity, 128, 203
In Search of the Miraculous, 71
Institute for Harmonious Development, 24, 129–130.
  See also Gurdjieff Work
Intellectualizing, xiv, xv, 122
An Introduction to the Study of Hindu Doctrines, 12, 101
Introspection, 90
Introversion, 72
Intuition, 7, 37, 47, 101
  aesthetic experience and, 119–120
  pure, 120
  René Guénon and, 106
  woman's, 59
Intuitionism, 109
Ionesco, Eugene, 55
Irreverence, 55–56
Islam, 13

Isolation, 32, 33
"It Only Takes a Word," 161

Jainism, 92
James, William, 109
Jarry, Alfred, 7, 10, 32, Fig. 5, 44, 47, 79
  absurd humor and, 48, 54
  and *La Grande Beuverie*, 48, 181.
  See also Pataphysics
Jnana. *See* Knowledge, sacred
Journal of the College of Pataphysics, 56
Joyce, James, 192
Judaism, 13, 122
Jugend (review), 24

Kabir, 121
Kali-Yuga, age of, 115, 116, 183
Karma-sannyasa (action-renunciation), 90.
  See also Renunciation
kavi (poet/priest), xiii, 114
"The Keys to a Great Poetic Game," 162, 168, 175, 207
Knowledge, sacred (*jnana*), 88, 89
  and introspection, 90
  mantra and, 115
  and *rasa* (as emotional consciousness), 117
  selfless action and, 90
Kramer, Hendrick, 15, 27, 60
Krishnamurti, 23, 105
Kwajagans, 128

"La Bête Noire," 105
la disponibilité (openess/readiness), 18, 22, 53, 59
La Grande Beuverie (A Night of Serious Drinking), xii, xiv, 14, 26, 172–173
  characters in, 19, 48, 183–190, 194–195, 205, 215–216
  gunas qualities and, xiv
  mind experimentation and, 9, 39–40
  nonsensical pataphysics and, 55
  parody and, 105, 183, 185
  and renunciation, 188
  style of, 189–196
La Grande Triade, 199
La Langue Sanscrite, 14
Lamartine, 97
"La Mort du Grand Jeu," 78

Lams, Marianne, 68
Langherhans, Emily, 148
La Nouvelle Revue Française (journal), 14
La Porte Etroite (The Narrow Door), 39
"La Révolte et l'ironie," 34
"La Révolution et les intéllectuals," 74
La Révolution Surréaliste, 47, 52, 57, 73
"The Last Words of the Poet, 173
Laughter, 53, 54
Lautréamont, Lecomte de, 57
Lavastine, Philippe, Fig. 11, xvi, 15, 21, 22, 23, 58
  and Gurdjieff, 143, 149
  and multiplicity, 104
  and Vedanta, 90–91
L'Aventure des Surréalistes, 73
"La Vision Extrarétinienne," 62
La Vision Extrarétinienne et le Sens paroptique, 62
Laws of Manu, The, 92
Le Contre-Ciel (The Counter-Heaven), xii, 14, 55, 161–162, 189
  gunas qualities and, xiv
  and *Prix Jacques Doucet*, xiii, 14, 161
Le Grand Jeu (The Big Game), xiii, 9, 11, 21, Fig. 8, 114, 179–196
  and absurdity of life, 53
  and André Breton, 60, 64, 65
  context for, 32, 43–44
  disintegration of, 68–69
  final meeting of, 13
  Gurdjieff and, 139–140
  inception of, 10
  members of/contributors to, 10, 13, 15, 17, 32, Fig. 4, 37, 60, 69, 74, 127
  and politics, 72, 73, 74
  publications, 44, 62, 65–67, 72, 102
  and religion(s), 83
  and René Guénon, 110
  surrealism and, 43–70, 64–70
l'Encyclopédie Francaise, 14
Le Quotidien des Livres, 10
Les Cahiers du Sud (journal), 14, 69, 99, 123
Les Grands Initiés (The Great Initiates), 98
Les Nourritures Terrestres (The Fruits of the Earth), 17, 18, 22, 104
Les Nouvelles Littéraires, 69
"Les Phrères Simplistes," 7, 8, Fig. 2
  and founding of *Le Grand Jeu*, 43–44
  and Pataphysics, 10, 50
  and surrealism, 45–46, 47, 50

Le Surmâle (The Supermale), 48
Le Surréalisme au Service de la Révolution, 57
Les Vases Communicants, 57–58
"Lettres de la montagne," 20
Leveque, Jean-Jacques, 10
L'Evidence Absurde, 9
L'Expérience spirituelle de Daumal et l'Inde (The Spiritual Experience of Daumal and India), 31
Lief, Geneviève, xvi, 25, 27, 110, 148, 156
Lief, Louis, 25, 27, 152, 155
Listening, 21–22, 56, 122–123, 171
Literary Origins of Surrealism, The, 97
Literature and the Sixth Sense, 73
"Living in a Surreality", 48
Lobet, Marcel, 181–182
Logic, 46, 99
L'Originel, 62
Lost Christianity, 94
Love, 58–59, 163, 164
Lucid dreaming, 7
Lycee at Reims, 6
Lycée Chanzy, 6
Lycée Henry IV, 9, 61

Maeterlinck, 7
Magic, 46, 60, 108
  word(s) and, 115
Mahabharata, 199
Maitri (mutual friendship), 178
Malin-Smith, Dennis, xvii
Man and His Becoming According to Vedanta, 12, 101, 106
Mandukya Upanishad, 106
Mantra (sacred utterance), 115
  and poetry, 167
Manusmriti, 88
Marxist dialectical theory, 53, 76
Master/disciple relationship, 128, 144–145, 149–150
Masui, Jacques, 31, 110, 127
Materialism, 73, 98, 109
Materiality, 31, 38
  spirituality and, 97–98
Maublanc, Professor René, 32, 62
Maxwell, Helen, xvii, 56
Meaninglessness, xii
Mechanical Man, 70, 107, 131–132
Meditation, 86
Mediumism, 60, 107

Meetings with Remarkable Men, 137
"Mémorables," 15, 28, 37, 51, 59, 78, 140
Mercure de France, 69
Meru, Mount, 199
Metanoia (religious conversion), 131
"The Metaphysical Intuition in History," 91
Metaphysics, xiii, 37, 43–44, 60, 102, 215
  and nature, 20
  and nondualism, 83–84
  pataphysics and, 56
  politics and, 72, 91–92
  surrealism and, 46
Meyrat, Robert, 6, 7, 8, 32, 50
  paranormal experience and, 61, 62
Michaux, Henri, 10
Michelangelo, 87
Militarism, 71
Milosz, O.V. de L, 38
Mind
  animistic, 60
  and automatic writing, 51–52
  and God, 99
  and hallucination, 9, 36–38
  parapsychic experimentation and, 7–8, 9, 11, 32, 35–39, 46
  and toxic substances, 9, 11, 35–39, 46
  and truth, 113
Mindfulness (*Dharmakaya*), 93, 129–130
Minet, Robert, Fig. 2
Mohamudgara (The Hammer of Stupidity), 90
Montparnasse, avante garde of, 10
Moore, James, 138
Moreau, Gustav, 45
Morise, Max, 51
Moses, 87
Mount Analogue, xii, xiv, 20, 29, 55, 111, 158, 197–216
  ascension and, 165
  characters in, 19, 201–206
  and love, 164–165
"Mugle," 19
Mujahede (holy war), 128
Multiplicity, 36–37, 86
Mundakya Upanishad, 113
Muscle relaxation exercises, 135
Musée d'Art Moderne, xi, xvii, 43
Musicians, 122–123
Mysticism, 56, 64, 72, 97–98
  monkhood and, 86
  René Guénon and, 104
  versus Gurdjieff teachings, 105

Nadeau, Maurice, 48, 59, 64
Nationale Revue Française, 26
Natya Sastra (Treatise on the Theater), xiv, 116
Naville, Pierre, 74
Nazism, 72
Near-death experience, xiii
Needleman, Jacob Dr., 13, 93
"Nénie," 19
Nerval, Gerard de, 48, 54, 57, 61, 97, 188
"Nerval Le Nyctalope," 61
A New Model of the Universe, 107
Nihilism, 45
Nonattachment, 31, 34, 83, 131, 165–166
  conscious states and, 35
Nonbeing, 86
Nondualism, 35–36, 83
  Hegel and, 99
A Novel of Symbolically Authentic Non-Euclidean Adventures in Mountain Climbing, 198

Objective Chance, 49
Occultism, 61, 98, 105, 107, 141, 173
Oneness, xii, 85–86
  soul friendship and, 8
  states of consciousness and, 36–38
"The Only One," 165
"On the Life of Basiles," 6
Opium, 9, 47
Oppression, 91–92
  religion and, 94
Ouspensky, P.D., 79, 107, 129, 134, 210
Out-of-body experience(s), 46, 61

Padmasana yoga, Fig. 12
"The Panic Sweat," 167, 172
Pantagruel, 181
Pantheistic, 104
Paranormal experience, 60–63.
  See also individual type by name
Paraoptics, 63
Pashyanti Vak, 115
Passageways, xv
Pataphotogrames, 54–55
Pataphysicians, 10, 49, 54
Pataphysics, 32, 36–37, 50
  and humor, 53, 54, 70, 170
"Pataphysics and the Revelation of Laughter" ("Le pataphysique et la Revélation du Rire"), 54

"Pataphysics of Phantoms," 55
"Pataphysics This Month," 14
Patriotism, 73
Paulhan, Jean, 20, 27, 110, 145
Pentland, Lord John, xv
Perception, xiii, 35
  consciousness and, 32, 60–63
  dream state and, 106
  dualism and, 53–54
  extra-sensory, 60–63
  mind-altering experiments and, 7–8, 9, 35–39
  and *rasa* (savor/tasting), 119–120
Perin, Luc, 6
Personality, xiii
Philosophy
  of the absurd, 34
  and communism, 71–79
  Hindu, 12–13, 78, 83–95, 113–124
  nondualist, 18
  and religion, 13
  surrealism and, 45
Physics, subatomic, 53
Picasso, Pablo, 45
Plato, 129, 196
"Poem to God and Man," 92
Poet(s)
  cursed (*poète maudit*), 69
  Hindu, xiv, xv, 12–13, 19, 75, 116, 120, 121
  inner state of, 114
  nineteenth-century, 45, 46, 48, 61
  party-line, 74
  role of, 172–173
  surrealist, 9, 20, 45–46, 47–48, 58
  twentieth century, xii, xvii, 33, 46
  vision(s) and, 38
Poetics, Hindu. *See* Hindu philosophy, and poetics
Poetry
  and art, xiv, 44, 45, 51
  Dadaists and, 44–45
  and God, 64, 92
  and Hindu poetics, 113–116, 121–122
  and mysticism, 12–13
  mythical woman and, 59
  omnipotence of, 45
  rasa (savor) and, xiv, 119–122
  and renunciation, 161–162, 165–166
  sacred nature of, xiii-xiv
  and the unconscious, 51, 52
  Vedic, 122, 208.
  See also Daumal, René, poetry by
Polizzatti, Mark, 156

Porphyrus, xv
Positivism, 109
"Powers of the Word in Hindu Poetics," 171
Powrie, Phil, 38, 169
Prasna Upanishad, 106
Prayer
  daring/pranks and, 50
  poetry as, xiii-xiv
Prenatal state, 60
Prévert, Jacques, 56
Prévost, Jean, 107
Pride, 32, 34
Proletarian revolution, 72, 77
Protestantism, 94
Psyche, 46, 108, 131
Psychoanalysis, xiii, 46, 107
Pure being, 17
Purgatory, xiv
Purity, 32

Quasha, George, xviii
Queneau, Raymond, 56
Quint, Leon Paul, 44

Rabelais, François, 48, 181, 189
Rahv, Philip, 73
Rajas guna (neutral quality), xiv
Random, Michel, 49
Rasa (Daumal), 12, 116
Rasa (savor/supernatural essence), xiv, xv, 116, 119–120, 178, 190
  communion and, 122–123
  and soul, of poetry, 120
  and theater, 117–119
Rationalism, 45, 109
Ravindra, Ravi, 139
Reality
  dream state and, 106
  mind-altering experiments and, 7–8, 9, 35–39
  perception and, xiii, 106
  surrealism and, 49
  toxic substances and, 9, 35–39
Reason, 99, 101, 134
Receptivity, 44, 47
Reign of Quantity and the Sign of the Times, 109
Religion
  agnosticism and, 9, 36
  Daumal and, 93, 122
  Gurdjieff and, 131, 139

Hindu teaching and, 13, 83, 90–91, 103
  and Marxism, 101–102
  power and, 91, 92
  René Guénon and, 103–104
  Simpliste acknowledgement of, 8–9
  study of, 12–13
  and surrealism, 45
  versus freemasonry, 5
Remembering, 129–130, 136
René Daumal: L'Etude d'une obsession, 38
"René Daumal et *Le Grand Jeu*," 74
René Dumaul: au-delà de l'horizon, xvii
"René Guénon Judged by Surrealism,"
  105–106
Renéville, Andre Rolland de, 16–17, 28,
  32, Fig. 4, 52
  and Alexander de Salzmann, 141,
    144–145
  and Hindu philosophy, 83–84
  and Le Grand Jeu, 69
  and poetic creation, 60, 121
  politics and, 75, 76
Renou, 12
Renunciation, xiii, 12, 21, 31–34, 188,
  215
  action and, 90
  and Gurdjieff Work, 131
  and nonbeing, 35
  poetry and, 161–162, 165–166
  and transformation, 83–95
Revelation, 9, 47
  drug-induced, 36–37
  and God, 39
Reymond, Liselle, xvi, 21, 86
Ribemont-Dessaignes, Georges, 9, 27, 64,
  74, 156, 210
Rig Veda, 84, 85, 188
Rilke, Rainer Maria, 23–24
Rimbaud, Arthur, 4, 7, 33, Fig. 6, 45, 69,
  140, 155, 172
  absurd humor and, 54
  dream exploration and, 57
  and nonduality, 83–84
Ritual, 84, 87–88, 188–189
Romains, Jules, 62
Romanticism, 45, 97
Roosevelt, 79
Rousseau, André, 199–200
Rugafiorri, Claudio, xvii, 15, 56, 179
Russian Revolution, 79

Sacredness
  and inner self, 32
  passageways and, xv
  sacrificial ritual and, 84
  Sanskrit and, 27
  seeing and, 130
Sacrifice, 84, 86, 131–132, 163, 188–189
Sahitya Darpana (Mirror of Composition),
  xiv, 116, 119–120, 177
Saint(s), 17, 37
Salvation, 34, 104
Salzmann, Alexandre de, Fig. 17, Fig. 18,
  xiv, 13, 23–24, 39, 127, 140–141,
  215.
  See also Gurdjieff, G.I.
Salzmann, Dr. Michel de, xviii, 24, 34,
  129–130, 144, 149
Salzmann, Madame Jeanne de, Fig. 19, xiv,
  xvi, 23, 24, 78–79
  and Daumal's letters, 143–144, 150–152
  and Gurdjieff Work, 135, 146–148
  and negative emotions, 132–133
Sankya, 19
Sannyasin (yogic teacher), 86
Sanskrit, xi, xiii, 115
  study of, 12–13, 113–116, 139
  treatises, xiv, 116–117
Sanskrit Poetics as a Study of Aesthetics, 120
Sattva guna (positive quality), xiv
Schlumberger, Jean, 26
Schopenhauer, 99
Schure, Edouard, 98
Science of Imaginary Solutions, 10
"A Season in Hell," 33
Second Manifesto, 64, 107–108
Seeing: The Endless Source of Inner Freedom,
  129–130
Seeking
  Hindu teachings/poetics and, 99, 114,
    209–210
  Le Grand Jeu and, 64
  methods/techniques and, 32
Self, 88, 89, 113, 122
Self-abnegation, xiii, 12, 33–34
  conscious states and, 35.
  See also Renunciation
Self-aggrandizement, 11
Self-awareness, 129–132
Self-confrontation, 13
Selflessness, 11
Self-negation, 32.
  See also Renunciation
Self-observation, 129–130
Sense(s), 19
  Gurdjieff Work and, 129–130
  and perception, 32

renunciation and, 90–91
surrealism and, 47–48
Shakespeare, William, 188
Shakyamuni, 92
Shankar, Ravi, 13, 100
Shankar, Uday, Fig. 13, xii, 13, 100
Shankara, 90
Shattuck, Roger, 48, 164–165
Silence, 176, 177
Sima, Joseph, 43, 68, 127
Simplicissimus (review), 24
Simplism, 8
Simplistes. *See Les Phrères Simplistes*
"Single Lady," 169
Sleep, 36, 57, 107
  alpha-, 62
  and Gurdjieff Work, 180
  pseudo-, 68
Sleeping Man, 70, 131
Social conscience, 74
Society
  artist and, 46, 51
  and class politics, 73–75
  and Communism, 71–79
  disillusionment with, 11–12, 72
  God and, 90–91
  and revolt, 32, 33
Solitude, 91
Soma, 199
Somnambulance, 61, 134
Sorbonne, 10, 13, 68, 213
Soul
  and automatic writing, 52
  collective, 8
  communion and, xiii, 35–36, 90
  dark night of the, xv
  and delusion, 89–90
  friendship and, 8
  Hindu philosophy and, 12, 90
  of poetry, 120
  renunciation and, 33–34, 90
  and search for purity, 32
  and society, 33
Sound, primordial, 115
  and God(s), 121
Space, xii, 36
  infinity of, 38
Spirit, 11, 57, 98
  and mind/time, 99
Spontaneity, 18
Stalin, 64, 73
Station Hill Press, xviii
Stein, Charles, xviii
Style, 123

Subconscious, 107
Suffering, 33, 69, 127, 131, 132, 155, 179
  and illusion, 132–133
  and sleeping, 180
Sufism, 84, 128
Suicide, 48, 52
Suicide by Hallucination, 48
Supraconsciousness, 108
"Sur la Musique Hindoue" ("On Indian Music"), 122
Surrealism, xiv, 45
  absurdity/duality and, 53–54
  and Le Grand Jeu group, 43–70
  mythical woman and, 59
  and poetry, 168–169
  and Sanksrit poetics, 12–13
  tenets of, 46, 53
Surrealists, xi, xii, 9, 17, 20, 21, 43–70
  and automatic writing, 51–53
  dream exploration and, 45, 51, 57–59
  and *Le Grande Jeu*, 64–70
  and politics, 23, Fig. 7, 64, 72, 73, 79
  René Guénon and, 105–111.
  See also each individual by name
Symbolism of the Cross, 101
Symbolists, 98
Symposium, 196

Table of Hydrogens, 98
Tad Atman, 103, 116
  experience of, xiii
Tagore, Rabindranath, 75
Tai Chi Chuan, xvi, 21
Taittiriya Upanishad, 123
Talent, 51
Tamas guna (negative quality), xiv
Taoism, 13, 84
Taste, of life, 119–120.
  See also Aesthetic experience; *Rasa*
Telepathy, 7, 46, 60, 107
Theater, 117–118
Theater of the Absurd, 48
Theosophism, 94, 100, 105
Theosophy, 98
Theresa, Saint, 34
Thomism (Saint Thomas Aquinas), 110
Thresholds, xv
Tibetan *Book of the Dead, The*, 122
Time, 36
  attitudes about, 122–123
  and God, 53
  infinity of, 38
Tiwari, Kapil, 88

"To Approach Hindu Poetic Art," 109
To Live Within (Reymond), xvi
"To Nothingness," 167
Torma, Julien, 56
Toxicomania, 69
Tracol, Henri, xvi, 149, 154
Transformation, 35–36, 83, 88–95, 123, 194, 197–198
Travers, P. L., 128
"Treatise of Patagrammes" (*Traité de patagrammes*), 54
Treatise of Pataphotogrammes, 5
Treatise of Sanskrit Grammar and Poetics, 173
Treatise of Style, 51
Trotsky, Leon, Fig. 7, 64, 73
Truth, 78, 103, 113, 116
Tzara, Tristan, 44, 51–52
    and Communism, 73

Ubu, Père, 48–49
Ubu Cuckolded, 48
Ubu Roi, 48
Union, 85, 90
    soul friendship and, 8
    states of consciousness and, 36–38
Universal analogy, 98
Universal soul, xiii, 35–36.
    See also Soul
Upanishads, 12, 87–88, 89, 123, 141, 193

Vailland, Roger, 6, 8, Fig. 2, 52
    and angel emanations, 61
    and Communist Party, 74
    and *Le Grand Jeu*, 69
Vakrokti, 177
Valery, Paul, 14, 161
Variétiés (journal), 14
Vasto, Lanzo del, 3, Fig. 21
Vatarasana (ascetic), 86
Vedanta, 90, 94
Vedas, 12, 83–84, 85, 118, 129, 199

Vedic Literature, 122
Vibration, 36
Vinaya (discipline/humility), 22
Virgil, 57
Visvanatha, xiv, xv, 116, 120–121, 122
Vitrac, Robert, 51
Void, the (*le néant*), xii
    mind experimentation and, 9
Voltaire, 196
Voluntarism, 109

Wagner, Richard, 117
Waking state, 106, 107, 134, 182
    Gurdjieff Work and, 136
War, 71
Water, xiv, 120–121
Weil, Simone, 9, 27
Weiner, Richard, 18
Whitehead, 91
"Willed Fire," 177
Willingness, 22
Wisdom, 115
Woman, cult of, 46
Woman, mythical, 59
Wonder, 22
Words(s), 115
Working class, 74
World War I, 5
Worthiness, 87
Wright, Frank Lloyd, 137
Writing, experimental, xiii

Yoga, 60, 115
    and *asanas* (yogic postures), 131
Yogi(s), 37, 104–105
You Were Always Wrong (*Tu tes toujours trompé*), 78, 92–93

Zeitgeist (Time-Spirit), 99
Zuber, René, xv